The Complete Guide to Writing Questionnaires

The Complete Guide to Writing Questionnaires

How to Get Better Information for Better Decisions

DAVID F. HARRIS

I&M Press • Durham, North Carolina

Permission to reproduce excerpted material on pages 166–167 and 194, 203 is gratefully acknowledged from the Higher Education Research Institute and from Gordon Willis & Sage Press.

Printed in the United States of America
Book design by Barbara E. Williams.
Cover Design by Pati Reis and Jeanne Taylor of Designing Solutions, LLC.
Typeset in Charis by BW&A Books, Inc, Durham, North Carolina

Library of Congress Control Number: 2014938165

ISBN 978-0-615-91767-2

This book is dedicated to all those who strive to create questionnaires that will help people and organizations make better decisions and effect positive change.

CONTENTS

ACKNOWLEDGMENTS

Many people helped as peer reviewers of the book and others generously gave me their support in the process of writing this book. I would like to thank Dianne Altman-Weaver, Betsy Bennett, Reba Burke, Hilary DeCamp, Leslie Doares, Jean Domanico, Terry Grapentine, Ed Gwodza, Sheza Healey, Una Healey, Omur Kayikci, Jessie Manthey, Susan McDonald, Lorna McLeod, Kim Olver, Nancy Roman, Paul Sackman, Wendy Smelzer, Lindsey Wagner, and Gordon Willis.

I am very thankful and appreciative of the editorial guidance of Mary Jo Tate in the development of this book. I also am thankful for the editing provided by Penelope Cray as we prepared this book for its readers.

I have much gratitude for the support and guidance of Jeanne Taylor, from Designing Solutions, LLC, and Barbara Williams, from BW&A Books, Inc. Their enthusiasm, guidance, and creative spirits were much appreciated.

Thanks to my sisters, Cathy, Carolyn, and Susan, and to my mom, Anne, for their friendship and support.

Many thanks and much gratitude to Janet Elbetri for her steadfast support in all phases of writing and developing this book.

Finally, I want to thank my son, Ben, for the many ways he contributed to this book. His edits to the manuscripts were impressive, but the larger contribution was his consistent support for writing this book. I thank him for his friendship and for all those evenings and weekends when we did our homework together.

David F. Harris
March 2014

INTRODUCTION

Questionnaires are the information-collecting tools of survey research in many disciplines. In the social sciences, we study health, income, family relationships, alcohol and drug usage, and more. In public-opinion research, we measure attitudes toward public policies and voting intentions. In both public and private organizations, we study the market potential of products and services, customer satisfaction, employee engagement and retention, advertising awareness, market segmentation, product positioning, and so on. The list goes on and on.

For many businesses and other organizations doing applied research, the information we collect with questionnaires shapes not only how we think about issues but, ultimately, also what we do. Our questionnaires on health issues affect who we think is at risk for disease and how and when to intervene. Our questionnaires on customer satisfaction shape our understanding of our company's performance and what we need to do to improve profitability and growth. Our questionnaires on new product opportunities shape our assessment of their potential and, ultimately, whether we invest financial and human resources in them.

This book was written with applied, rather than academic, research in mind. One of the key differences between academic research and applied research is that in academia you can pursue knowledge for the sake of knowledge; in applied research, you are almost always seeking information to aid decision-making, either short or long term. For example, you may work for a business that needs to improve customer satisfaction, decide which advertisement to put on television, or decide whether to invest in a new technology. The time and money invested in survey research is almost always aimed at improving something.

Other organizations, from colleges and universities to nonprofit organizations, are also doing research because they need to decide how to improve things. A university may want to decide how to reduce student attrition or a nonprofit may want to decide how to persuade people to donate to its cause. The point is that the need to make decisions is driving the need for the survey.

When you are doing research to support decision-making, it is critical to think through what those decisions might be and what information is needed to inform those decisions. Once you understand what information is needed, you can move on to writing the questionnaire.

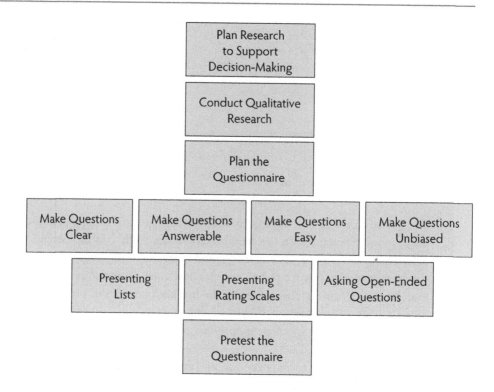

My purpose in writing this book is to provide a user-friendly, comprehensive guide for planning and writing questionnaires. This book offers a framework for writing questionnaires that begins with planning research to support decision-making, conducting qualitative research, and planning the questionnaire before you begin writing questions. We then provide guidelines for making questions clear, answerable, easy, and unbiased. We also provide guidelines for the three most common tasks we ask of respondents: selecting items from a list, rating items on a scale, and answering open-ended questions. Finally, we discuss how to properly pretest a questionnaire. Throughout the book I show how respondents misinterpret seemingly well-written questions; I then provide rewritten questions that follow the guidelines.

This book is for everyone involved in planning, writing, and reviewing questionnaires. You may write questionnaires yourself or you may hire others to write them. You may need questionnaires for measuring customer satisfaction, assessing new market opportunities, collecting information on your brand, getting opinions about health care, measuring employee engagement, or any number of other information-gathering research projects. Or you may be outside the direct circle of designing questionnaires and instead be involved in reviewing questionnaires written by others. Whatever your role in the world of questionnaires, this book will help you and your colleagues deliver accurate information that will support better decision-making.

Writing questionnaires is arguably one of the most challenging forms of writing. It is, in a sense, a conversation between you and hundreds, if not thousands, of diverse respondents. The conversation may take fifteen, thirty, or even forty-five minutes. And the questions have to be written so that every respondent can and will answer each question accurately, without misinterpretation and without bias. The challenge is daunting!

My goal in providing the framework and guidelines presented in this book is to help you with these conversations. While the guidelines hold true in the vast majority of circumstances, there are always exceptions. Ultimately, the quality of a question comes down to whether it is getting the right information for your organization and whether respondents can and will answer the questions without misunderstanding and bias. As discussed in part 4, pretesting questionnaires with respondents will help you determine whether people will understand the questions as you intended and, most important, take the time to answer them accurately.

I wrote this book to help you write better questionnaires. But my ultimate purpose is the same as the underlying purpose of any questionnaire: to help you and your organization get better information for better decision-making.

HOW TO USE THIS BOOK

Please read this book from beginning to end. This way, you will come to understand the importance of following a stepwise approach to conducting research and to writing questionnaires. The process begins with planning research, followed by qualitative research, and then planning the questionnaire *before* you write any of the questions. The guidelines on writing effective questions—that is, questions that are clear, answerable, easy, and unbiased—are best mastered before the guidelines on asking respondents to select from a list (chapter 10), to rate items on a scale (chapter 11), and to answer open-ended questions (chapter 12). And all of these aspects of questionnaire writing need to be understood before readers proceed to part 4 on pretesting and revising the questionnaire.

Once you have read the book from beginning to end, you can dip back into it, much as you would a reference guide. Each step in the process of planning research, planning the questionnaire, writing questions, and pretesting and revising the questionnaire can then be revisited as needed.

This book contains a lot of information. There are a total of sixty-five guidelines organized into a framework of eleven conceptual steps. To help you understand the material, we offer this table to show the relationships between the parts of the book, the framework, and the guidelines associated with each step in the framework. After you read the book from beginning to end, referring to this table will help you find the guidelines you need at any stage in the process.

The example questions used in this book were created to illustrate how to write better questionnaires. The details associated with these questions, such as the items on lists, brand names, or the exact words and phrases that respondents who would be surveyed would use, for example, are not intended to be factual.

Guidelines for Writing Effective Questionnaires

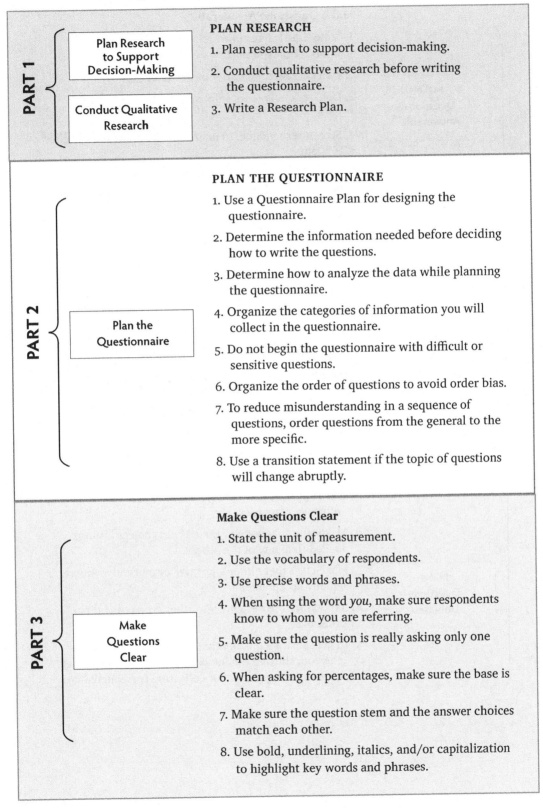

PART 1

Plan Research to Support Decision-Making

Conduct Qualitative Research

PLAN RESEARCH

1. Plan research to support decision-making.

2. Conduct qualitative research before writing the questionnaire.

3. Write a Research Plan.

PART 2

Plan the Questionnaire

PLAN THE QUESTIONNAIRE

1. Use a Questionnaire Plan for designing the questionnaire.

2. Determine the information needed before deciding how to write the questions.

3. Determine how to analyze the data while planning the questionnaire.

4. Organize the categories of information you will collect in the questionnaire.

5. Do not begin the questionnaire with difficult or sensitive questions.

6. Organize the order of questions to avoid order bias.

7. To reduce misunderstanding in a sequence of questions, order questions from the general to the more specific.

8. Use a transition statement if the topic of questions will change abruptly.

PART 3

Make Questions Clear

Make Questions Clear

1. State the unit of measurement.

2. Use the vocabulary of respondents.

3. Use precise words and phrases.

4. When using the word *you*, make sure respondents know to whom you are referring.

5. Make sure the question is really asking only one question.

6. When asking for percentages, make sure the base is clear.

7. Make sure the question stem and the answer choices match each other.

8. Use bold, underlining, italics, and/or capitalization to highlight key words and phrases.

PART 3 (continued)

Make Questions Answerable

Make Questions Answerable

1. State time frames in which people can recall the information you need.

2. Don't assume regularity of behavior.

3. Don't ask people for information they simply don't have.

4. Screen respondents to make sure each question applies to them.

5. Make *"Don't know"* an answer choice if some respondents simply don't know the answer to your question.

Make Questions Easy

Make Questions Easy

1. Keep the question stem under twenty-five words.

2. When writing questions, say the question out loud as if you were talking to someone.

3. Limit the length of the questionnaire.

4. Don't ask for more detail than you really need.

5. Soften questions with phrases such as *approximately, your best estimate,* or *as best you remember.*

6. Don't ask questions in the form of complex grids.

7. Add labels to answer categories.

Make Questions Unbiased

Make Questions Unbiased

1. Do not introduce ideas or opinions in questions that will influence responses.

2. Make sure that none of the answer choices is more loaded than any of the others.

3. Make clear that either a positive or a negative answer is equally acceptable.

4. Randomize answer choices if there is a possibility of order bias.

5. To get sensitive information, consider disguising the question, shifting the focus away from the respondent, softening the question, or collecting correlated data.

PART 3 (continued)

Presenting
Lists

Presenting Lists

1. Make sure the list includes all possible answer choices.

2. Make sure numeric categories are as broad and detailed as needed.

3. Make sure items on the list do not overlap.

4. Consider using forced choice instead of *"Check all that apply."*

5. Use the question to direct respondents to the list.

Presenting
Rating Scales

Presenting Rating Scales

1. Make the scale match how people think about the topic.

2. Ask the question before describing the scale.

3. Consider using bipolar scales, unless what you are measuring does not have a clear opposite.

4. For bipolar scales, decide if you want a midpoint and what to call it.

5. Whether to name the middle points is usually a practical decision.

6. Limit the number of times you ask respondents to rate things.

7. Make the scale length reasonable—shorter is usually better.

8. Don't make the endpoints too extreme.

9. Make sure bipolar scales are balanced.

10. Replace agree/disagree scales with direct questions about what you really want to measure.

11. If you are naming only the endpoints, present the scale horizontally with the positive endpoint and higher numbers to the right.

12. When naming all the points on the scale, put the more positive labels at the top when displayed vertically or to the right when displayed horizontally.

PART 3 (continued)

Asking Open-Ended Questions

Asking Open-Ended Questions

1. Format and label answer boxes to help respondents understand the response task.

2. Provide an appropriate space for answers.

3. Do not use exploratory open-ended questions as a substitute for qualitative research.

4. Recognize the limitations of exploratory open-ended questions.

5. Make exploratory open-ended questions specific.

6. Consider adding an introductory statement to improve the quality of responses.

PART 4

Pretest the Questionnaire

PRETEST AND REVISE THE QUESTIONNAIRE

1. Make sure the skip patterns work properly.

2. Examine the questionnaire with colleagues to find and fix flaws.

3. Develop a plan for pretesting.

4. Pretest the questionnaire in the mode in which it will be given to respondents.

5. Pretest the questionnaire with 3 to 10 respondents per segment, and consider more than one round of pretesting.

6. Conduct a soft launch of the questionnaire as a final step in quality control.

PART 1. PLAN RESEARCH

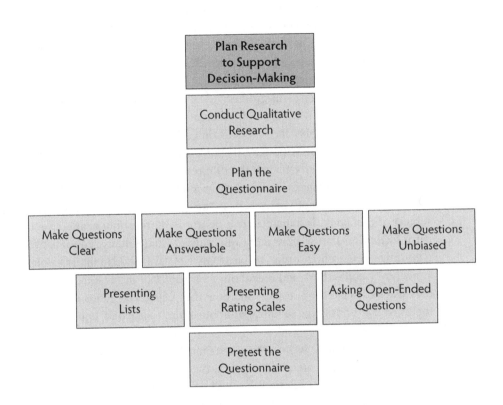

When you take the time to plan your research, you create a blueprint for your entire research process. The planning stage is crucial; it is here that you determine the potential final results of your research. Just as you should not build a house without a blueprint, you should not conduct research without a plan. Not only will you will waste time and money and possibly lead the organization in the wrong direction, but failing to plan your research can also cause you to miss opportunities. We have seen too many research studies presented, only to hear someone in the organization say, "Great study, but it doesn't help me with my decision." This happens all too often when research is not planned and the decision-making the research will support is not identified up front.

Planning research involves three key steps: identifying the decisions the research will support, identifying the information needed to make those decisions, and designing a study that will collect the information you identified.

These three steps—identifying decisions, identifying the information needed to make those decisions, and designing the study—must occur in order. The information you need to collect will depend on the decisions you intend to make. If you change those decisions, you will also change the information you need to collect. Furthermore, changes to the first two steps—identifying decisions and identifying information needs—often yield dramatic changes in the study's design. For example, when a research team more clearly defines the decisions its study will address, not only will the information required to make those decisions change but the people the team wishes to survey may also change or the survey itself may change from a quantitative survey to a qualitative exercise involving interviews or focus groups.

As you determine what type of information is needed to support your decisions, you will invariably face the question of whether that information is qualitative or quantitative. Although this book is not about qualitative research per se, it is helpful to briefly review the differences between qualitative and quantitative information needs, as researchers must be able to identify which tool to use and when to use both approaches. The questionnaire, which is the primary subject of this book, is a quantitative instrument and simply cannot be used to get information that is inherently qualitative. Additionally, you must conduct qualitative research in order to write an effective questionnaire. Unless you know how people think and feel about your topics of interest, what vocabulary they use to discuss these topics, and how they categorize items related to these topics, you are not going to know what questions to ask and, equally important, how to ask them.

We also urge you to write a Research Plan. The mere process of writing down the decisions the research will support, the information needed to make those decisions, and the study design that will collect that information leads to more precise thinking. Drafting a research plan invariably helps the research team define its project more clearly and work together more effectively. It also helps ensure that, in the end, all the effort invested in the survey will yield information that makes a difference.

Three Guidelines for Research Planning

1. Plan research to support decision-making. (Research Planning #1)
2. Conduct qualitative research before writing the questionnaire. (Research Planning #2)
3. Write a Research Plan. (Research Planning #3)

CHAPTER 1

Plan Research to Support Decision-Making

Organizations conduct research to support a larger purpose. They collect information to determine how to better allocate resources, improve product performance, retain customers, or take some other action. Because the cost of doing survey research is significant, few, if any, organizations commission survey research simply for the sake of understanding something. Even when the research is exploratory, most organizations will use its results to consider some future course of action.

Understanding the decisions that your research will support and designing your research to support that decision-making is necessary if that larger purpose is to be accomplished. We know that many of you will not be the final decision-makers for the topic at hand. Rather, your role may be to provide the information that someone else will use to make decisions. Still, knowing the decisions that are on the table allows you to get the information others need to make the right call. This is how you provide value in the research process.

Planning research to support decision-making requires taking on more responsibility, yet it also brings a greater sense of value and purpose. The best way to help organizations succeed in their research design is to first identify the key decisions they need to make. As with any exercise that introduces more responsibility, this exercise is not without its challenges. But in the long run, it leads to better, more accurate, less costly, and more useful information and, most importantly, to sound decision-making.

Information Requests, Study-Type Requests, and Decision Requests

Planning research to support decision-making can be quite challenging. Most people, when they think of doing survey research, think of *what they want to know* or the *study type* they want to administer rather than the *decision* they will need to make when the survey is completed.

The problem with beginning with what you want to know, or what we call your information needs, is that it provides little guidance about what to ask in the questionnaire. A survey can include an almost limitless number of questions. Without a clear decision in mind, the person writing the questionnaire will likely pass it around to various people who will, in turn, add questions to it to make sure they have enough information after the study is completed. This process will yield a questionnaire that is too long and contains unnecessary questions that may fatigue or perplex respondents and encourage guessing. At worst, a poorly designed questionnaire can lead the organization to make decisions based on faulty information.

Approaching survey research by thinking in terms of *study type* is equally common and unproductive. People might say, "We need to do an ad-tracking study" or "We need to do depth interviews with experts." Like information requests, these study-type requests do not consider what decisions will need to be made when the study is completed. Are we considering an ad-tracking study, for example, to decide whether to stop running the ad, change the contents of the ad, or place the ad at different times of day and on different TV shows? We need to know what decisions are being considered in order to know how to design the research and what information to collect.

Defining decisions first is critical to getting the right information and designing the right study. We cannot know what information to get or what kind of study to design until we clearly specify what we plan to *do* with that information. Unless we have clearly articulated the decisions or choices the organization needs to make, we cannot know what to explore or quantify.

Identify Decisions → Determine Information Needed → Choose Study Type

Let's look at a few examples of information requests, study-type requests, and decision requests.

Information Requests

An information request simply asks for information. An organization commissioning a questionnaire might say:

- We need to test for customer satisfaction.
- We need to understand the market dynamics for this disease.
- We need to see why consumers are using this brand more than the others.
- We need to track uptake of the product.

These requests say nothing about what will be done when the information has been collected or how much information is needed to make a decision. Without knowing the ultimate decision, questionnaire writers tend to collect a lot of information just to cover their bases.

Study-Type Requests

A study-type request focuses on what type of study will be conducted. An organization might say:

- We need to conduct *focus groups* with customers who do not use our brand to see what is going on.
- We need to do *depth interviews* with experts.
- We need to conduct a *satisfaction study* with our customers.
- We need to do a *tracking study*.

Focus groups, depth interviews, satisfaction studies, and tracking studies are general categories that define the *nature* of the work performed. They do not address what information will be measured or how it will be used. Without a plan that includes such details, how can the researcher know what questions to ask?

Decision Requests

A decision request, on the other hand, begins with the heart of the matter. Organizations who focus on decisions first often use declarative statements like these:

- We need to *decide* whether to license this product for our company.
- We need to *decide* which of three product concepts to move forward to advertising development.
- We need to *decide* which element of our brand campaign to adjust in order to improve market performance.

Once these key decisions have been identified, the kind of information needed and the kind of study most appropriate for gathering that information will be far easier to determine. After these questions have been answered, you are ready to write a questionnaire, if indeed a questionnaire is warranted.

Why Isn't Planning Research to Support Decisions the Norm?

Gathering information without knowing what will be done with it is costly. When the decision-making time finally arrives, the organization, despite much time and effort, may still not have the necessary data. Planning your research to support specific decisions is in everyone's best interest. When our clients are uncertain about the purpose of their information or study-type request, opening the process with a discussion often highlights those decisions that are looming on the horizon awaiting more data to inform them. We can then demonstrate that the research will be much more valuable if we first outline those decisions before spending thousands of dollars.

Given these distinct time- and money-saving advantages, you might ask why organizing research to support decision-making is not the norm. Why do people instead tend to frame research in terms of information or study-type requests? Here are several hypotheses.

The decision-making process in organizations is often unclear. Many of the people who are asked to do research are not the actual decision makers and are not clued in to the ultimate decision-making process, which, in turn, is often not clearly defined. In these situations, the people charged with doing research often do not feel comfortable consulting with internal clients or management on the decisions the research will support. They may also feel that it is not their responsibility. Just doing the research project seems to make more sense.

Assuming responsibility for decision-making in organizations can be risky. Organizations do not always reward people for assuming responsibility. Moreover, people like to associate themselves with success. When things go well, so much the better. But people may fear that when things do not go well, they will be unable to distance themselves from the failure. Therefore, a person assigned to do research may feel safer proceeding without reference to the decision-making underlying that research.

Identifying and clarifying decisions is hard to do and involves a thought process that has to be learned. Thinking about information needs or study types is easy. Thinking through the decisions the organization will need to make, along with the information needs, is hard work. Few people are trained to think through this process. One reason we wrote this book was to show survey researchers how to clearly define decisions and to ensure that their questionnaires will support making those decisions.

Many organizations that provide survey research reinforce the idea of organizing research simply to get information or to perform a particular type of study. Being a research supplier is hard work. Often, research suppliers are asked to just run the study. They are not often asked to consult with key decision makers about how to organize the research to support the key decisions the company needs to make. As a result, their products and services cater to the information and study-type requests, not to the ultimate needs of their clients.

The term *decision* is somewhat loaded. When we ask people about the decisions their research will support, we find that they often take a step back or fold their arms. However, when we ask people what they hope to do when the study is complete or what choices are on the table, their response is more positive. For whatever reason, the term *decision* in the context of survey research is intimidating to many people.

Despite these obstacles, decision-oriented research is superior to the approach of gathering information simply for the sake of having more information. Decision-oriented research provides better, clearer data and consistently saves time and money. The truth is that at some point, almost all research is used to do something. Figuring out what that something is ahead of time tells you what information you need—and what type of study to conduct.

For readers in academic settings who believe that many questionnaires are designed to generate knowledge, not to support decision-making, we offer two points of view. First, most research that involves surveys is used in the context of more applied disciplines such as education, public health, applied sociology, and so on. At some point down the road, someone will possibly be using your research to make decisions.

Second, even if your questionnaire is being used only to gather information and there is no decision in sight, thinking about what you will conclude or hypothesize when the study is done can be quite helpful. Writing down statements like "We will *create hypotheses about* who is most at risk for alcohol abuse" or

"We will *create hypotheses about* what leads to dropping out of high school" will yield a better questionnaire.

Research Planning #1: Plan Research to Support Decision-Making

Before you begin any research project, you must first address the fundamental issue of what decisions your research will support. The decisions that are on the table determine both the kind of study needed and whether a questionnaire will meet those objectives. If a questionnaire is suitable, then the decisions will guide what questions to ask.

To understand this first guideline, let's look at a typical research request that demonstrates how many studies begin.

Sarah, a director of marketing for a company that makes food products, approaches you with the following request: "I want to understand the dynamics of the market for weight control products."

This kind of request, which does not specify a decision, is common. The request is simply for information. Usually, however, lurking behind information requests are decisions the person or organization needs to make. To determine how to deal with situations like these, let's apply Research Planning #1 to Sarah's situation.

What does Sarah really need? It's hard to know from her request; we need more specific information. Maybe she needs to decide whether to license a new line of diet foods? Maybe she wants to decide whether to adjust the messaging for an existing brand of diet food? Since we don't know the decisions, we don't know what information she needs.

As we talked to Sarah, we discovered that she needed to determine the key benefits *men* want in dietary products in order to develop a new line of products specifically for men. We also discovered that her company had not yet talked with customers or potential customers to get a deep understanding of the benefits sought or to identify the demographic and attitudinal profiles of potential customers.

We developed a few decisions for her and her team to consider:

- We will determine the key benefits that men seek from dietary products.
- We will determine the demographic and attitudinal profiles of men to target with the new dietary products.

Since they had not talked to existing or potential customers, administering a questionnaire would be premature. We suggested beginning with qualitative research wherein we would interview men who were interested in dietary products and then moving to a quantitative approach informed and guided by the qualitative exercise.

Let's look at another example. Suppose Ted, a director of institutional research at a university, comes to you with the following request: "We need to do a survey of students who have dropped out of the university."

This is a study-type request. We don't know the decisions motivating the study, so let's apply Research Planning #1 to Ted's situation.

Why is the university interested in a survey of students who have dropped out? Is the university thinking about implementing changes to keep students after they matriculate? What is being considered? Are they thinking about changing the admissions policies to reduce the number of students who are at risk for dropping out? Until we understand what the university is willing to do, we won't have a full picture of what to measure.

Ted's request is for a particular type of study—a survey of students who have dropped out. We talked with Ted about possible decisions the research would support. What was the university willing to do to reduce the attrition rate? Would they be willing to adjust their admissions policy, financial aid decisions, and course requirements? If the issues were social in nature, would they be willing to change to improve the social environment? Might they adjust their policies around housing? And what about the faculty? Is it possible that the university might change some aspect of the way the faculty is supported or managed? Getting all the possible decisions out on the table helps us determine what to ask in the questionnaire.

One simple method we use to support our clients in this process is asking them to complete the following three fill-in-the-blank statements:

We will decide _____ .
The information we will use to make this decision will be _____ .
The threshold for making the decision will be _____ .

This usually starts the process of thinking about the decision or set of decisions the research will support. Then you can move on to what information is needed and what type of study will supply that information.

In Ted's case, we would start by offering a few possible decisions for discussion, such as these:

- We will decide how to adjust the admissions process to reduce the attrition rate.
- We will decide how to intervene during the freshman and sophomore years to reduce student attrition.

These sorts of specific decisions help generate conversations about what the organization is interested in doing. Further, it focuses all involved on what information to collect. Ultimately, upfront thinking like this is necessary for the research to make a real impact on the organization.

Note that once you determine the actual decisions the research will support, you might decide to survey different groups. Ted had originally asked to survey students who had dropped out. In addition to conducting research with students who have left the school, it might make sense to survey students during their freshman and sophomore years, when attrition is at its highest, to get additional insight into the problem so that the university can take more effective actions.

Until you have clearly specified the decisions the research will support, you won't know what information to collect, and in some cases, whom to get the information from. Identifying decisions is the essential starting point for every good research study.

Consulting Skills for Decision-Oriented Research

Focusing your team on the decisions your research will support is often challenging. Many people think in terms of information needs or study types—not decision-making. It may appear that your role in the organization, or as a consultant, is simply to do as you are told and to get the data or do the study. Sometimes that is all you can do, but it's best to avoid this situation.

In most cases, your team members will ultimately, if not immediately, appreciate your support in working through the decisions they will need to make when the research is complete. It is helpful to approach this topic from a number of angles. Very rarely is it sufficient to ask, "What decisions are you going to make when the study is complete?" You can start with that question, but that likely will be just the beginning.

If your team is resistant to talking about decisions, then there are probably other people and departments with a stake in the game. Find out who else is involved in the project and might have a role in decision-making. You may need to bring them to the table.

Sometimes people feel put on the spot when asked about decisions they will make. In cases like these, you can try to approach the subject in another way. Ask questions like:

- What are you hoping to find when the study is complete? If you found that, how would it help you?
- What choices are you and the team considering when the study is finished?

Another approach is to offer possible decisions and then ask for feedback. Here are some hypothetical examples:

- Are you considering changing the positioning and messaging for the product?
- After the customer satisfaction survey, are you considering a training program for employees to improve customer satisfaction or providing employees with better support?

As you can see, designing decision-oriented research studies requires good consulting skills. But the extra effort is well worth it. You will end up helping your organization or client much more than if you were to just do what you are told.

CHAPTER 2

Qualitative versus Quantitative Research

"Not all things that count can be counted,
and not all things that can be counted count."

—Albert Einstein

To plan research, and to write good questionnaires, you need to be well versed in qualitative research. Most serious research efforts involve both qualitative and quantitative needs and approaches. Qualitative research offers numerous ways to explore topics that are both different from and complementary to those of quantitative research. Knowing the benefits of qualitative research and how to apply them to your quantitative work will greatly enhance both your understanding of what you are researching and your ability to write an effective questionnaire.

Performing qualitative research is almost always the first step in any research process. On the most basic level, you need the insights and information qualitative research provides to know *what to ask* and *how to ask it* in a questionnaire. Imagine trying to write a question that asks respondents to select which of several items were their reasons for cancelling their service with your company. How would you know what to put on the list without first talking to people? Or suppose you want to assess the attitudes of patients who drop out of an addiction treatment program and compare them to the attitudes of those who complete the program. You need to discover what these attitudes are and how these patients describe them before you can measure them. To write an effective questionnaire, you need first to explore the issues it addresses.

On a deeper level, to develop a thorough understanding of a topic, you need the insights that only qualitative research can provide. Can you imagine developing a sophisticated understanding of *how* families decide which car to buy, *why* some people resist taking prescription medicines, or the *process* alcoholics go through to eventually make the decision to seek treatment without first talking to members of these groups? Planting a few open-ended questions in your questionnaire just won't do it. Qualitative research offers the tools and flexibility to dig into topics that quantitative research simply lacks.

To develop a thorough understanding of a topic and to write an effective questionnaire, you have to begin with qualitative research.

What follows is a brief introduction to qualitative and quantitative research, their differences, and how they complement one another. Since this book focuses on how to write questionnaires to get the information you need for decision-making, we highlight the differences between qualitative and quantitative information needs. Qualitative research is the right tool for some information needs, while quantitative research is the right tool for other information needs. When planning research and writing questionnaires, it is critical to be able to distinguish between qualitative and quantitative information needs so that you can pull out the right tool for the job.

Qualitative Research

Qualitative research involves talking with people in such formats as one-on-one interviews and focus groups. This can be done in person, over the phone, or over the Internet. As Alfred Goldman and Susan McDonald state in their book *The Group Depth Interview: Principles and Practice* (1987), "Whether one chooses to conduct group or individual interviews, the underlying goal of qualitative investigations is always the same: to explore in depth the feelings and beliefs people hold, and to learn how these feelings shape overt behavior." Qualitative research aims not to make estimates for the population, as you might with quantitative work, but to carefully explore a set of issues in order to better understand them.

> **Interviewer:** a qualitative researcher who is interviewing one person
> **Moderator:** a qualitative researcher who is conducting a focus group with several people

Unlike quantitative research, qualitative research is interactive. Questions can be modified depending upon how people respond. In quantitative research, we have to ask each question in exactly the same way to get statistically reliable data. With qualitative methods, we can rephrase a question if the original way of asking it proved ineffective or ambiguous. We have the flexibility to modify questions, follow an unexpected train of thought, and interpret reactions.

Qualitative research provides the flexibility to explore issues in depth, to dig below the surface. We can probe deeper into a discussion with statements like "Tell me more" or "Why do you say that?" When people tell us they want to buy a certain brand, we can ask a series of questions to uncover what benefit they feel the brand offers them. Is it reliability, safety, status, or some other underlying benefit that we, as outsiders, never thought of? Qualitative researchers can ask, "Why is that important to you?" and "What else might that do for you?" Sometimes people are not fully conscious of the rationale—both intellectual and emotional—for their thoughts and feelings. Exploring with probing questions gives us the ability to more thoroughly understand what people say.

In this way, qualitative research offers a kind of sensitivity that quantitative research does not. Interviewers and moderators develop rapport with the people they interview to facilitate openness and self-disclosure. They pay attention to every hesitation, nuance, facial expression, and silence. They can also explore unexpected topics that come up in the course of the conversation. In focus groups, they can observe and interpret social interactions among group members. Well-trained interviewers and moderators are able to detect thought processes, emotions, and underlying motivations that would go undetected if the only tool in the toolbox were a questionnaire.

Qualitative researchers also have a number of techniques for further exploring thoughts and feelings that may be otherwise hard to uncover. Ethnographic research, for example, allows the researcher to simply observe situations, such as car buying or floor cleaning, to look for insights that they would otherwise miss. Researchers can use projective techniques to engage people in some task wherein they reveal their underlying beliefs, feelings, or motivations. These and many other techniques can be employed to enhance our understanding of the subject matter.

During this qualitative information-gathering phase, we probe topics, develop new hypotheses, record the terms and phrases people use to describe things, and develop a deeper understanding of our target group's thoughts, beliefs, and emotions. However, because we have not engaged in any structured way with a representative sample of this target group, we cannot project our findings onto the target population. Our next step, then, is to quantify what we discovered in our qualitative research. Put another way, we use qualitative research to *find out* what matters so that later we are sure to *quantify* what matters.

Quantitative Research

As the name suggests, quantitative research is about counting things. It uses numerical representations of perceptions, attitudes, and behaviors as well as statistics to make estimations for the target population. In qualitative research, you might ask people to discuss why they do not feel valued at work; the information is represented in words. In quantitative research, you ask people to select from a list of items the ones that represent their reasons for not feeling valued at work; this information is represented in numbers and graphs.

While qualitative research is exploratory, quantitative research is largely confirmatory: It helps us confirm or reject the hypotheses we developed from our qualitative research. For example, while our qualitative research may have *suggested* that women are more interested than men in a new treatment for a certain medical condition, we won't know if that is true until we *quantify* interest in the new treatment with a representative sample of men and women.

Qualitative research and quantitative research are complementary in nature. Take a classic segmentation study as an example. You need to identify different groups of customers who might be interested in different products from your company. Toothpaste is a good example. Toothpaste marketers can identify groups of people that are looking for different benefits: teeth whitening, fresh breath, better taste, gum protection, and so on.

In this case, our quantitative segmentation study is largely confirmatory. We are analyzing the data to determine whether there are different demographic or attitudinal groups who each want a certain type of toothpaste. However, before we begin our quantitative segmentation study, we first need to engage in qualitative research to explore attitudes and perceptions about toothpaste and, from there, to determine what to include in the segmentation study. In other words, what we ask and how we ask it needs to be informed by our qualitative study. The quantitative study will then allow us to confirm or reject our hypotheses. Essentially, what we ask in the quantitative segmentation questionnaire will have come from what we learned in the qualitative segmentation study.

What we do with the data we gather during our quantitative research falls into three categories: estimating population parameters, looking for differences between groups, and looking for associations. We might, for example, be *estimating* the percentage of adolescents who have tried drugs, *looking for the differences* between how men and women respond to an advertisement, or *looking for the associations* between each of several factors and customer satisfaction. We return to these categories in greater depth in chapter 4, Questionnaire Planning #3.

In quantitative research we are concerned with *sampling error* and *measurement error*. Minimizing these two types of error is critical to the accuracy of quantitative research. Sampling error occurs when the sample size is too small or our method of getting the sample for the study introduced bias. Measurement error is a measure of the extent to which we are actually capturing what we think we are capturing. Writing an effective questionnaire is key to reducing measurement error. Using questions that are clear, answerable, easy, and unbiased improves the accuracy of our measurement. And, as we now know, doing qualitative research first will improve our ability to figure out what really counts so that we can count it accurately.

While most research initiatives start with qualitative research, when there is a lot at stake and important decisions are on the table, we need to follow up with quantitative research. Imagine you are conducting research to help a company decide whether to purchase a new product. Qualitative exploration will be essential to understanding the market and learning how potential customers think, feel, and behave. But while you might guess from qualitative research whether the potential for the new product is large or small, only quantitative research can tell you with any assurance how large or small that potential really is. A prudent decision maker will want to quantify the opportunity. What price might customers pay for it? What features of the new product are most important to customers, and what features are drawbacks? What is the competition, and how well do customers like the competition? You need to quantify what you learned qualitatively so that the company can make sound decisions.

It is important to understand the complementary roles of qualitative and quantitative research. Let's consider an extended example based on work with a college that had a high attrition rate. The attrition rate not only was costly to the school but also created a difficult situation for many of the students and their families. We have changed some of the details to preserve the confidentiality of the college as well as to make the example more comprehensive and useful.

When we began our research initiative with the college, one of the hypotheses circulating among some faculty and administrators was that the students who left just could not handle the academic pressure. Given this hypothesis, they felt that perhaps the solution lay with admissions policies, course-load requirements, or academic support. To address their hypothesis, we began with qualitative research to explore the role of academic pressure and other issues that might be at play.

When we interviewed recent dropouts, however, they talked about their dissatisfaction with the social environment. Many talked about feeling alone and isolated. We also found that some students felt the school had a problem with reverse discrimination. The school was known for having a very liberal student body, and some former students said they felt shunned or looked down upon because they wore an Izod shirt—not the standard "I am super-liberal" attire. We were hearing that it was the social environment, and not academic pressure, that was causing the high attrition rate.

These interviews revealed information that could only be accessed and understood through talking to people. We had to hear the students' voices, stories, and frustrations. The insights and understanding we developed from these interviews could not have come from reading percentages, correlations, and histograms. And in fact, we could not have known what percentages, correlations, and histograms to make unless we first took the time to talk to people and find out what data to collect.

The qualitative work we undertook had a profound effect on our subsequent quantitative research. We now knew what to ask when we surveyed recent dropouts. We also gleaned insights that changed our overall quantitative approach. We decided, for example, to survey current students to get an accurate read on the experience of freshmen versus upperclassmen. Could we also get an accurate read on when students were more at risk for leaving the college? Could we get more accurate information about how and when to intervene? The answer was yes.

Quantitative research confirmed that academic pressure was not the primary source of the high attrition rate. Rather, the social environment was driving the high attrition rate. However, our most interesting finding was that dissatisfaction with the social environment did not begin until the sophomore year and beyond. Freshmen were quite happy with their experience at the school. How could this be?

As it turned out, this college had on-campus housing for freshmen only. As students progressed beyond their freshman year, they had to find off-campus housing within a two- or three-mile radius of the school. While students were living in dorms and eating in the dining hall with their peers, they were happy with their social lives and more accepting of one another. Yet when they lived ten or more minutes away from campus, their connection to others and to the college community was hampered, and they felt more isolated and less connected.

While we cannot detail every outcome of our work with the college, one obvious recommendation was for the college to increase the availability of on-campus housing. Our research (both qualitative and quantitative) found that students who lived on campus were much happier with the social environment. The college also made other changes to improve the social life of students. We are happy to say that the college now has a much better retention rate.

This scenario is a good example of the respective roles of qualitative and quantitative research. The qualitative research gave us insight into the experience of students who had dropped out of the college. It taught us what to ask in the questionnaire. It also inspired us to expand the original Research Plan to include surveying current students by year in order to assess which factors might be contributing to the problem. Exploring the issues qualitatively and then quantifying our insights with a larger sample allowed us to much better understand the problems the college faced. Ultimately, the college understood the issues and was able to take action to reduce the attrition rate.

Qualitative research is the starting point for developing more precise quantitative measurements. Quantitative research is then essential for drawing conclusions based on your qualitative research. In cases involving important decisions—and as we saw in chapter 1, most research is related to important decisions—you would not want to take action without first following up on your qualitative exploration with quantitative verification.

Qualitative versus Quantitative Information Needs

One of the keys to writing a good questionnaire is knowing the difference between information needs that require a qualitative approach and information needs that require a quantitative approach. Many questionnaires suffer from the lack of qualitative information, which forces the questionnaire to extract information that requires qualitative exploration. This approach, while seeming to save time and money at the outset, is backward at best and just doesn't work. Using a quantitative method to seek qualitative information creates an awkward questionnaire that does not deliver the insights you need.

In Figure 2.1 we show some of the basic differences between qualitative and quantitative information needs.

Figure 2.1

Qualitative Information Needs	Quantitative Information Needs
Why do so many people want to avoid taking prescription drugs?	**How many** people self-treat with herbal or other natural remedies (not prescription)?
How do families **decide** what car to purchase?	**What is the difference** in perception of safety between Honda and Toyota?
What do employees **mean** when they say they want to be valued?	**What is the level** of employee satisfaction this year compared to last year?

Qualitative information needs are exploratory in nature. They require conversation because the answers are often not clear-cut. Whenever we want to understand *why* people have a certain attitude or *why* they behave in some way, we need to bring out our qualitative tools. It is hard to begin to understand why many people avoid taking prescription drugs without first developing rapport with people and talking about it. We may suspect that they have strong feelings about their own sense of health, the pharmaceutical industry, and giving up control. But the fact is we don't really know, which is why we need to conduct qualitative research.

When we need to understand a complex *decision process,* or *how* something is done, we need to use our qualitative tools. We begin by spending time with people, developing rapport, and using our exploratory skills to uncover how things are really done and how attitudes and past experiences play a role in this doing. Often, people are not fully conscious of all the issues and contingencies involved. They may act without thinking or assume that what they do is "only natural." In the case of how families decide what car to purchase, the sheer number of variables, such as safety, status, reliability, car color, quality of service, and usability for family events and vacations, makes the decision very complex. A husband and wife might have different views on how the decision is made. Using a questionnaire to ask about how the decision is made without talking to couples first wouldn't work very well.

When we need to understand *meaning,* we need to conduct interviews or focus groups. Imagine all the different dimensions related to what it means to feel valued at work. The feeling of being valued is emotional and it isn't the same for everyone. Qualitative research allows the interviewer or moderator to probe for a deeper understanding of what feeling valued means. Insights are unearthed. A twenty-minute survey, on the other hand, would simply ask respondents to rate something on a rating scale we define or select one or more items from a list.

To understand the meaning of feeling valued at work, we must do qualitative research. To see the extent to which our insights hold true for the entire work force, we must follow up with quantitative research.

Research Planning #2: Conduct Qualitative Research before Writing a Questionnaire

Before writing a questionnaire, we need to understand the topic from the perspective of the people we will survey. In the research-planning process, we determined which decisions the research will support. Then we identified what information was needed in order to make those decisions. Some of the information needs we identify will be qualitative, and some will be quantitative. The qualitative information will improve our understanding of the subject matter and help us determine what to ask and how to ask it in the questionnaire.

Let's explore this guideline with a few examples.

Suppose we are planning to conduct a survey to help a bank determine how to retain more customers. The bank has seen an unusual rise in the number of customers who have left the bank. They are considering making changes to their products and services as well as other changes that might help the situation.

Figure 2.2: Topic Guide versus Questionnaire

Discussion Guides versus Questionnaires

When planning qualitative research, you will need to prepare a discussion or topic guide for the issues you want to explore. Preparing a discussion guide is quite different from designing a questionnaire.

A discussion guide is a tool used by the interviewer or moderator in the course of conducting an interview. It provides a list of topics to be discussed, with notes about where to probe or explore more deeply. Most important, a discussion guide is flexible. It allows the interviewer or moderator to follow the respondents' train of thought rather than simply asking static questions. The interviewer can modify the discussion as the conversation progresses by rewording the questions and following the trains of thought that appear most useful.

By contrast, a questionnaire is inflexible. It comprises a fixed series of questions that will be read or asked in the same way. It does not offer the flexibility to reword questions on the fly or to explore issues that come up along the way.

Figure 2.2 provides a side-by-side comparison of a topic guide and a questionnaire using an employee engagement study as the setting.

Topic Guide	Questionnaire
1. Tell me about your job. In particular, I'd like to hear about your responsibilities.	1. Below is a list of possible job responsibilities. Please check all that apply to your job. ☐ Managing direct reports ☐ Organizing meetings ☐ Performing quantitative analysis ☐ Providing strategic input
2a. What do you like best about your job? (Probe: What makes this the best? What else?) 2b. What do you like least? (Probe: What specifically is the problem? Probe for additional issues.)	2. Please rate the extent to which you like or dislike the following job responsibilities. Use the scale from 1 to 5, where 1 = dislike very much and 5 = like very much. Managing direct reports 1 2 3 4 5 Organizing meetings 1 2 3 4 5 Performing quantitative analysis 1 2 3 4 5 Providing strategic input 1 2 3 4 5
3. What would make your job more satisfying? (Probe: In what areas would you like your job to be different?)	3. Please select the statements below that best describe how to make your job more satisfying. (Please check all that apply.) ☐ I would like more recognition. ☐ I would like to be included in decision-making. ☐ I would like to manage more people. ☐ I would like to work from home more often.

To make sound decisions about important changes such as these, the bank will need quantitative data. But what would we ask in the survey? Suppose we wanted to ask respondents to select from a list of possibilities their reasons for leaving the bank. What would we put on the list? Do you think we could come up with all the possible reasons without talking to customers? Do you think our bank could figure this out without talking to customers like you?

We talked with someone who took a survey about why she left her bank. The main reason she left her bank was that she could not get anyone from her branch on the phone, but that reason was not on the list of items to select from.

Suppose you also want to know what products and services are important to customers. What products and services would you put on the list in the questionnaire? It is impossible to answer this question effectively without first finding out where the former customers are taking their business. It may be possible that other banks, or credit unions, are offering products and services that encourage switching. Perhaps employers are offering special rates at other banks.

These are topics we would need to explore before writing a questionnaire. While the bank ultimately needs quantitative data based on a large enough sample to make decisions about changing products or services, or other significant aspects of the organization, we can't know what to quantify until we explore the topic with the people we want to learn about. In this case, we might also want to talk with customers who are not leaving, possibly to determine whether there are meaningful differences between loyal customers and those who leave, and whether what works for one group doesn't work for another. After we conduct such qualitative research, we will be in a good position to write a questionnaire to either confirm or reject our hypotheses about why the bank is losing customers and what changes it can make to retain them.

Consider another example. Suppose we are helping a company decide whether to develop a nonprescription herbal treatment to prevent migraine headaches. Ultimately, the decision about whether to develop the new product will involve making quantitative estimates of the financial opportunity the new treatment represents. However, assessing this financial opportunity first requires learning more about potential customers for the treatment and the marketing challenges associated with attracting them.

Before we design a survey, we will need to find out who the potential customers are. How are they currently trying to prevent migraines? How satisfied are they with these current treatments? What are the attitudes toward herbal treatments among migraine sufferers? Who would be most likely to purchase an herbal preventive treatment? Are the most likely purchasers in a certain demographic group? We don't even know whom to survey until we know more about the potential customers.

Furthermore, we will need to find out how migraine sufferers assess the benefits and risks of treatments. Do they use preventive treatments of any kind? Why or why not? If they use preventive treatments, do they treat continuously, sporadically, or in some other way? Their answers to these questions will have implications for what we ask in the questionnaire and for our assessment of the financial opportunity. For example, if migraine sufferers are inclined to treat episodically, such as before family and work events, the financial opportunity would not be as large as if they were to treat continuously.

Deciding whether to develop a new treatment for migraine headaches requires a huge investment of time and resources and would certainly require quantification. We would conduct survey research to ask potential customers about their interest in the new product and their likelihood of purchasing it, as well as to quantify other factors, such as what features of the product are most likely to attract new customers, whom migraine sufferers consult for treatment, and where they shop. This information will help the organization decide whether and how to develop the new product. We need to explore the landscape qualitatively, and thoroughly, before investing additional resources in survey research.

Any serious effort to understand a topic for the purpose of decision-making requires that we use all of our tools. Because of its flexibility, sensitivity, and exploratory nature, qualitative research will give us insights and information that quantitative methods simply cannot provide. When it comes time to write a questionnaire, we will know a lot more about not only what to ask and how to ask it but also *whom* to ask.

CHAPTER 3

The Research Plan

One of the most important documents you will write is the Research Plan. Organizations use these plans to ensure that research dollars are spent wisely and that the research provides information that will lead to sound decision-making. We have seen these documents called research plans, project plans, marketing-research plans, marketing-research request forms, and so on. The name is not important. The contents of the document, however, are vital.

Research projects begin when an organization or individual feels the need to make improvements in some dimension. A company may want to assess the market opportunity for a new product. A government agency may want to survey homeowners about mortgage-lending practices. A division of an international company may want to track satisfaction among customers in each of five segments. People ask for research to gain insights or measure some behavior and predict future action so that they can make effective decisions.

All the research projects mentioned in the preceding paragraph represent requests for information or for certain types of studies. The requests do not yet specify the decisions the research will support. But you know by now that you need to determine what will be done when the information is collected in order to know what information to collect.

Research is a *process*. There is a sequence of activities—each activity having its own set of decisions about the research—that is best executed in a logical order. A well-thought-out Research Plan is your blueprint for the quality of the research project. Just as you would not build a house without a blueprint, you would not want to spend time and money on research without a plan for achieving the desired outcomes.

The Research Plan is also an excellent consulting document. It helps ensure that everyone's thinking is precise and that all people associated with the project know what is being done and have the opportunity to see whether improvements are needed.

Research Planning #3: Write a Research Plan

Ensure careful planning and agreement by writing down the decisions, information needed, and study design before proceeding with research. This will improve the quality of the research, coordinate teamwork, and hone the team's focus. It will also help you save time and money.

A Research Plan should be clear and concise. One page or so is sufficient. The essential components are described in Figure 3.1.

Figure 3.1   The Research Plan

Background

The background is a paragraph or two that builds the story and sets the tension. Why does this research make sense? After reading the background, others associated with the project should be able to say, "I understand the context and why we need to spend the money to do this research."

Decisions

The decision section is a clear statement about what will be done when the research is completed.

Information Needed

This is a list of the key information you will collect to make the decisions.

Study Design

A study design includes such details as:
• Qualitative or quantitative approach
• Sample frame and sample size
• Data collection method (Internet, phone, mail, in-person, etc.)

Timing

Key dates for deliverables

Signatures

_____ (name and title)
_____ (name and title)

This planning document will help ensure that the research is focused on decisions, that the right information is collected for those decisions, and that the right study methods are used to get the information needed.

Writing a clear, concise Research Plan is critical to any research project, be it qualitative or quantitative. In fact, in the process of writing Research Plans, we have seen many quantitative projects turn into qualitative projects and vice versa. Every project we have worked on has been improved significantly through the use of this document as a thinking and planning tool.

Sample Research Plans are provided in Figures 3.2 and 3.3. Both explore obesity—Figure 3.2 from a qualitative perspective and Figure 3.3 from a quantitative perspective.

Notice how the decisions help guide what kind of information is needed. Also note the relationship between this initial qualitative project and the subsequent quantitative project outlined in Figure 3.3.

Figure 3.2   The Research Plan—Obesity Qualitative Research

Background

Body mass index (BMI) is a number calculated from a person's weight and height. A BMI of 30 or greater indicates that a person is obese. There are about 36 million people in the United States with a BMI over 30, yet less than 2 percent are on prescription therapy. Of the $33 billion per year spent on weight-loss products in 2013, only about $500 million represents prescription therapy. The most prevalent consumers of diet products (both Rx and non-Rx) are adult females.

Our company is interested in a compound that produces a sense of fullness within one hour of ingestion, which in turn should lead to a greater sense of control over eating. The compound has fewer adverse GI effects than do competitive products. Previous research shows that while physicians appear reluctant to treat obesity, they do recognize the potential benefit of our compound and will honor a request from a patient for treatment. To fully assess the market potential, we need to assess interest from consumers. We will begin with qualitative research to understand the market potential from the consumer perspective.

Decisions

1. We will decide how to design subsequent quantitative studies to assess the market opportunity.
2. We will determine the vocabulary of consumers in order to design questionnaires.
3. We will determine what to measure in order to understand demand with respect to how consumers think about their condition and alternative treatments.

Information Needed

1. Among obese people, what are the behaviors, beliefs, attitudes, and emotions toward treatments?
2. What is a successful treatment outcome for patients, and how do they measure and describe it?
3. What are the benefits and risks associated with current treatments? What words and phrases do consumers use to describe benefits and risks? How do they measure benefits and risks?
4. For patients on competitive treatments, what are the unmet needs?
5. What is required for our product to achieve differentiation that would lead to the desired consumer behavior (seeking treatment, requesting, switching, etc.)?

Study Design

- Males and females over 21 with a BMI of 30 or greater
- 3 focus groups with males, 3 focus groups with females
- 20 individual depth interviews (10 females, 10 males)
- Groups and depth interviews conducted in 3 cities

Timing

Focus groups and interviews will take place during the first three weeks of March.

Signatures

_____ Jamie "Decision-Maker" Thompson (Vice President, Marketing)
_____ Jim "Decision-Support" Reed (Director, Research)

Figure 3.3   The Research Plan—Obesity Quantitative Research

Background

Body mass index (BMI) is a number calculated from a person's weight and height. A BMI of 30 or greater indicates that a person is obese. There are about 36 million people in the United States with a body mass index (BMI) over 30, yet less than 2 percent are on prescription therapy. Of the $33 billion per year spent on weight-loss products in 2013, only about $500 million represents prescription therapy. The most prevalent consumers of diet products (both Rx and non-Rx) are adult females.

We are interested in a compound that produces a sense of fullness within one hour of ingestion, which in turn should lead to a greater sense of control over eating. The compound has fewer adverse GI effects than do competitive products. Previous research shows that while physicians appear reluctant to treat obesity, they do recognize the potential benefit of our compound and will honor a request from a patient for treatment. To fully assess the market potential, we need to assess interest from consumers. At this point we will quantify what we learned in previous qualitative research.

Decisions

1. We will decide which elements of our value proposition to pursue to gain the most leverage.
2. We will determine our target market based on its acceptance of our value proposition and its size.

Information Needed

1. How many target consumers have favorable perceptions and attitudes toward our value proposition relative to competitive brands?
2. Which of the differences between brands is most critical to consumers' decisions to take the action we desire (seek diagnosis, ask for our brand initially, or switch?)
3. How persuasive is our value proposition?
4. For what type of consumer is our value proposition most persuasive?
5. How many of these consumers exist in the market?

Study Design

- Males and females over 21 with a BMI of 30 or greater
- Internet panel members sampled
- Sample size to be determined later

Timing

Survey will be administered the first two weeks of May.

Signatures

_____ Jamie "Decision-Maker" Thompson (Vice President, Marketing)

_____ Jim "Decision-Support" Reed (Director, Research)

Writing a Research Plan ensures that you and your other team members are clear about what decisions the research will support and what information is needed to make those decisions. Later, when you move to planning the questionnaire and writing questions, the Research Plan will keep everyone focused on the purpose of the research.

PART 2. PLAN THE QUESTIONNAIRE

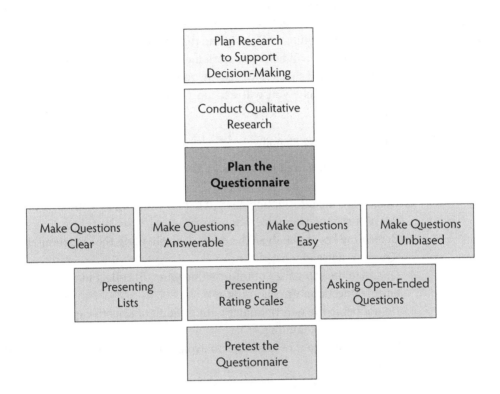

Research planning helps you determine which decisions the research would support, the information needed to make those decisions, and an appropriate study design. Writing the Research Plan enhances the precision of your thinking and agreement among team members. Even when agreement is not reached initially, the written document helps to expose areas of disagreement and, hopefully, ease consensus on the purposes of the research.

By the time you start writing the questionnaire, you will have explored the subject matter qualitatively and better understand what to ask in the questionnaire and how to ask it.

Now it is time to *plan* the questionnaire. We emphasize *planning* the questionnaire before *writing* the questionnaire for several important reasons. First, you need to determine the order in which to present the questions in the questionnaire so that the flow of questions does not confuse respondents. You have to think through issues such as order bias and where to put difficult or sensitive questions that might cause respondents to drop out of the survey.

Questionnaire writing is far more complicated than most people realize. Before you write any questions, you first need to think carefully about what information you really need to gather. Once that is determined, there are usually many ways to ask the question. Furthermore, many kinds of information cannot be obtained from a single question but rather require asking several questions and analyzing the data together. You need to think about how you will analyze the data as you translate the information needed into specific questions.

Questionnaire planning is a discipline that is well worth the effort. The process we will describe will help you work more effectively with your colleagues. You will end up with a shorter, less-costly questionnaire that gets more accurate information. Ultimately, you will end up with better information for making better decisions.

Eight Guidelines for Questionnaire Planning

1. Use a Questionnaire Plan to design the questionnaire. (Questionnaire Planning #1)
2. Determine the information needed before deciding how to write the questions. (Questionnaire Planning #2)
3. Determine how to analyze the data while planning the questionnaire. (Questionnaire Planning #3)
4. Organize the categories of information you will collect in the questionnaire. (Questionnaire Planning #4)
5. Do not begin the questionnaire with difficult or sensitive questions. (Questionnaire Planning #5)
6. Organize the order of questions to avoid order bias. (Questionnaire Planning #6)
7. To reduce misunderstanding in a sequence of questions, order questions from the more general to the more specific. (Questionnaire Planning #7)
8. Use a transition statement if the topic of questions will change abruptly. (Questionnaire Planning #8)

CHAPTER 4

The Questionnaire Plan

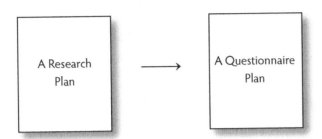

Writing a Questionnaire Plan is an excellent practice for developing an effective questionnaire. Questionnaire writing has many moving parts. You have to determine all the information that the questionnaire needs to collect, which is no simple task. You have to decide how to order the questions within the questionnaire. If questions jump around from topic to topic, respondents will get confused and either give erroneous answers or quit the questionnaire.

One of the keys to designing effective questionnaires is making the distinction between *the information you need* and *how to ask the questions*. Most clients who ask you to write a questionnaire will tell you something like, "Ask them how interested they are in the new product." But is this the information the client really needs? Maybe what the client needs to know is whether potential customers intend to buy the product, and if so, how much? *Interest* in a product and *likelihood to buy it* are different things. Distinguishing between the information needed and how to ask the question is critical. The Questionnaire Plan helps you make this distinction.

Sometimes the information needed from a survey requires several questions that need to be analyzed in a creative way. For example, you might need to know how income, gender, and opinions towards certain public policies are related to each other. Or you might need to know how interest in purchasing your product is related to a variety of demographic and attitudinal measures. The Questionnaire Plan hleps you make sure you get all the pieces of information needed and that you have thought through how you plan to analyze the data once it is collected.

Questionnaire Planning #1: Use a Questionnaire Plan for Designing the Questionnaire

Questionnaire planning requires producing a written document to help with the order of questions, communicating with colleagues, and articulating your plans for how to analyze the data. We call this written document the Questionnaire Plan.

The Questionnaire Plan can take many different forms, but the essential components remain the same, as shown in Figure 4.1. The first row restates the decisions the research will support, which can be copied from the Research Plan. These decisions are your anchor. They need to be front and center for everyone working on the project.

Figure 4.1   The Questionnaire Plan

Decisions:		
Information Needed	**How to Ask the Question**	**How to Analyze the Data**

Information Needed

The first column is where you record the information you need to collect. Determine what this the information is before you decide how to ask the question. This is particularly important as you work on the questionnaire design with other people, most of them being either experts on the topic or in charge of making the decisions the research will support. Work with these other team members to discover what information they need. This is a complicated and challenging process in itself.

Once you have determined the information needed, you can use the Questionnaire Plan to record various ways to ask the questions. You can then circle back to team members and walk through what you are trying to get (i.e., the information needed) and how you are trying to get it (i.e., through the questions).

Later in this chapter we will discuss the three kinds of information we ask of respondents: their history, their attitudes and perceptions, and their intentions.

How to Ask the Question

The second column is where you record the best way to ask the questions that will obtain the information you need. Sometimes you might write down two or three ways to ask a question that will elicit this information. We typically ask respondents to perform three kinds of tasks: answer an open-ended question, select from a list, or rate something from a scale we provide. If you ask respondents to rate something on a scale, which scale will you use (e.g., satisfaction, likeability, interest, etc.)?

Part 3 of this book offers guidelines on how to ask questions. There is much to consider when you get to the point where you are writing questions. By the time you reach this point, it is critical that you have already determined the information each question needs to collect.

How to Analyze the Data

The third column is where you state how you plan to analyze the data. In the case of some questions, you may simply need the data to see if people are eligible for the study. In the case of other questions, you may want to estimate a population value or see how well the data from one question correlates with the data from another question.

Thinking carefully about how you plan to analyze the data is very helpful to the design of the questionnaire. You will find that planning how to analyze the data will help you determine what questions to ask.

Later in this chapter we discuss the three things we do with data: estimate population parameters, look for differences between groups, and look for associations between variables in our data (see figure 4.8 on page 45).

Organize the Flow of Questions

Another benefit of drafting the Questionnaire Plan is that doing so will help you organize the flow of questions throughout the questionnaire. Figure 4.2 provides another view of the Questionnaire Plan that shows how it can help you organize the flow of questions. We return to the example we use in Figure 4.2, namely, advertising tracking, in chapter 5, "Organize the Order of Questions."

Screener: The section of the questionnaire in which you ask respondents questions to determine whether they are an appropriate audience for your survey. For example, if you wanted to survey women who have children between the ages of ten and eighteen, you would ask respondents their gender, whether they have children, and if so, their children's ages. Most surveys open with at least a few screening questions to see whether each respondent meets the qualification requirements.

Figure 4.2   The Questionnaire Plan

Decisions:		
Information Needed	**How to Ask the Question**	**How to Analyze the Data**
Screener Information		
Unaided Advertising & Brand Recall		
Prompted Brand Awareness		
Action & Intention		
Demographic Questions		

We use Microsoft Excel to create a Questionnaire Plan, but you could use other software.

We will have more to say about Questionnaire Plans throughout the book. They are invaluable tools for working with team members and ensuring that the questionnaire delivers the information needed. Once you have completed the Questionnaire Plan, you can easily copy the questions from column two into whatever software program you are using to write or program the questionnaire. Column three, how to analyze the data, is helpful once the data has been collected and the analysis process begins.

Questionnaire Planning #2: Determine the Information Needed before Deciding How to Write the Questions

Almost everyone who writes questionnaires simply jumps in and starts writing questions. First making the distinction between the information needed and how to ask the questions to get that information is rare. Typically, someone writes a draft of the questionnaire and then circulates it to the team for edits. Team members edit the questions, delete some questions, and add more questions. The questionnaire is then re-edited and circulated for yet more edits. This process is often repeated several times, and it can be very time-consuming. Most questionnaires produced this way are poorly written and poorly organized. You end up with a long questionnaire that confuses respondents and does not help organizations make the right decisions.

By using a Questionnaire Plan and first thinking through the information you need to collect, you will be in a better position to write an effective questionnaire.

Let's look at a few examples of how thinking about the information first is a good practice.

Consider a question generated through the method we described above, where the writers did not think carefully about what information they really needed to collect. A large manufacturing company gave this questionnaire to its employees after their computers had been repaired by the IT department.

Q: How would you rate the technical skills of the technician who repaired your computer? (*Please circle one number.*)

Poor 1 2 3 4 5 Excellent

During pretesting of the questionnaire, one of the respondents said, "All I know is that this guy with a cart took my computer away and another guy brought it back. How would I know how to rate the skills of the technician?"

We went back to the team that wrote the question and asked them what information they were trying to get. They said, "We just wanted to know if people are satisfied with the way their computer was fixed."

Surely whoever wrote the question was trying to do a good job. But asking about the technical skills of the person who repaired the computer does not elicit information about satisfaction with the repair process.

Using the Questionnaire Plan, we would work with team members to home in on the information needed, as demonstrated in Figure 4.3.

Figure 4.3   Questionnaire Plan—Computer Example

Decisions: We will determine how to improve IT support . . .		
Information Needed	**How to Ask the Question**	**How to Analyze the Data**
Overall Satisfaction		
A measure of overall satisfaction with computer repair.	How satisfied were you with the repair of your computer? Not at all Very satisfied 1 2 3 4 5 satisfied OR How satisfied or dissatisfied were you with the repair of your computer? Very Very dissatisfied 1 2 3 4 5 satisfied	

By talking with colleagues about the information they need—and not about how to ask the question—you get a better sense of the kind of information you need to collect. You can then work on ways to ask the question.

Here is another example where the question writer skipped thinking about the information needed and just wrote down questions.

Q: Is your dog a vegetarian?
☐ Yes
☐ No

What information do you think the questionnaire writers were intending to get?

The people who wrote the question worked for a company that made dog food. They were on a team charged with deciding whether to come out with a line of products for pet owners who do not want to feed their dog meat. What they wanted to know was the percentage of dog owners in the United States who feed their dog a meatless diet.

We might try asking the question as shown in Figure 4.4.

Figure 4.4   Questionnaire Plan—Dog Diet Example

Decisions: We will determine whether to continue to develop a meatless dog food brand . . .		
Information Needed	**How to Ask the Question**	**How to Analyze the Data**
Dog Diet		
Whether the dog owner feeds their dog meat.	Thinking about the past 30 days, did you feed your dog any meat or meat products? ☐ Yes ☐ No	

We would need to consider whether a 30-day period is the appropriate time frame and what to do about people who have more than one dog. We will address those kinds of issues in chapter 6, "Make Questions Clear."

If we were working with this client, we would first find out what information it needed to make its decisions. In this case, we would suggest getting information about interest in a meatless diet. There may be some portion of people who feed their dog meat but would like to avoid meat if at all possible. Simply asking a respondent whether he or she feeds a dog meat would miss this group of potential consumers. The company might ultimately make decisions based on faulty information and miss market opportunities. Thinking about what information you need before writing the questions helps you do a thorough job of covering the bases.

As a final example, consider a question a team wrote for a health-care survey aimed at doctors before figuring out what information they needed.

> **Q:** What percentage of time do you practice in each of the following settings?
> _____ % Office
> _____ % Hospital/Clinic
> _____ % Other

We asked the team members who had written this question what they wanted to know (i.e., the information needed) and what they planned to do with the data (i.e., their analysis plan). They said they just needed to screen for doctors who treated at least 50 percent of their patients in a hospital or clinic setting. That was the real reason for the question. (Note that we were working with them on the information they needed and what they planned to do with the information, not on how to ask the question.)

In the Questionnaire Plan, we might write this up as shown in Figure 4.5.

Figure 4.5   Questionnaire Plan—Doctor Example

Decisions: We will decide on the price of our new product for type 2 diabetes.		
Information Needed	**How to Ask the Question**	**How to Analyze the Data**
Screener Information		
Screen for doctors who see at least 50% of their patients in a hospital or clinic setting.	Do you, yourself, see 50% or more of your patients in a hospital/clinic setting? ☐ Yes ☐ No OR Thinking of the patients you, yourself, see, what is your best estimate of the percentage you see in a hospital/clinic setting? ____%	

In this example, we show two ways to ask the question. Sometimes we are not sure which way is best. It helps to collaborate with subject-matter experts. We can show them two or sometimes three ways to ask the question and discuss the strengths and weaknesses of each.

As these examples suggest, determining what information you need before attempting to write the question makes sense. The information you need and how you ask the question are different concepts. Identifying the information you need before writing the questions makes the process of writing a questionnaire more efficient and effective.

Using the Questionnaire Plan to talk with other team members about the information needed is a very effective way to begin designing your questionnaire. Most people are better at *telling* you what they need than they are at writing questions. Few have been trained to write good questionnaires. By talking with people about what information they need to make the decisions that are on the table, you are in a much better position to craft the questions.

Questionnaire Planning #3: Determine How to Analyze the Data While Planning the Questionnaire

While you are figuring out what information is needed, think also about how you plan to analyze the data. The Questionnaire Plan facilitates this thinking. Knowing what you plan to do with the data after it is collected can influence what questions you ask and how you ask them.

Let's revisit the example about dog owners who feed their dogs a meatless diet. For the purposes of illustration, let's say that the decisions this research was designed to support included determining the target audience for a meatless dog food and how to reach this target audience through advertising.

Determining the target audience requires collecting a host of demographic data. One piece of information the company surely needs is the age of those dog owners who are most likely to feed their dog a meatless diet. To determine how to reach this target audience, the company also needs to know which magazines might make sense for advertising. These are just two pieces of information, among many, that the company would need in order to make a sound decision.

Figure 4.6 provides an example of how we would use the Questionnaire Plan to address decisions related to both the demographic and advertising information needs.

The third column is where we record what we plan to do with the data. In this brief example, we have included estimating a population value, looking for a difference, and looking for an association.

Planning your data analysis in the Questionnaire Plan will help ensure that you get the data you need for decision-making. It will also help you limit the questions you ask to the ones that really matter.

Let's look at another example. In many businesses, marketing teams that are promoting a product will survey their customers a few times a year to see how the various elements of their advertising campaign are doing. These surveys are

Figure 4.6   Questionnaire Plan—Dog Diet Example for Analysis

Decisions: We will determine the target audience for a meatless dog food and how to reach the target audience through advertising.		
Information Needed	**How to Ask the Question**	**How to Analyze the Data**
Dog Diet		
Whether the dog owner feeds their dog meat	Thinking about the past 30 days, did you feed your dog any meat or meat products? ☐ Yes ☐ No	Determine the percentage of dog owners who feed their dog a meatless diet. This constitutes estimating a population value.
Magazine Subscriptions		
Information about magazine subscriptions	To which of the following magazines do you currently subscribe? ☐ Dog Times ☐ Pet Care ☐ Other	Look for a difference between these magazine subscriptions and feeding dogs a meatless diet.
Demographic Information		
Age of the dog owner	In what year were you born? _____	Look for an association between the age of the respondent and whether he or she feeds the dog a meatless diet.

often referred to as tracking studies. The decisions they support include, for example, whether to change the messages of the advertising campaign.

Suppose you are designing a tracking study and you need to know whether the key messages for the campaign are having a positive influence on purchasing. The product marketing team needs this information to decide whether to change these key messages. As we have mentioned, you cannot obtain this information simply by asking, "Are the following messages influencing your decision to purchase this product?" It would be naive to assume that people would, and could, answer this question accurately.

The information needed includes:

• Are consumers actually receiving the key messages?
• Are these messages differentiating the company's brand from that of the competition?
• Does receiving these messages influence purchasing or intent to purchase the brand?

Keeping the decision in mind, you would include these information needs in your Questionnaire Plan, along with a plan to analyze the data by seeing if the key messages are more associated with your brand than with its three compet-

Figure 4.7   **Questionnaire Plan—Tracking Study**

Decisions: We will decide which product messages, if any, need to be adjusted to improve the effectiveness of the marketing campaign.

Information Needed	How to Ask the Question	How to Analyze the Data
Message Reception		
Find out whether customers are receiving our brand messages.	Please rate how well each statement describes each brand on a scale of 1 to 5, where 1 means "Does not describe at all" and 5 means "Describes very well." Statement 1 Brand A 1 2 3 4 5 Brand B 1 2 3 4 5 Brand C 1 2 3 4 5 Statement 2 Brand A 1 2 3 4 5 Brand B 1 2 3 4 5 Brand C 1 2 3 4 5	Measure message association so we can correlate message association with previous purchase or intent to purchase.
Purchase History		
Measure purchase history.	Have you yourself purchased Product X within the past 30 days? ☐ Yes ☐ No *(If Yes)* In the past 30 days, how many units of Product X have you yourself purchased? ☐ 1 ☐ 2 ☐ 3 ☐ 4 or more	See if those who associate our messages with our brand are more likely to have purchased our brand.
Purchase Intention		
Measure purchase intention.	How likely are you to buy Product X in the next 30 days? ☐ Definitely will buy ☐ Probably will buy ☐ May or may not buy ☐ Probably will not buy ☐ Definitely will not buy	See if those who associate our messages with our brand are more likely to intend to purchase our brand.

itors. This will tell you whether the messages are getting through to customers and whether they are differentiating your brand from the competition. You will also determine whether associating these messages with your brand is correlated with increased purchasing rates and an increased intention to purchase the brand. Figure 4.7 provides an example of how we would use the Questionnaire Plan for a tracking study.

In this example, the information needed cannot be obtained from a single question. We need to measure message association *and* purchase history and purchase intention to see whether the messages are affecting what people buy or intend to buy.

These are rather simple examples of how to use a Questionnaire Plan to plan your analysis. In most questionnaires, there are many more questions and useful ways to analyze the data. But using a written Questionnaire Plan will undoubtedly help you with the process of designing your questionnaire.

Figure 4.8   **Analysis Planning: The Three Things You Do with Data**

Estimate Population Values	Look for Differences	Look for Associations

There are three things you can do with the data you collect with a questionnaire:

1. Estimate a population value
2. Look for a difference between groups
3. Look for an association between things

What you plan to do with the data is more formally referred to as analysis planning.

Quite often, questionnaires are used to *estimate population values*. You might want to know the average amount of alcohol consumption among college students. You might want to know the percentage of new mothers who say they intend to buy a new brand of baby formula. Or you might want to estimate how many people between the ages of twenty-five and sixty suffer from depression.

Some questionnaires look for *differences*. You might look for differences between males and females on a variety of topics to see whether it makes sense to develop a different ad campaign for each gender. Or you might look for differences in the product evaluations of various demographic groups to determine the best target audience.

Finally, some questionnaires are often designed to look for *associations*. For example, you might want to identify which demographic factors are associated with interest in a new product. You might be interested in seeing what behavior is associated with poor glucose control among type 2 diabetics. Or you might wish to look for an association between voting intentions and attitudes toward public policies.

As you plan the questionnaire, think about whether you need to estimate a population parameter, look for differences between groups, or look for associations. This thought process will help you determine what kinds of questions you need to ask. Hopefully, keeping these categories in mind will make writing a Questionnaire Plan a little easier.

CHAPTER 5

Organize the Order of Questions

A Questionnaire Plan is a helpful way to determine the order in which you will collect the information throughout the questionnaire. This attention to the ordering of information collection is necessary if you are to avoid order bias and confusing respondents by jumping from topic to topic. It also helps you avoid asking difficult or sensitive questions too early in the questionnaire. Such questions can lead some people to drop out of the questionnaire.

This chapter and chapter 9, "Make Questions Unbiased," deal directly with the effect that each question has on the next question or set of questions. By using a Questionnaire Plan and being aware of how questions can affect each other, you will be in a better position to write an effective questionnaire.

Order Bias and Order Misunderstanding

There are two ways that questions can influence subsequent questions: order bias and order misunderstanding.

Order bias results when we order questions such that the first question influences the response to the second question and thereby leads to inaccurate responses to that second question. A classic example is to be found in a Gallup poll conducted in September 1997 (Moore, 2002). The poll asked the following two questions:

"Do you generally think Al Gore is honest and trustworthy?"

"Do you generally think Bill Clinton is honest and trustworthy?"

When asked about Al Gore first, 68 percent of respondents indicated that Al Gore was honest and trustworthy. However, when asked about Bill Clinton first, only 60 percent of respondents indicated that Al Gore was honest and trustworthy.

Understanding the question was not the problem. The problem was that the question about Bill Clinton affected responses to the question about Al Gore. The effect was not random but directional. It is a clear case of order bias.

Order misunderstanding occurs when respondents misunderstand a question because they bring forward the parameters of a previous question or set of questions. The transition from one question to the next, in other words, is not clear.

Consider the following two questions:

1. Did you, yourself, take an aspirin within the past 7 days?
2. How many vitamin bottles are in your household?

The first question asked about "you, yourself," while the second question did not make clear whether the question was still about you only or whether it referred to everybody in the household. Some respondents will answer for everyone in the household, while others will carry forward the mindset from the previous question and think only about themselves. The respondent misunderstands the second question because it does not clearly indicate who is being addressed.

The second question, in other words, did not do enough to establish its own mindset. The wording did not make it clear enough that the components of the question had changed. This is a clear case of order misunderstanding.

In cases of order bias, respondents *understand* the question but allow the first question to influence their response to the next question. In cases of order misunderstanding, some respondents don't understand the second question. The transition between the first and second questions is not clear enough.

Fatigue and Confusion

Order bias and order misunderstanding are direct ways that questions affect subsequent questions. There are also two indirect ways that questions can affect subsequent questions: fatigue and confusion.

When there are too many questions, respondents will tire and start giving answers without much thought and attention, reducing the quality of the information gathered; some may even drop out of the survey. If some questions are unclear, respondents will become confused about what is really being asked and may not provide accurate answers. Confusing questions can also reduce respondents' willingness to answer subsequent questions simply because they become frustrated.

Planning the order of information requests with a Questionnaire Plan helps reduce respondent fatigue and confusion.

Practical Issues

We can offer a few practical tips for ordering your questions to your best advantage. Start the questionnaire with easy questions that people are willing to answer. Hitting respondents early in the questionnaire with difficult or sensitive questions will increase dropout rates. Get them involved in the questionnaire first before addressing issues that are difficult or sensitive. We also suggest using transition statements when the topic of the questionnaire changes abruptly to help avoid order misunderstanding.

Organizing the information you will ask of respondents makes a lot of sense. There are just too many ways in which questions can affect one another. And the people answering the strings of questions in surveys have the difficult challenge of understanding what you are really asking about and coming up with accurate answers. The clearer you can make that journey for them, the better.

Questionnaire Planning #4: Organize the Categories of Information You Will Collect in the Questionnaire

Using the Questionnaire Plan to organize the categories of information you will collect in the questionnaire helps avoid order bias, order misunderstanding, fatigue, confusion, and high dropout rates.

Most questionnaires collect between three and seven categories of information.

A pricing study, for example, might collect information in the following five categories:

1. Screener
2. History of Purchase Behavior
3. Presentation of Product Concepts with Different Prices
4. Intended Purchase Given Price
5. Additional Demographic Questions

A customer-satisfaction study might collect these five information categories:

1. Screener
2. Overall Satisfaction
3. Measures of Competitors
4. Satisfaction with Specifics Associated with the Product or Service
5. Additional Demographic Questions

When companies advertise brands, they often use a survey to track the effectiveness of the advertisement. The tracking study can help them determine whether the advertisement is working, which will in turn help them decide whether the advertisement needs to be changed or adjusted to achieve its goals.

An advertising tracking study might have to collect as many as six major categories of information. Figure 5.1 shows how to use headings in the Questionnaire Plan to organize these categories. For this example, we have assumed that the goal of the advertisement is to increase awareness of the brand and that increasing awareness helps increase purchasing of the brand.

Figure 5.2 displays the three types of information we collect from respondents in questionnaires—history, perception and attitude, and intention. Figure 5.3 shows examples of questions that elicit one of these three types of information.

Organizing the categories of information to collect in the questionnaire has several important benefits. First, it helps the questionnaire-writing team stay focused on the information needed instead of just jumping in to write questions. Second, it helps arrange the flow of questions to make it easier for respondents to answer—and this minimizes fatigue and confusion. Third, it helps control order bias.

Figure 5.1 Questionnaire Plan—Advertising Tracking

Decisions: We will decide which product messages, if any, need to be adjusted to improve the effectiveness of the marketing campaign.

Information Needed	How to Ask the Question	How to Analyze the Data
Screener		
Select males between ages 50 and 70.		
Unaided Brand Awareness		
Determine who is aware of the brand, unaided.		
Find out if they recall the main message of the advertisement for the brand.		
Prompted Brand Awareness		
For those who do not mention the brand unaided, see how many recognize the brand name.		
Prompted Ad Recognition		
Determine how many recognize the advertisement.		
Action and Intention		
Determine how many have purchased the brand.		
Determine how likely they are to purchase the brand.		
Demographics		
Determine relevant demographic information.		

Figure 5.2   Three Types of Information You Collect from Respondents

History	Perception & Attitude	Intention

As you plan your questionnaire, it is useful to think about the following types of information that can be collected from respondents. Any question you might ask always falls into one of these three types:

History
Perception and attitude
Intention

The first type is *history*. You ask people what they recall doing in the past. You might ask, "In what year did you buy your washing machine?" "What was the first brand of computer you owned?" and so on. You might ask physicians questions about the number of patients they have treated, the number using certain drug therapies, and the brands prescribed.

The second type is *perception and attitude*. Perception is simply what people believe about something, while attitude is the value—positive or negative—they put on that belief. The statement "I believe IBM is a big company" is a perception. The statement "I like big companies because they contribute to society" indicates an attitude. In questionnaires, you ask people to share their perceptions about and attitudes toward products, political issues, customer service, companies, and so on.

The third type is *intention*. In most research, you want to use the results to predict what people will do in the future. Will people buy this product? What features do you need to add or delete to increase purchases? Will customers recommend your service to a friend?

While it is relatively easy to measure what respondents say about their intentions, it is difficult to understand and predict how those intentions will result in real behavior in the marketplace. Companies that do this best have extensive databases of studies of intention and measurements of actual marketplace performance.

Figure 5.3   Sample Questions for Three Types of Information

History	• During your most recent stay at the Merlin Hotel, how many times did you order room service, if any? • In the past 30 days, how many times have you, yourself, mowed your lawn? • As best you can remember, which of the following brands of shampoo have you, yourself, used to wash your hair in the past month?
Perception & Attitude	• Please rate your satisfaction with your most recent stay at the Merlin Hotel. • Do you believe that your neighbors should use chemical pesticides in their yards? • Which of these two brands would you say gave you the most lather when you used them?
Intention	• How likely are you to select the Merlin Hotel on your next visit to Charleston? • How likely are you to purchase a new lawn mower before the end of next summer? • If the price of this brand was $4.95, how likely would you be to purchase it the next time you needed shampoo?

Knowing that there are three types of information will help you organize your questionnaire in a way that makes sense to respondents. Ask yourself questions like:

- What is it about the respondent's history that will help us make this decision?
- Which are the key perceptions and attitudes we need to measure?
- What will people do in the future with our product or service?
- Which perceptions and attitudes are associated with the intent to use our product or service?
- What kinds of historical behavior are associated with interest in our product or service?

In subsequent guidelines we will talk about organizing the flow of questions in a way that make sense to respondents. For now, just being aware of the fact that there are only these three types of information will make writing a questionnaire easier and more effective.

Please note that each of these types of information may comprise several questions that you would want to group together in the survey. Accordingly, when you use Questionnaire Planning #4 and organize the categories of information in the questionnaire, you may find you have more than one category for attitude and perception. You might, for example, ask respondents about their attitudes toward their company, and then later ask them about their attitudes toward a set of new policies at the company.

Questionnaire Planning #5: Do Not Begin the Questionnaire with Difficult or Sensitive Questions

Two of the more difficult aspects of survey research are getting respondents to agree to take the survey and keeping them in the survey once they start. Finding respondents is costly. Getting them to take the survey is costly. Having respondents terminate the survey not only costs money but also biases the data. One way to reduce cost and bias is to keep respondents in the survey once they agree to respond to the questionnaire.

Difficult questions and questions that people find sensitive and are reluctant to answer—for whatever reason—cause some respondents to terminate the survey. Take special care not to begin any questionnaire with such questions.

Difficult Questions

Difficult questions can take many forms. Here is a classic example of a difficult question:

Q: Please tell us why you chose Ramis College over the state university.

For many people, open-ended questions like this are difficult. Explaining why they made a particular choice is challenging. If you need to collect this kind of information, it would be better to save it for the latter part of the questionnaire. As we said in chapter 2, "Qualitative versus Quantitative Research," you will gain greater insight into this issue with a qualitative approach.

Here is another question that would not be a good candidate for the first question in a survey:

Q: Please rate our performance on each of the following criteria. Please use the scale below, where 1 = poor and 7 = excellent.

	Poor						Excellent
	1	2	3	4	5	6	7
Cleanliness	○	○	○	○	○	○	○
Service	○	○	○	○	○	○	○
Food quality	○	○	○	○	○	○	○
Check-in	○	○	○	○	○	○	○
Room service	○	○	○	○	○	○	○
Bed comfort	○	○	○	○	○	○	○
Parking	○	○	○	○	○	○	○

This question is too detailed to serve as an initial question. Starting off with a simpler question would make things easier for respondents.

Although these two examples may not seem difficult to the questionnaire writer, they are for some respondents—sometimes so difficult that they decide not to take the survey. Start off with easy questions. Once people have answered a few easy questions, they are at least partially invested in finishing the questionnaire and more likely to answer difficult questions later.

Sensitive Questions

It's generally a good policy to avoid starting with questions that people are reluctant to answer. There are a whole host of topics that people are reluctant or unwilling to discuss. These include obvious things such as sexuality, drug usage, alcohol usage, and other emotionally loaded topics. Other topics might not appear sensitive to some people but are indeed sensitive to others. These include age, income, the number of times people have been married, and whether they pay alimony, to name a few.

The key is to avoid addressing sensitive issues at the beginning of the questionnaire. If you must collect sensitive information, do so later in the questionnaire after your respondents have some investment in finishing it.

If you must ask for sensitive information early in the questionnaire, make the question as general as possible to avoid causing respondents to drop out early. As an example, suppose you need to ask for respondents' age in order to screen people into the study. Let's say you need people between the ages of 30 and 64.

The following three questions might seem like obvious choices but in fact ask for more specific information than you require:

Q: What is your age? _____
Q: In what year were you born? _____
Q: Which of the following categories best represents your age?
  ☐ Under 21
  ☐ 21-30
  ☐ 31-40
  ☐ 41-50
  ☐ 51-64
  ☐ 65+

Instead, why not just ask:

Q: Are you between the ages of 30 and 64?
    ☐ Yes
    ☐ No

Or ask:

Q: What is your age?
    ☐ Under 30
    ☐ 30 to 64
    ☐ 65+

This way, people are less likely to terminate the survey. If you need more detail about age, ask for it at the end of the survey after respondents have completed most of the questions.

It's difficult to anticipate the full range of topics that might be sensitive for any given group. As always, we urge you to do qualitative research first and to take note of topics that might be considered sensitive. You may also pick up on sensitivities to certain questions when you pretest the questionnaire.

In summary, avoid asking difficult or sensitive questions early in the questionnaire. Such avoidance will help you retain respondents, provide more accurate data (by avoiding bias associated with people dropping out), and prevent the unnecessary costs associated with people terminating the survey.

Questionnaire Planning #6: Organize the Order of Questions to Avoid Order Bias

While writing the Questionnaire Plan and laying out the order of categories and types of information to collect, you will need to think about order bias. In chapter 9 we offer specific guidelines for making individual questions unbiased. Here we address the potential biasing effect of one question on another.

"Figure 5.4: Questionnaire Plan—Advertising Tracking for Awareness" provides a good example for talking about order bias. One of the measures of advertising success is unaided awareness of a brand. For example, say I asked you, "When you think of television sets, what brands come to mind?" You might say, "Sony, LG, Mitsubishi," and maybe several others. If we were advertising a new brand, we would want to know whether the unaided awareness of our brand was increasing because of our advertising.

Another measure of an advertising campaign's success is aided brand awareness. In the television example, you could *recall* only three brands. But you might *recognize* additional brands if you heard them. If I said, "Have you heard of the brand Toshiba?" you might say yes because although you could not recall the brand name, you recognized it when I mentioned it.

Clearly, you need to measure unaided brand awareness (recall) before measuring aided brand awareness (recognition). Asking about aided awareness first would influence or bias your questions about unaided awareness.

Figure 5.4 shows how we organized the questionnaire to ask for unaided awareness before aided awareness.

Figure 5.4　　　　Questionnaire Plan—Advertising Tracking for Awareness

Information Needed	How to Ask the Question	How to Analyze the Data
Decisions: We will decide which product messages, if any, need to be adjusted to improve the effectiveness of the marketing campaign.		
Screener		
Select males between the ages of 50 and 70.	Are you between the ages of 50 and 70?	
Unaided Brand Awareness		
Determine who is aware of the brand unaided.	When you think about treatments for Condition X, what brands come to mind?	
	(IF YES) In the past month, have you seen or heard any advertising about Condition X?	
	What brand was the advertisement for?	
Find out if they recall the main message of the advertisement for the brand.	Thinking about the advertisement you saw or heard for [insert brand name], what was the main idea presented?	
	Where did you see or hear that advertising?	
Prompted Brand Awareness		
For those who do not mention the brand unaided, see how many recognize the brand name.	(IF BRAND NOT MENTIONED) Have you ever heard of Brand X for treating Condition X?	
Prompted Ad Recognition		
Determine how many recognize the advertisement.	Now I am going to read you a description of an advertisement. (READ AD).	
	Have you seen the advertisement I just described?	
	(IF YES) What is the brand being advertised?	

Action & Intention		
Determine how many have purchased the brand.	As a result of seeing the advertisement for _____, did you _____?	
Determine how likely they are to purchase the brand.	How likely are you to purchase this brand? ☐ Definitely will purchase ☐ Probably will purchase ☐ Might or might not purchase ☐ Probably will not purchase ☐ Definitely will not purchase	
Demographics		
Determine relevant demographic information.	In what year were you born?	
	Are you of Hispanic or Latino origin? ☐ Yes ☐ No	

The order of questions also matters in satisfaction research. You usually should ask about overall satisfaction before asking about satisfaction with specific aspects of the product or service. This is because asking about specific aspects of the product or service influences how people answer questions about overall satisfaction. Moving from general questions to more specific questions can often help in avoiding order bias.

Order bias is important to consider when setting up the categories of information you plan to collect, and when ordering the questions within those categories. Here's a good rule of thumb: When you are concerned that a question may influence the next question, consider reversing their order. If this arrangement does not seem to produce its own order bias, it may be the better way to order the questions.

How To Determine Whether Order Bias Exists: Do an Experiment

Often, we do not know whether our ordering of questions contains order bias. One way to test for order bias is to add an experiment to the survey when it is administered. You could split the sample and let half of the respondents see question A and then question B and let the other half see question B and then question A.

An example of this kind of testing for order bias is the study we mentioned earlier about the respective trustworthiness of Bill Clinton and Al Gore. Half of respondents were asked for their views on the honesty of Bill Clinton and then of Al Gore, while the other half were asked about the honesty of Al Gore and then Bill Clinton.

You will find many situations where you simply do not know if there is order bias. Experimenting when you administer the survey is always an option.

Questionnaire Planning #7: To Reduce Misunderstanding in a Sequence of Questions, Order Questions from the General to the More Specific

Within each category of information, it is important that questions flow in an order that makes it easy for respondents to think of the answers. Moving from general to more specific questions makes it easier for respondents by forming a pattern that facilitates their thinking of the answers.

Here is a set of questions from a survey of restaurant waiters.

Q1: Of those customers you personally served a meal to today, how many ordered beer with their meal? _____

Q2: Question 2. How many of the customers that you personally served a meal to today ordered an alcoholic beverage with their meal? _____

Q3: Question 3. Thinking about today only, how many customers did you personally serve a meal? _____]

This is what two respondents thought when trying to answer these questions.

Brad:	Graham:
For question three I am not sure if they just mean customers who also ordered alcoholic beverages or if they want me to include the people who did not have any alcohol.	I am not sure if question two means alcoholic drinks other than beer. They already asked me about the beer drinkers.

When a questionnaire appears to be illogically organized, it is harder for the respondent to answer.

Let's apply this guideline to this sequence of questions. Compare the original sequence of questions to the following improved sequence.

Improved Question Sequence:

Q1: Thinking about today only, how many customers did you personally serve a meal? _____

Q2: How many of the (INSERT NUMBER) customers that you personally served a meal did you also serve an alcoholic beverage? _____

Q3: Of those (INSERT NUMBER) customers you personally served an alcoholic beverage with their meal, how many had a beer? _____

The improved sequence goes from broader questions to more specific questions. It starts with a question about all the customers whom they served a meal, then those who ordered an alcoholic beverage with their meal, and finally, of those who ordered an alcoholic beverage with their meal, how many ordered a beer. This sequence of asking questions, moving from general to more specific, helps respondents understand what you are asking about.

Here is a sequence of questions from a survey of people with headaches.

Q1. How many headaches have you had in the past 30 days?
_____ number of headaches

Q2. Did you take any medicine for your most recent headache?
☐ Yes
☐ No

Q3. Did you see a doctor for your most recent headache?
☐ Yes
☐ No

Q4. How many of the [INSERT ANSWER FROM Q1] headaches you had in the past 30 days would you say were mild, moderate, and severe?
_____ Mild
_____ Moderate
_____ Severe

This sequence is a little awkward. It shifts from asking about the number of headaches over a 30-day time frame, to a couple of questions about a most recent headache, and then back to another question about headaches over a 30-day time frame.

Here is an improved version of this set of questions:

Improved Question Sequence:
Q1. How many headaches do you recall having in the past 30 days?
_____ number of headaches

Q2. As best you can remember, how many of the [INSERT ANSWER FROM Q1] headaches you had in the past 30 days would you say were mild, moderate, and severe?
_____ Mild
_____ Moderate
_____ Severe

Now we would like to ask you a few questions about your MOST RECENT headache.

Q3. Did you take any medicine for your most recent headache?
☐ Yes
☐ No

Q4. Did you see a doctor for your most recent headache?
☐ Yes
☐ No

Notice that we added a transition statement (see Questionnaire Planning #8 below) when we moved from asking about all headaches over the past 30 days to asking about respondents' most recent headache. This makes the questions easier for respondents to understand and, in turn, answer.

Remember that you will first organize your categories of information in the questionnaire. Then, within each category, you should move from asking for general information to asking for more specific information. This will not only make answering the questionnaire easier but will also reduce the chances that some respondents will make mistakes in their answers or just give up.

Questionnaire Planning #8: Use a Transition Statement If the Topic of Questions Will Change Abruptly

As you move from one category of information to another, it may be necessary to alert respondents to the change in the topic of conversation. This will help them clear their minds from the previous set of questions and move on to the new topic.

For example, after asking a series of questions about the entire family, let's assume you want to ask a set of questions about only the person taking the survey. Add the following transition statement to the questionnaire:

Now we are going to ask a few questions about you personally.

This will help ensure that respondents do not carry forward a family-oriented mindset from the previous sequence of questions.

Another situation that might benefit from a transition statement is moving from asking about past behavior to asking about future behavior. You might add the phrase:

Now we are going to ask some questions about what you might or might not intend to do in the future.

Another example comes from employee engagement and retention surveys. After asking a number of questions about the company, the questionnaire might move to a series of questions about the department where the employees work. A transition statement like this would help ensure that respondents know that the focus of the questions has changed:

We now need to ask you a few questions about your department.

Transition statements like these help respondents shift their focus from the previous set of questions to a new set of questions. The result will be more accurate answers.

PART 3. WRITE QUESTIONS

"Language is the source of misunderstandings."
—Antoine de Saint-Exupéry

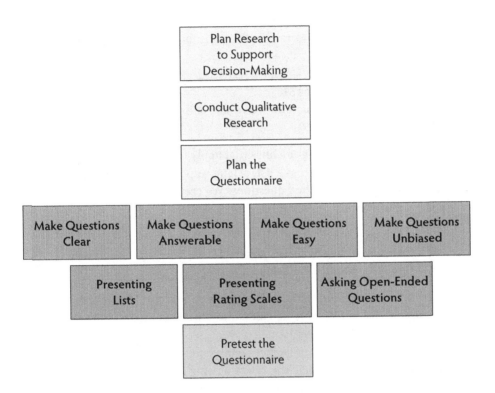

We cannot overemphasize the importance of planning the research and planning the questionnaire before you write the questions. If you have skipped parts 1 and 2 of this book, we caught you! Writing a questionnaire without knowing what decisions the research will support, identifying the information needed to make those decisions, and constructing a thoughtful plan for ordering your questions is like writing a book without an outline or writing a screenplay without a plot. To create an effective questionnaire, you need to have your house in order—with a Research Plan and a Questionnaire Plan in place—before you write your questions.

If you have been following the steps outlined in parts 1 and 2 of this book, you now have a Research Plan that states the decisions the research will support and the information needed to make those decisions. You have done enough qualitative research to understand how people think about the issues you are about to quantify with a questionnaire. You know what to measure and how to measure it. And you have a Questionnaire Plan that outlines the categories of information you need to collect and in what order. This provides a basic structure for the kinds of information you need and the order in which you will collect the information.

Now you are ready to start writing questions. In part 3, we'll present four basic guidelines for writing questions:

1. Make Questions Clear—Be precise and unambiguous. (Chapter 6)
2. Make Questions Answerable—Ask for information people have. (Chapter 7)
3. Make Questions Easy—Make questions less complicated to avoid tiring respondents. (Chapter 8)
4. Make Questions Unbiased—Make sure the wording does not influence responses. (Chapter 9)

In addition, we present guidelines that apply to three specific situations: asking respondents to select from a list, asking respondents to rate something on a scale, and asking open-ended questions. We created three additional chapters for these guidelines.

1. Presenting Lists (Chapter 10)
2. Presenting Rating Scales (Chapter 11)
3. Asking Open-Ended Questions (Chapter 12)

Writing an effective questionnaire is no easy exercise. The goal is to provide a framework along with specific guidelines for making the writing of questionnaires easier and more effective.

The four fundamental guidelines—make questions clear, answerable, easy, and unbiased—are ultimately the key to writing good questions. The guidelines for lists, scales, and open-ended questions represent additional special cases for ensuring that questions of these types remain clear, answerable, easy, and unbiased.

The best way to present guidelines is to first provide a sample question, ask what might be wrong with it, and share how two respondents interpreted and responded to the question. This inductive approach works well because it generates deeper understanding by allowing you to discover what might be wrong with the question and how it needs to be fixed before we introduce the guideline in detail.

One student said it best. She explained that this way of presenting the guidelines is like the way material is presented in school. You get a problem and try to solve it yourself. Then the answer key is provided to show what you may have missed.

Writing a questionnaire is an arduous task that has all sorts of pitfalls along the way. A questionnaire is, in a sense, a conversation in which all respondents—be there 300 or 3,000—need to understand each question and be able to give you the answer without much effort or bias. Unlike a live conversation, a questionnaire does not afford you the luxury of being there with each respondent to clarify any ambiguities. Therefore, your questions have to be written almost perfectly.

For that reason, questionnaire writing is at least as difficult as any other form of writing, if not more. The guidelines provided in these chapters will help you communicate better with each respondent. A better questionnaire provides more accurate data and, ultimately, supports better decision-making for your organization.

Finally, virtually all the questions you will attempt to write for your questionnaires will benefit from the application of several guidelines. Consider the following first draft of a question:

Q: How frequently do you go to the grocery store?
   ☐ Very frequently
   ☐ Frequently
   ☐ Neither frequently nor infrequently
   ☐ Infrequently
   ☐ Very infrequently

This seemingly simple question contains several significant pitfalls. First of all, it lacks a unit of measurement; frequency is a vague term that has a different meaning to different people (Clear #1). The question also lacks the time frame in which you want people to recall the information you need (Answerable #1).

Q: In the past 30 days, how many times have you gone to the grocery store? ___

This is better. We have replaced "frequency" with "how many times" (a countable concept) and added a time frame of 30 days. Now, we need to clarify the referent of "you" (does it refer to the generic you or to the respondent?) (Clear #4) and label the answer box to make clear that we want a single number, not a range of numbers (e.g., 5–10) or a text response like "ten" or "a lot."

Q: In the past 30 days, how many times have you, yourself, gone to the grocery store? _____ # times gone to grocery store

We also need to think carefully about the concept *grocery store* (Clear #3). Would we want respondents to include visits to gas stations or drugstores to pick up a few grocery items? What information do we really need (Questionnaire Planning #2)?

Q: In the past 30 days, how many times have you, yourself, gone to the grocery store to purchase groceries? *(Please do not include visits to gas stations or drugstores to pick up food items.)* _____ # times gone to grocery store

Most of the examples in this book illustrate one or two problems that could be fixed using only one or two guidelines. For learning purposes, that made the most sense.

When you write questionnaires from scratch, however, you will need to keep *all* of these guidelines in mind. Using all the guidelines associated with planning research, planning the questionnaire, and writing questions will help create a good questionnaire. In part four, we will explore the final step—using the guidelines associated with pretesting—in making the questionnaire truly excellent.

The Anatomy of a Question

Using consistent terminology for the various parts of questions in questionnaires makes it easier to discuss them. Note that not every question will include all of these parts. Below are the terms we will use and their definition:

Transition statement: what you say to make sure respondents understand that the focus of the next set of questions is different from that of the last set.

Introductory statement: what you say to prepare the respondent for the question.

Question stem: the initial question statement.

Answer choices: a list of possible answers or responses.

Question instructions: directions such as *"Check one only."*

The question: all the components of the question (question stem, instructions, answer choices, etc.), not including the transition statement. Since transition statements appear between two sets of questions, they are technically not part of either set.

Here are three examples:

Transition Statement	Now we are going to ask you some questions about <u>your NEXT</u> home purchase.
Question Stem	**If you were selecting a house that had both a living room and a family room, which <u>one</u> of the following would you prefer?**
Question Instructions Answer Choices	*(Check one only.)* ☐ Equal sized living room and family room ☐ Larger living room and smaller family room ☐ Smaller living room and larger family room ☐ A great room combining the living room and family room into one

Question Stem	**Which of the following best describes your opinion of the movie you just saw?**
Question Instructions Answer Choices	*Please select one number from 1 to 5:* Very poor 1 2 3 4 5 Very good

Introductory Statement	We want to understand what we can do to improve the swim and tennis club, so your perspective is very important to us.
Question Stem	**Please tell us why you chose to cancel your membership to the swim and tennis club.**
Question Instructions Answer Box	Please be as specific as possible. _____

When writing questions, it can help to use **bold**, CAPITAL LETTERS, <u>underlining</u>, and *italics* to emphasize key words and phrases in the question. This is particularly important when something in the question, such as the time frame, has changed from that of a previous question. We discuss this issue in chapter 6 in Clear #8.

Make Questions Clear

"Everything is vague to a degree you do not realize till you have tried to make it precise."

—Bertrand Russell

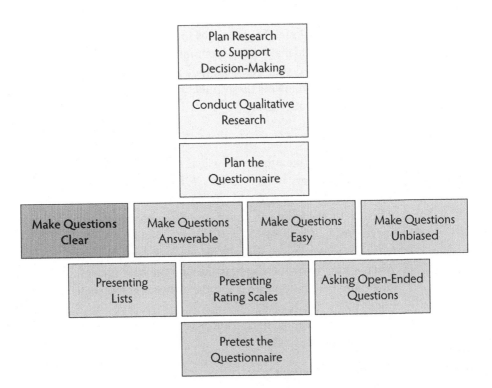

Communication always has its challenges. How often have you thought you said something clearly to a family member or a coworker, only to find out later that they thought you meant something else? Even when talking face-to-face with the full benefit of cues such as tone of voice, inflection, facial expression, and context, we can still miss the true meaning of what another person intended to say.

Conversation provides an opportunity to seek clarification. If someone asks if you have a subscription to the *Wall Street Journal*, you could ask, "Do you mean me personally or my family?" If someone asks, "What percent of the time do you read e-mails?" you could respond, "Do you mean at work, at home, or both?" You might also inquire, "Do you mean percent of a twenty-four-hour day or percent of my work week?" You can move toward an understanding of what the question means.

Now imagine yourself taking a questionnaire. You are answering questions written by a team of people you've never met whose objectives you'll never know. They are asking about your experiences and views about topics such as health care, parenting, your stay at a hotel, or your decision to cancel your cable service. They don't know much about your situation or your point of view. How can they even know how to frame the questions?

A questionnaire is a conversation with hundreds or maybe thousands of respondents that contains no opportunity for rephrasing a question or asking for clarification. You have to get the questions in the questionnaire right the first time.

This chapter provides eight guidelines for helping you clearly define the information you need and making sure your questions are clear and unambiguous. When respondents read your question, they should be able to say, "I know what they want from me." Following these guidelines will help you communicate with respondents and get better data.

Eight Guidelines to Make Questions Clear

1. State the unit of measurement. (Clear #1)
2. Use the vocabulary of respondents. (Clear #2)
3. Use precise words and phrases. (Clear #3)
4. When using the word *you*, make sure the respondent knows to whom you are referring. (Clear #4)
5. Make sure the question is really asking only one question. (Clear #5)
6. When asking for percentages, make sure the base is clear. (Clear #6)
7. Make sure the question stem and the answer choices match each other. (Clear #7)
8. Use bold, underlining, italics, and/or capitalization to highlight key words and phrases. (Clear #8)

Clear #1: State the Unit of Measurement

Here is a question from a survey of women who just gave birth to a healthy baby at a hospital:

Q: How long was your baby in the hospital?

Some women answered in days, while others answered in inches!

How long is not a unit of measurement with a precise meaning. You need to state in the question a unit of measurement that will have the same meaning for all respondents. If you want to ask about days, ask "How many days was your baby in the hospital?" If you want to ask about inches, ask "How many inches long was your baby at the time of birth?"

Here is another question that might seem clear and straightforward:

Q: When did you get married? _____

Here is what two people thought when they read the question:

Ted:	Dana:
My first thought is "before I was ready!" My gosh, I got married in high school.	*Do they want the month, day, and year, or just the year, or my age? I'll just put down my age.*

A question about marriage can bring forth all sorts of associations. Ted's first thought was more about being unprepared for marriage. Dana wondered if they wanted the day, month, and year, or maybe just her age. Specifying a unit of measurement will clarify how respondents should answer.

Let's assume we wanted the *year* a respondent got married:

Improved Question A:

Q: In what year did you get married?
_____ Year

Now let's assume we wanted a respondent's *age* when he or she got married:

Improved Question B:

Q: What was your age when you got married?
_____ Age

The unit of measurement is often unclear in questions about frequency, like this one:

Q: How frequently did you visit the post office in the past 30 days?
- ☐ Very frequently
- ☐ Frequently
- ☐ Somewhat frequently
- ☐ Infrequently
- ☐ Very infrequently

Here is what two respondents thought when they read the question:

Ryan:	Miriam:
I had to go there three times this month because they lost my package. That's too many times. I'll say "very frequently."	*I go there once a week to pick up stuff from my husband's post office box. That's just our system, so I guess that means "somewhat frequently."*

In this question, the word *frequently* is not well defined. Miriam actually goes to the post office more often than Ryan does, but their perspectives are different and so, in turn, are their answers, which are impossible to interpret. Stating a specific unit of measurement (in this case, the *number* of visits) will make the question clear.

Improved Question:

Q: How many times did you visit the post office for any purpose in the past 30 days?

_____ # times visited post office in past 30 days

This version of the question does not ask respondents to interpret what we mean by *frequently*.

Please note that when you ask for a unit of measurement, you usually need to specify a time frame that people can remember (see chapter 7, Answerable #1). Most questions require the use of more than one guideline.

Asking about Frequency Requires Respondents to Do Two Things

Asking someone to tell us how frequently they went to the post office requires them to recall first *how many times* they went to the post office in that time frame, and then translate that answer into a level of frequency. Essentially, this is asking them to do two things in one question. It is like saying, "How many times did you go to the post office in the past 30 days? And what frequency estimate would you attach to the number of times you went to the post office?" As you will see later, this is in clear violation of guideline Clear #5.

Here is a question given to physicians about discussing side effects for a particular drug for asthma:

Q: When you start patients on albuterol for the first time, how often do you personally discuss the possible side effects?
☐ Very often
☐ Somewhat often
☐ Not very often
☐ Not often
☐ Never

Dr. Davis:
I always discuss side effects when patients start on albuterol, but I've started only two patients on albuterol in the past few weeks, so I guess the answer is "not very often."

Dr. Marler:
I've started only two patients on albuterol in the past month, but I always discuss side effects. I assume that is what they are after, so my answer is "very often."

These two respondents had different ways of interpreting *how often*. Although Dr. Davis always discusses side effects when she starts patients on albuterol, she answered "not very often" because her frame of reference was all the patients she had seen in the past few weeks. Dr. Marler also always discusses side effects when starting a patient on albuterol. He answered "very often" because his frame of reference was only the patients he had started on albuterol, not all the patients seen in the past month. Even though they had started the same number of patients on albuterol and always discussed the side effects, their answers were different and the data were useless.

Specifying a unit of measurement will improve this question. Let's assume we wanted to know the frequency of discussions about side effects when the doctor starts a patient on albuterol.

Improved Question:

Q: Thinking of the last 10 patients you started on albuterol, with how many of these 10 patients, if any, did you personally discuss possible side effects?
_____ Number of patients

Before you write a question, ask yourself what unit of measurement you really need. Then consider the time frame in which respondents could recall the information you need, and that gives you the data you want.

Related Guidelines

Clear #1	Answerable #1
State the unit of measurement.	State time frames in which people can recall the information you need.

These guidelines are often used together to make a question clear and answerable. Instead of asking someone how frequently they have visited the post office, you have to ask for *a specific unit of measurement* over a *time frame that people can remember.* So ask about the *number of times* respondents have visited the post office over *the past 30 days,* if that is what they can remember. We discuss additional guidelines for making questions answerable in chapter 7.

Units of Measurement

Questions that begin with phrases like *how frequently* and *how often* fail to specify a unit of measurement. They also tend to ask people to calculate some sort of number and then interpret where that number falls on the frequency scale.

Other terms that fail to specify a unit of measurement include *regularly* and *usually.* Asking someone if they regularly read the newspaper or if they usually eat dinner at home gives you data that you can't interpret. Each respondent has her or his own interpretation of what is regular or usual.

Think about the unit you want to measure and ask for that unit of measurement. Just make sure you also specify a time frame.

Here are some specific units of measurement:

- How many days
- How many hours
- How many months
- How many years

Here are some common question openers that lack a unit of measurement:

- How much time
- How often
- How frequently
- How long
- Do you regularly
- Do you usually

Clear #2: Use the Vocabulary of Respondents

The following question appeared in a survey sent to patients discharged from a county hospital that serves as the major treatment center in the county for people with no insurance.

Q: When you left the hospital, did someone from the accounting department tell you that your treatment was pro bono?
☐ Yes
☐ No

Here are the reactions of two patients:

Tristan:	Anna:
They told me it was my gall bladder. I better put no. I am glad it was free because I have no money.	*No, they didn't tell me that. They just said that I didn't owe anything.*

Clearly, these people did not understand the question.

Learn the respondents' vocabulary during qualitative research before you write a questionnaire. When talking to respondents in interviews or focus groups, pay attention to how they understand concepts and the words they use to describe them. This will help you figure out how to ask the questions.

Let's suppose that, in this case, we had conducted qualitative research prior to drafting a questionnaire. Let's walk through three alternate ways of asking the question. Remember, we are trying to figure out whether they were told they had to pay for their treatment or not.

The first option eliminates the unfamiliar term *pro bono*.

Improved Question A:

Q: When you left the hospital, were you told that you had to pay for your treatment?
☐ Yes
☐ No

This looks like a better way to ask the question. Yet we were somewhat concerned that this way of asking the question contained bias. As you will see in chapter 9, Unbiased #3 tells us to make clear that either a positive or a negative answer is equally acceptable. The next two versions of the question accomplish that goal:

Improved Question B:

Q: When you left the hospital, were you told that you had to pay for your treatment or that you did <u>not</u> have to pay for your treatment?
☐ I was told that I had to pay for my treatment.
☐ I was told that I did <u>not</u> have to pay for my treatment.

Improved Question C:

Q: Which of the following statements best describes what you remember being told when you checked out of the hospital?
- ☐ I was told that I had to pay for my treatment.
- ☐ I was told that I did <u>not</u> have to pay for my treatment.
- ☐ I do not remember being told anything about paying or not paying for my treatment.

Without first pretesting these questions with respondents, we can't be sure which option will work best. They may both work pretty well. Notice the subtle difference between options B and C. Option B asks the respondent *what they were told*, whereas option C asks them *what they remember* being told. Option C is a little easier for respondents because it is not asking them to report the facts; rather, it is simply asking them what they remember.

Here is another question in a health survey for men:

Q: Have you ever been diagnosed with:

Dislipidemia	Yes	No
BPH	Yes	No
Hypertension	Yes	No

In the general population, many people do not know terms like *dislipidemia*, *BPH*, or *hypertension*. These terms come from the vocabulary of doctors or the pharmaceutical industry, not from ordinary people.

Let's revise this questionnaire with terms that probably make more sense to respondents:

Q: Improved Question: Have you ever been diagnosed with:

High cholesterol	Yes	No
Enlarged prostate	Yes	No
High blood pressure	Yes	No

The following question is from a survey of people working at a large company. It seemed reasonable to the people who wrote it.

Q: Did your company conduct any DAR advertising tests in 2009?
- ☐ Yes
- ☐ No
- ☐ Don't know

The problem is that respondents may not know what DAR stands for. Asking the question so that everyone taking the survey will understand it almost always requires spelling out the acronym.

Improved Question A:

Q: In 2009, did your company conduct Day After Recall (DAR) advertising tests in which recall of the brand name was measured 24 hours after the advertising appeared on television?
- ☐ Yes
- ☐ No
- ☐ Don't know

Using technical terms that people do not understand results in poor data. Make sure the answer choices match the point of view of the respondents.

These examples represent common mistakes. Using the vocabulary of respondents, not the vocabulary of your discipline or industry, is critical to getting quality data. Don't use industry jargon, acronyms, or vocabulary at a higher level than is necessary.

To use the vocabulary of respondents, you will need to do qualitative research before writing a questionnaire. This is only way to understand the words people use and how they think about the issues. At a later stage, when you pretest the questionnaire, you can fine-tune the wording of the questions to match the vocabulary of respondents.

Clear #3: Use Precise Words and Phrases

Even when you use the vocabulary of respondents, questions still may not be clear.

Consider this question sent to households about trash:

Q: Who in your home handles trash in your home? (*Please check one only.*)
   ☐ Me
   ☐ Spouse or partner
   ☐ Child(ren) under 18 years of age
   ☐ Cleaning service/housekeeper
   ☐ Other adult living in the home

Here is what two respondents thought when they read the question:

Ellen:	Craig:
We don't have a cleaning service, but we all put stuff in the trash, so I have to check all of these possible answers except one.	*What do they mean by* handle? *Do they mean who empties the trash or takes it outside to the trash bin? I have no idea what to say.*

The problem with this question is that respondents do not know what is meant by "handles trash." Does the phrase refer to the person who puts trash in the trash can, who takes the trash to the outside bin, who takes the trash out to the street for pickup, or something else? In this context, the word *handle* is unclear and open to varied interpretations.

Let's make an assumption about what information is needed to write an improved version:

Improved Question:

Q: Who in your home is the one person most likely to take the trash from your home to some outside place to be taken away?
   ☐ Me
   ☐ Spouse or partner
   ☐ Child(ren) under 18 years of age
   ☐ Cleaning service/Housekeeper
   ☐ Other adult living in the home
   ☐ No one person does it most often

This version more clearly describes the information we want.

Here is another question from a survey for business owners:

Q: How many customers do you have?

_____ # customers

Many business owners would find it hard to answer this question because the term *customers* can have many definitions. Are they supposed to count everybody who walks into the store or only people who make a purchase? What's the time frame? Is it for this year only? Are they supposed to consider both retail customers and businesses they might have as key accounts? Is a customer someone who has ever purchased their product or service, someone who will likely repurchase it, someone who has purchased it within the past 6 months, or what? As you can see, there are many ways to define the term *customers*.

This question can be clarified by defining what is meant by *customers* and by specifying a time frame, as we learned in Answerable #1. We will use two different definitions—one focused on who has purchased products or services and the other on who has visited the store.

Improved Question A:

Q: How many customers have purchased any products or services from your company in the past 5 days?

_____ # customers who have purchased any products or services from our company in the past 5 days

Improved Question B:

Q: How many customers have visited your store in the past 5 business days, whether or not they bought anything?

_____ # customers who have visited our store in the past 5 business days

You can also use question instructions to help define a question's terms. Here is an example from the American Community Survey from the U.S. Census Bureau. This question follows other questions about a person living in the household.

Q: Has this person ever served on active duty in the U.S. Armed Forces, military Reserves, or National Guard? *Active duty does not include training for the Reserves or National Guard, but DOES include activation, for example, for the Persian Gulf War.*
☐ Yes, now on active duty
☐ Yes, on active duty during the last 12 months, but not now
☐ Yes, on active duty in the past, but not during the last 12 months
☐ No, training for Reserves or National Guard only
☐ No, never served in the military

The instructions for this question define what is meant by the term *active duty*. We know that the U.S. Census Bureau takes great care to pretest their questions. This question was surely pretested with many respondents and written to ensure that people understood what *active duty* meant.

Using precise terms and phrases that we believe all respondents will interpret in the same way helps respondents understand what we want. They can answer our questions more easily and accurately, and we get better data. When terms and concepts are not defined clearly, respondents' answers will be based on varied interpretations, and we will end up with data that is, as statisticians say, full of noise or error and therefore flawed.

Defining terms is certainly one of the biggest challenges for questionnaire writers. As Jean Converse points out in *Survey Questions: Handcrafting the Standard Questionnaire*, we can take pains to define the term *family* as anyone living in the household or the term *neighborhood* as people living within three blocks of your home, but some respondents will still use their own definitions of such terms. The best we can do is to make our terms precise, knowing all the while that perfection is unattainable.

Avoid Using Vague Modifiers

Questionnaire writers are often tempted to use vague words that, although commonly used in conversation, do not have precise meanings. Be careful about using these types of modifiers.

Here is a question we saw in a questionnaire:

Q: Do you regularly read the newspaper?
☐ Yes
☐ No

The problem with this question is that what *regularly* means is unclear to many respondents. Does it mean every day, or most days?

Here is another question with a vague term:

Do you generally exercise in the morning?
☐ Yes
☐ No

What does it mean to generally exercise? If you want to know how many times a person exercises in the morning, specify a time frame. Ask how many times in the past 7 days he or she has exercised in the morning.

We found the following question in a survey given to psychiatrists:

Thinking of your typical depression patients, for what percentage do you prescribe Paroxetine?

Psychiatrists do not know what is meant by "*typical* depression patients." The question would probably stump most respondents, and their answers would represent different interpretations of the term *typical*.

Related Guidelines

Clear #2	Clear #3
Use the vocabulary of respondents.	Use precise words and phrases.

Both of these guidelines explain how to communicate clearly with respondents. Clear #2 reminds us to use the words our respondents use. Avoid industry jargon, technical terms, and acronyms.

Clear #3 tells us that even when we use the vocabulary of respondents, the terms may still be ambiguous. The example "How many customers do you have?" makes that point clear. While respondents are familiar with the term *customers*, that word can have many meanings. Do we mean people who visited the store, or do we mean people who bought something? These two interpretations of the term result in very different answers!

Clear #4: When Using the Word *You*, Make Sure Respondents Know to Whom You Are Referring

This question may seem clear enough, but consider how these two respondents interpreted it differently.

Q: Which of the following magazines do you have a subscription to, if any? *(Please check all that apply.)*
 ☐ *Time*
 ☐ *Newsweek*
 ☐ *People*
 ☐ *The New Yorker*
 ☐ *Sports Illustrated*
 ☐ *Vogue*
 ☐ None of these

Reba:	Betsy:
My husband subscribes to Time *and* Sports Illustrated, *so I'll check those.*	*My husband subscribes to* Time *and* Sports Illustrated, *but I don't have any subscriptions, so I guess I should not check anything.*

Even a simple word like *you* can be ambiguous. Without clarification, some respondents may think it is singular and refers to them individually, while others may think it is plural and refers to them and their family, them and their company, and so on.

As this example demonstrates, respondents need your help defining *you*. Phrases such as *you personally* or *you, yourself* can make the intent more clear.

Let's apply this principle to our example:

Improved Question A:

Q: Which of the following magazines do you personally have a subscription to, if any?
 (Please check all that apply.)
 ☐ *Time*
 ☐ *Newsweek*
 ☐ *People*
 ☐ *The New Yorker*
 ☐ *Sports Illustrated*
 ☐ *Vogue*
 ☐ None of these

If we wanted the question to refer to the entire household, we might ask it this way:

Improved Question B:

Q: Which of the following magazines do you or someone else in your home have a subscription to, if any? *(Please check all that apply.)*
 ☐ *Time*   ☐ *Sports Illustrated*
 ☐ *Newsweek*   ☐ *Vogue*
 ☐ *People*   ☐ None of these
 ☐ *The New Yorker*

The word *you* is ambiguous not only for families but also for organizations. This question was given to business owners:

Q: Do you spend more than 1 hour a week talking to suppliers of cleaning products for your janitorial service business?
☐ Yes
☐ No

Jim:	Ava:
We sure do. I have a person on my staff that spends most of her time doing this, at least an hour a week, so the answer is yes.	*My staff spends well over an hour a week on that stuff, but I don't, so I'll say no.*

Depending on the information being sought, this question could be improved in various ways.

Improved Question A:

Q: Do you personally spend more than 1 hour a week talking to vendors of cleaning products for your janitorial service business?
☐ Yes
☐ No

Improved Question B:

Q: Do the people in your company collectively spend more than 1 hour a week talking to vendors of cleaning products for your janitorial service business?
☐ Yes
☐ No
☐ Don't Know

Here is an example from a survey that was given to physicians. Let's assume we determined in qualitative research that these types of physicians have a steady flow of patients from week to week and that the phrase *typical week* makes sense.

Q: In a typical week, how many HIV patients do you treat?
_____ # HIV patients

Some physicians in group practices will answer for all the physicians in the practice, while others will answer for themselves only. We can easily make this question clear.

Improved Question:

Q: In a typical week, how many HIV patients do you yourself treat?
_____ # HIV patients

The key is to be very clear about who is meant by the term *you*. Because of the various interpretations of the term, it is often necessary to use the phrases "you, yourself" or "you personally." If you have any reason to believe that some respondents might interpret "you" to include a group to which they belong, such as a family or a set of coworkers, then replace "you" with "you, yourself" or "you personally."

Clear #5: Make Sure the Question Is Really Asking Only One Question

Here is a question from a survey on a political issue:

Q: Do you think the government should provide tax incentives and reduce regulations to encourage small business growth?

John:	Beth:
Small businesses need tax incentives, but we still need regulations. So I am going to say NO.	*Small businesses need tax incentives, but we still need regulations. I agree with the first part of the question, so my overall answer is YES.*

These two respondents had identical reactions to the question, but they gave opposite answers because they had different ideas about how to deal with the word *and*. This question is really asking two questions—one about tax incentives and one about regulations.

Fixing this question is easy. Separating it into two questions will result in better data.

Improved Questions:

Q: Do you think the government should provide tax incentives to encourage small business growth?
☐ Yes
☐ No

Q: Do you think the government should reduce regulations to encourage small business growth?
☐ Yes
☐ No

Here is an example from a questionnaire given to people who had a company design and build a deck for their residential home:

Q: Would you recommend our company to your friends for the design or construction of decks?
☐ Definitely would not
☐ Probably would not
☐ Neutral
☐ Probably would
☐ Definitely would

Although it uses the word *or* rather than *and*, this question is also asking about two things—whether you would recommend the company to friends for the design of decks and whether you would recommend the company for the construction of decks.

The best way to solve these sorts of issues is to ask one question at a time.

Improved Questions:

Q: Would you recommend our company to your friends for the <u>design</u> of decks?
☐ Definitely would
☐ Probably would
☐ Neutral
☐ Probably would not
☐ Definitely would not

Q: Would you recommend our company to your friends for the <u>construction</u> of decks?
☐ Definitely would
☐ Probably would
☐ Neutral
☐ Probably would not
☐ Definitely would not

This two-question version will give the organization better information about how customers view the company and will help in deciding whether design or construction should be the focus of any improvements.

This example comes from an employee-satisfaction survey:

Q: How important are each of the following issues to you at our company? *Please use the scale below, where 1 = not important and 5 = very important.*
Commitment to learning and continuous improvement
Not important   1   2   3   4   5   Very important
Etc.

This is really two questions—one about the importance of commitment to learning and one about the importance of commitment to continuous improvement. The clue is the word *and*. Once again, there is a simple fix: just ask two separate questions:

Improved Question:

Q: How important are each of the following issues to you at our company?
Please use the scale below, where 1 = not important and 5 = very important.
Commitment to learning
Not important   1   2   3   4   5   Very important
Continuous improvement
Not important   1   2   3   4   5   Very important

These three examples show the most obvious way two questions are combined into one. The use of the words *and* and *or* are dead giveaways. But there are other, less obvious ways a question can ask more than one question. Let's look at a few examples where the second question being asked is not so obvious.

Q: Please indicate whether you agree or disagree with the following statement:
I am concerned about my health, so I often take vitamins.
☐ Agree
☐ Disagree

The problem with this question is that it contains two subjects: (1) I am concerned about my health and (2) I often take vitamins. It is quite possible to be concerned about one's health and not take vitamins, or to be unconcerned about one's health and take vitamins.

It would be better to ask about health concerns and taking vitamins separately. Improved Questions:

Q: How concerned are you about your health? *Please use the scale below, where 1 = Not at all concerned and 5 = Very concerned.*

Not at all concerned   1   2   3   4   5   Very concerned

Q: Thinking about the past 30 days, about how many of those days did you take vitamins?

_____ Number of days I took vitamins in the past 30 days

Here is a question from a survey one of us received after staying at a hotel in New York City:

Q: For each item below, please tell us if we met your expectations.
1 = Less than expected   2 = As expected   3 = Better than expected

Friendliness of front desk staff	1 2 3
Efficiency of check-in	1 2 3
Room cleanliness	1 2 3
Comfortable bed	1 2 3

I took the questionnaire, and most of my responses were "As expected." My colleagues had told me the hotel was excellent, and I thought it was excellent, so it met my expectations.

Within a week I received a call from the manager of the hotel, who wanted to know what went wrong and how they could improve their performance. I told her nothing had gone wrong. I expected excellence, and everything was excellent. Therefore, their performance met my expectations!

The problem with this question is that it is really asking for two pieces of information. It is asking respondents to rate their experience at the hotel and to rate their experience relative to their expectations.

If I had expected the place to be terrible and it was only somewhat terrible, I would have had to say that my experience was "better than expected." In my case, I had expected the place to be great and it was great, so it simply met my expectations.

This question can be clarified by asking for each piece of information separately. Below is one way to split this question into two questions.

Improved Questions:

Q: As best you can remember, how did you expect us to perform on the following items prior to arriving? *Please use the scale below, where 1 = poor and 5 = excellent.*

	Poor				Excellent
	1	2	3	4	5
Friendliness of front desk staff	○	○	○	○	○
Efficiency of check-in	○	○	○	○	○
Room cleanliness	○	○	○	○	○
Comfortable bed	○	○	○	○	○

Q: Now please tell us how we performed. *Please rate our performance using the scale below, where 1 = poor and 5 = excellent.*

	Poor				Excellent
	1	2	3	4	5
Friendliness of front desk staff	○	○	○	○	○
Efficiency of check-in	○	○	○	○	○
Room cleanliness	○	○	○	○	○
Comfortable bed	○	○	○	○	○

This would at least tell the hotel staff directly how they performed. They could also compare the performance scores to their customers' original expectations.

Questions that contain more than one question are often referred to as "double-barreled" questions. Make sure each of your questions is really asking only one question. Sometimes the second item in the question is hidden or not obvious. As you gain experience writing questionnaires and following this guideline, you will become quite adept at spotting double-barreled questions.

Appropriate Use of *Or*

As we have seen, it's important to be careful about using the words *and* and *or*. However, they do not automatically indicate a faulty question. Consider a question from the 2008 National Survey on Drug Use and Health:

Q: How old were you the <u>first time</u> you smoked part or all of a cigarette?

The survey researchers needed only their age when either the whole or part of a cigarette was smoked, so this is an appropriate use of the word *or*.

Here is a question from a survey of people who suffer from a medical condition that used the slash (/)to communicate a concept:

Q: Who did you talk to about this new treatment for migraine headaches? (Select all that apply)
- ☐ Friend
- ☐ Relative
- ☐ Doctor
- ☐ Pharmacist
- ☐ Nurse/Physician Assistant (PA)
- ☐ Nutritionist/Dietician

For the type of respondents that this survey went to, the use of the slash was probably helpful. Most people who suffer from migraine headaches probably don't know whether their nutritionist is a dietician or whether the dietician is actually supposed to be called a nutritionist. The slash in this case is used to say, "We're not sure what the person is actually called, so either name will do."

Clear #6: When Asking for Percentages, Make Sure the Base Is Clear

Percentages are a special kind of unit of measurement. Because they are often used in questionnaires and can generate flawed data, we have decided to treat them in a separate guideline.

Let's begin by looking at what can go wrong when asking for a percentage. This question comes from a survey given to technicians who install and repair office equipment for residential customers:

Q: Thinking of the past 5 business days, what percent of your time did you personally spend on installing new equipment for residential customers?

Joe:

I think I spent five hours doing new installations. I work at least fifty hours a week. That's about 10 percent.

Mike:

I spent about five hours doing new installations. Overall, I spend about twenty hours a week with residential customers doing new installations and repairs, so I guess five hours out of twenty is about 20 percent. Most of my workweek these days seems to be filling out paperwork and selling stuff—not installations or repairs.

Both of these respondents spent five hours on new installations, but they used a different base, or denominator, to compute the percentage. Joe assumed the percentage of time was to be based on his entire workweek of fifty hours, while Mike assumed the percentage of time was to be based only on the twenty hours a week he spends with residential customers.

Also note that Mike did not do the math properly. Five hours out of twenty is actually 25 percent! Don't make it your respondents' job to do division to come up with a percentage. Some calculations are harder than these. What is seven divided by thirty-three? It takes a little effort, or a calculator, to come up with the correct answer.

In many cases, another unit of measurement will do, like the number of hours spent installing new equipment.

Improved Question A:

Q: Thinking of the last 5 business days, about how many hours did you personally spend installing new equipment for residential customers?

_____ # hours

This version also defines the time frame as "the last 5 business days," which is clearer than "last week."

Both Joe and Mike would have said five hours, and that might have been enough information.

If we really need to know what percentage of their time is spent on new installations for residential customers, we could directly ask for the unit of measurement we wanted to use as the denominator. Suppose we wanted the percentage to be of all hours spent at the homes of residential customers. We could simply ask for the denominator first, and then ask for the numerator. We can have the computer calculate the percentage.

Improved Question B:

Q: Thinking of the last 5 business days, about how many hours did you personally spend at the homes of residential customers?

_____ # hours at homes of residential customers

Q: About how many of the (INSERT # HOURS FROM PREVIOUS QUESTION) hours did you personally spend on installing new equipment?

_____ # hours installing new equipment

Since we now have both the numerator and the denominator, the computer can calculate the percentage. Computers tend to do the math better than respondents do!

When considering a question that asks for a percentage, think carefully about whether another unit of measurement (e.g., hours, days, number of customers, etc.) would suffice. Also consider the education level of the people taking the survey. Some people are not clear on the concept of a percentage. You can also ask for the numbers you need to calculate the percentage rather than asking respondents to do that work.

There are, however, some situations where asking for percentages is desirable. These are usually situations where it is easier for respondents to provide a percentage as an estimate than to provide estimates for both the numerator and denominator. When you do ask for a percentage, be sure to make clear what the denominator is.

Let's look at a few examples.

Here is a question from a survey of physicians.

Q: What percent of your patients is on prescription lipid-lowering agents?

Here, it is far easier for the physicians to provide an estimate than it is to provide an exact number.

However, what group of patients constitutes the base? Some doctors might answer for all of their patients, some might answer for patients who have high cholesterol and might need a lipid-lowering agent, and others might answer for some other group of patients.

A better way to ask this question would be to make the base clear.

Improved Question:

Q: Thinking of all the patients you yourself have seen in the past 30 days, about what percent are on prescription lipid-lowering agents?

_____% on lipid-lowering agents

Assuming all you need is an estimate, this question is probably fine as is.

Here is another example:

Q: Thinking of all the customers who have come to your store in the past 30 days, about what percent were female?

_____% female customers

Providing this percentage would certainly be easier for respondents than providing an estimate of the number of total customers and the number of those customers that were female.

Here is a question given to technicians who install and repair air conditioning units:

Q: Thinking of the past 12 months, what is your best guess as to the percentage of new installations that required at least one follow-up repair?

_____% requiring at least one follow-up repair

Asking for the information this way may be fine. We have made the base clear.

Note how we establish the base. Starting the question with "Thinking of . . ." is a common way to clearly specify the base when asking for a percentage.

Stating a Base of Ten As a Way to Estimate a Percentage

One way to make the base clear is to start with a base of ten, as in the following question:

Q: Thinking of the LAST 10 TRIPS to the grocery store, on how many of these trips did you purchase milk?

___ # times purchased milk

This technique forces respondents to give a number between 0 and 10, which you can then use to estimate a percentage. It is also a way to make a question easier for respondents to answer.

Related Guidelines

Clear #6	Clear #5
When asking for percentages, make sure the base is clear.	Make sure the question is really asking only one question.

Asking for a percentage is really asking the respondent to do three things: determine the denominator, determine the numerator, and calculate a percentage. This is why asking for a percentage is challenging.

In a sense, Clear #6 is a special case of Clear #5. By making sure the denominator is clear, you are reducing the number of tasks the question is asking the respondent to perform.

Clear #7: Make Sure the Question Stem and the Answer Choices Match Each Other

Consider two respondents' interpretation of this question from a public health study:

Q: How likely are you to have a flu shot before the end of the year?
☐ Extremely interested
☐ Interested
☐ Slightly interested
☐ Not at all interested

Mari:	Jim:
I am interested but not likely to get the flu shot. Not sure how to answer this.	*Actually I am not at all interested, but my wife insists that I get one, so I will. I am going to be truthful and say I am not interested.*

The shift from "likely" in the question stem to "interested" in the answer choices is confusing. The data this question collects will not reveal how likely a respondent is to obtain a flu shot. We need to reword the answer choices.

Improved Question:

Q: How likely are you to have a flu shot before the end of the year?
☐ Definitely will have a flu shot
☐ Probably will have a flu shot
☐ Might or might not have a flu shot
☐ Probably will not have a flu shot
☐ Definitely will not have a flu shot

Here's an example from a social services study:

Q: Please tell us how much you liked the meal you had at the restaurant.
☐ Very satisfied
☐ Somewhat satisfied
☐ Neither satisfied nor dissatisfied
☐ Somewhat dissatisfied
☐ Very dissatisfied

The question stem asks about *liking* the meal, while the answer choices are distributed along a *satisfaction/dissatisfaction* scale.

Improved Question:

Q: Please tell us how satisfied or dissatisfied you were with the meal you had at the restaurant.
☐ Very satisfied
☐ Somewhat satisfied
☐ Neither satisfied nor dissatisfied
☐ Somewhat dissatisfied
☐ Very dissatisfied

Now the entire question makes sense.

Here is one more example:

Q: Please rate the extent to which you agree or disagree with the following statement.
I oppose capital punishment.

Strongly Disagree	Disagree	Neither agree nor disagree	Agree	Strongly Agree
1	2	3	4	5
○	○	○	○	○

Asking people to rate a statement like this on an agree/disagree scale introduces a mismatch between the question and the response scale. Respondents have to assess how much they do or do not oppose capital punishment and then convert that answer into a level of agreement or disagreement.

Here is an improved version of the question:

Q: Please rate the extent to which you favor or oppose capital punishment using the scale below. *Please check one box below.*

Strongly oppose	Somewhat oppose	Neither favor nor oppose	Somewhat favor	Strongly favor
1	2	3	4	5
○	○	○	○	○

When the question stem and the answer choices match each other, questions are clearer and easier for respondents to answer. Don't require respondents to perform mental gymnastics to figure out what you want.

Related Guidelines. You may have noticed a similarity between the following two guidelines:

Clear #7	**Clear #5**
Make sure the question stem and the answer choices match each other.	Make sure the question is really asking only one question.

When the question and the answer choices do not match, the question is really asking about two things. In the flu shot example, the question is asking them "how likely" they are to get a flu shot, but the answer choices are asking them "how interested" they are in getting a flu shot. These are two different questions!

If we follow Clear #5 and make sure the question is really asking only one question, then we will certainly make sure the question stem and the answer choices match each other. Clear #7 is really one way to make sure you follow Clear #5. Put another way, one way to make sure a question is really only one question is to have the question stem and the answer choices match each other.

Clear #8: Use Bold, Underlining, Italics, and/or Capitalization to Highlight Key Words and Phrases

When you talk to people, you can use your voice to emphasize particular terms and phrases. Obviously you can't do this in a written questionnaire. Other techniques are needed to draw attention to specific terms and phrases. Questionnaire writers use bold, underlining, italics, and/or capital letters. These techniques are particularly important when you want to be sure respondents understand the distinction between a new question and a previous set of similar questions or when you want to emphasize a key component of a question or answer choices.

Here is a question that follows a set of questions about the entire family:

The next few questions are about **only** your **oldest child**.
[Questions about the oldest child would then fall here]

In this case the questionnaire writers used bold to help respondents understand that the transition away from the entire family and to the oldest child.

Here is another example, which we will explore further in Easy #1. In this case, the questionnaire writers used capital letters to draw attention to the key components of the answer choices:

Q: Have you ever personally used the types of washing machines listed below to wash clothes?

A washing machine you load through a DOOR YOU OPEN IN THE FRONT of the machine

☐ Yes

☐ No

A washing machine you load through a LID YOU OPEN IN THE TOP of the machine

☐ Yes

☐ No

This example from the American Community Survey from the U.S. Census Bureau presents key terms in the instructions in full capitals:

Q: How many separate rooms are in this house, apartment, or mobile home?
Rooms must be separated by built-in archways or walls that extend out at least 6 inches and go from floor to ceiling.
INCLUDE bedrooms, kitchens, etc.
EXCLUDE bathrooms, porches, balconies, foyers, halls, or unfinished basements.
_____ Number of rooms

For the paper version of the questionnaire, the American Community Survey is using the approach of consistently bolding the question and offering instructions in italics. Key words are highlighted with capitalization. It is a very effective approach.

There is no consensus or standard on how to use bold, underlining, italics, and/or capitalization to make questions more clear. The key is to be consistent throughout the questionnaire.

CHAPTER 7

Make Questions Answerable

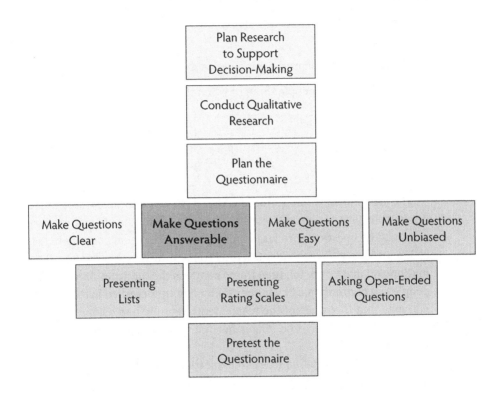

One of the most common mistakes in questionnaire writing is asking people questions they can't answer. Sometimes we ask people for information they simply do not have. Other times we ask for information from a time period that is impossible for people to recall. Or we ask questions that are appropriate for some respondents but not for others. Finally, we may ask people for information where "don't know" is a legitimate response but fail to offer it in the answer choices.

In this chapter we present five guidelines for asking questions that people can answer.

Five Guidelines to Make Questions Answerable

1. State time frames in which people can recall the information you need. (Answerable #1)
2. Don't assume regularity of behavior. (Answerable #2)
3. Don't ask people for information they simply don't have. (Answerable #3)

4. Screen respondents to make sure each question applies to them. (Answerable #4)

5. Make "Don't Know" an answer choice if some respondents simply don't know the answer to your question. (Answerable #5)

Answerable #1: State Time Frames in Which People Can Recall the Information You Need

The following question reveals an important principle for writing questionnaires:

Q: Have you experienced a computer crash?

Here is what two people thought when they took the questionnaire:

Alison:	Doug:
In my lifetime?	*It has been over a year since my computer crashed, so I'll say no.*

The problem with this question is that it provides no time frame. Alison wondered if she was supposed to consider her entire lifetime of computer use. Doug assumed the questionnaire was looking for a more recent computer crash.

You need to give respondents a time frame in which they can recall the information and make sure the time frame contains the information you need. While people can certainly recall whether their computer crashed in the past 24 hours, you may find that none of the respondents actually had a computer crash. You need the time frame to be longer but not so long that people can't recall the information.

Let's use this guideline to fix this question. First of all, let's assume that we know something about the frequency of computer crashes and the time frames in which people can remember a computer crash. A short time frame, like the past 30 days, may not give us enough respondents who had computer crashes. We will use a longer time frame.

Improved Question A:

Q: In the past 12 months, have you experienced a computer crash?

We might want to modify this question further by narrowing its scope to home computers and by more clearly defining the concept of a "computer crash." This change comes from Clear #3, "Use precise words and phrases."

Improved Question B:

Q: In the past 12 months, has your home computer had any problems that resulted in the need for a repair?

Another question that reveals the need to establish clear time frames comes from a questionnaire for psychiatrists.

Q: In the past 12 months, how many patients have you personally diagnosed with depression?

_____ # patients

A 12-month time frame may work well for recalling computer crashes. Other infrequent events, such as vacations and weddings, will support similarly long time frames. However, for busy psychiatrists who see many patients each week, recalling the number of patients they diagnosed with depression over a 12-month time frame is difficult, if not impossible. A shorter time frame would make it easier for psychiatrists to accurately recall and provide the information we need.

Let's use this guideline and shorten the time frame:

Improved Question:

Q: In the past 30 days, how many patients have you personally diagnosed with depression?

_____ # patients

This question will elicit much more accurate data because respondents will be able to recall the information in that time frame.

Making the Time-Frame Question Easier by Posing a Situation

Some questions about specific time frames are difficult. Consider the following two questions for doctors about prescribing a diabetes drug, metformin, and discussing its side effects:

Q: In the past 30 days, how many patients have you STARTED on metformin for the first time?

_____ # patients STARTED on metformin

Q: Of the (INSERT NUMBER) patients you started on metformin for the first time, with how many did you personally discuss the possible side effects?

_____ # patients discussed possible side effects

Recalling specific numbers of patients is challenging. An easier way to pose the question would be as follows:

Q: Thinking of the last 10 patients you started on metformin, with how many of these 10 patients, if any, did you personally discuss possible side effects?

_____ # of patients discussed possible side effects

This allows the respondent to give you an answer while thinking of the last 10 patients, not the last 30 days. This may be easier for respondents.

You can use this technique for many other situations, such as the last 5 trips to the grocery store or the last 3 times you filled your car up with gas.

We talk extensively about how to make questions easier to answer in chapter 8.

In some questions, the time frame implicitly covers an entire lifespan. For example, asking someone if they have ever been diagnosed with cancer or served in the military is appropriate. But for the majority of survey questions, specifying time frames is necessary, and you often need to make them short time frames.

Another way survey researchers can ask respondents to recall events is to ask them to make a generalization about a time frame. For example, you might ask about a *typical* or *average* week, month, or year.

Q: In a typical week, about how many times do you go to the grocery store?
Q: On average, how many times per month do you mow your lawn?

This method of asking about events assumes that the pattern of behavior—going to the grocery store or mowing the lawn—stays fairly constant. Is there such a thing as a typical week for the respondent who is being asked about going to the grocery store? If so, the question is probably fine.

What about mowing the lawn? Can respondents provide an average number of times they mow their lawn per month? For most climates, this would be a poor way of asking the question, since grass grows faster during certain times of the year. If you ask respondents to make a generalization about time frames, make sure in qualitative research that they can do it and that the question collects the information you need.

Another issue to consider is whether respondents understand terms like *typical* or *average*. For some, asking "on average" makes sense, but for others, "on average" may not be understood. This is an issue that needs to be worked out in qualitative research and pretesting.

Determine the information you need before deciding whether asking about an average or typical week, month, or year makes sense. If the information is consistent over time, respondents understand the term, and all you need is an estimate of what is indeed average or typical, you may be fine.

However, if you need the entire range of the number of times people go to the grocery store in a week, you will not want them to do their own averaging. You will want to know the highest and lowest numbers for that group. To get an estimate of the distribution—which includes busy weeks and not-so-busy weeks—asking about the past 7 days or the past 30 days would be a better way to get the information you need.

Unfortunately, many questionnaires ask questions with no time frame at all. Faced with this ambiguity, some respondents will think about a short time frame, others will think of a longer time frame, and others might consider their entire lifetime. What you can be sure of is that the data collected will be flawed. We also see plenty of questionnaires with time frames that are too long for people to accurately recall the information. As a general rule, find the shortest time frame that will deliver the information you need. Before writing the questionnaire, use qualitative research to find out what time frame makes sense to respondents. During pretesting, you can further explore how people came up with their answers to your questions. That will often reveal what time frames people actually use when they think about the events you ask them to consider.

Asking about Time Frames

Researchers often need to ask questions about events that took place over a week, month, or year. The problem is that these terms can be misinterpreted.

When you ask about the past month, some people will assume you mean the last calendar month, others will assume you mean the current month up until the moment they are taking the questionnaire, and others will assume the last four weeks. If you ask about a year, people may not know whether you mean the last calendar year, the most recent 12 months, or some other variation of a year.

Instead of this:	Ask this:
In the past week . . .	In the past 7 days . . .
In the past month . . .	In the past 30 days . . .
In the past year . . .	In the most recent 12 months . . . Or In the calendar year 2011 . . .

Define time frames clearly and concretely. That way you will avoid the problems associated with respondents' various interpretations of terms like *past week*, *month*, or *year*.

Answerable #2: Don't Assume Regularity of Behavior

This question states a time frame, yet it contains a subtler problem:

Q: Thinking of the past 12 months, how often have you baked a cake?
☐ Less than once a month
☐ 1 to 3 times a month
☐ More than 3 times a month

Cathy:	Carolyn:
I bake cakes when there is a birthday party. We've had three in my family this year, all in November. Does that mean three times a month?	*I bake one or two cakes every month during the school year. I don't bake any during the summer. I do pies during the holidays. I am not sure how to answer the question.*

This question assumes that people bake cakes on a regular schedule. But neither of these respondents bakes cakes according to the regular schedule offered by the question.

When you are not sure behavior is regular, ask the question in a way that does not assume regularity. Set a time period, such as a week, month, or year, and ask for the number of times the respondent performed the task in that time period.

Improved Question A:

Q: Thinking of the past 12 months, how many times did you bake a cake?
_____ # times baked cake in past 12 months

Improved Question B:

Q: Thinking of the past 12 months, about how many times did you, yourself, bake a cake?

_____ # times baked cake in past 12 months

Our revised question asked about the number of times the respondent baked a cake in the 12-month period and eliminated the idea of regularity of behavior from month to month.

Some people feel uncomfortable answering a question like this when they are unsure of the exact number. Therefore, in Improved Question B, we added the word *about* to let respondents know that their best guess is fine (Easy #5). We also helped clarify what we mean by *you* by changing it to *you, yourself*. Remember that some people will interpret *you* as meaning the whole family or some other group with which they identify (Clear #4).

Here is another question that incorrectly assumes regularity of behavior.

Q: Thinking of the past 12 months, how often have you traveled by air?
☐ Daily
☐ Weekly
☐ Monthly
☐ A few times
☐ Once
☐ Never

For many people, air travel does not follow a regular pattern. Here is an improved version of the question:

Q: Thinking of the past 12 months, about how many times have you, yourself, traveled by air?

_____ # times traveled by air in past 12 months

An early draft of the 2007 Complementary and Alternative Medicine Module for the National Health Interview Survey asked this question:

Q: On average, how much do you spend on vitamins and minerals per month?

The people pretesting the questionnaire found that not all respondents buy vitamins and minerals on a consistent schedule that allows for averaging. They recommended rewording the question without assuming regularity of behavior.
Improved Question:

Q: How much did you spend on vitamins and minerals in the past 30 days?

Unless you know that a behavior follows a consistent pattern, it is best to avoid asking respondents to make a generalization. Phrases such as *how often* and *on average* are tip-offs that you may be asking for a generalization that is not consistent from time period to time period. While some behaviors are somewhat regular, be sure you check this out when you do qualitative research before designing the survey and asking respondents to make a generalization. Chances are most behaviors do not follow a consistent pattern for all of your respondents.

Answerable #3: Don't Ask People for Information They Simply Don't Have

Consider this question given to physicians:

Q: Of the last 100 patients you have personally seen for weight control, how many are currently following the American Heart Association (AHA) exercise program?

_____ # of the last 100 patients are on the AHA exercise program

Dr. Bolton:	Dr. Edwards:
I know what I recommend, but I have no way to really know what they are actually doing. They want a number, so I'll say 10.	*Even if I don't recommend the American Heart Association exercise program, I wonder if some of my patients are following it because someone else recommended it or they found it on the Internet?*

In retrospect, it seems obvious that doctors would not know what their patients are actually doing.

To apply Answerable #3 to this question, let's first go back to basics. What *information* do we really need? Let's assume that we want information about how frequently doctors are *recommending* the American Heart Association exercise program. Note the fundamental change: We'll ask what the physician did, *not* what the patient may have done. That way we are asking physicians something they know.

Second, we won't ask about 100 patients. That is just too many for a physician to recall. We will narrow the scope to the last 10 patients.

Improved Question A:

Q: Thinking of the last 10 patients you personally saw for weight control, for how many of these 10 patients did you recommend the American Heart Association exercise program, if any?

I recommended the American Heart Association exercise program for_____ of these 10 patients.

Or we could ask the question this way:

Improved Question B:

Q: Thinking of the last 10 patients you personally saw for weight control, for how many of these 10 patients did you make any of the following recommendations?

I recommended the American Heart Association exercise program for _____ of these 10 patients.

I made other exercise program recommendations for _____ of these 10 patients.

I did not recommend a specific exercise program for _____ of these 10 patients.

These versions of the question are better because we are asking for information the doctor actually has.

Remember Questionnaire Planning #2: Determine the information needed before deciding how to write the questions. If the questionnaire writers had followed this step, they would have recorded in their Questionnaire Plan that they needed to know how frequently doctors are recommending the American Heart Association exercise program. Then, when they later worked on how to write the question, they probably would have asked it in one of the improved ways.

Even after considering all of these issues, we still know that the answers are approximations until the respondents actually check their records. However, an approximation is usually good enough for most purposes. If we need exact records, we will take a different research approach and audit the records.

Here is another example from a health-care survey. In this survey, all respondents had been screened into the survey for having cold sores.

Q: In what year did you get your first cold sore?

_____ Year got first cold sore

This is a tough question. Few people remember when they got their first cold sore.

The other problem with the question is that we need to frame it from the point of view of respondents. In other words, the question needs to reflect how they think about the topic, not how we think about it. We doubt people think about the year they first contracted the virus that causes cold sores. They might think about their *age* when they first *noticed* a cold sore.

Here is an improved version of the question:

Q: What was your age when you first remember having a cold sore? Please give us your best estimate.

_____ Age first noticed cold sore

This way of asking the question probably reflects better the frame of reference of people taking the survey. They know when they remember getting a cold sore. They may not know when they first got a cold sore, which could have been years before they actually remember their first cold sore.

Here is a question in a survey of motorcycle riders:

Q: In the past 30 days, how many hours did you ride your motorcycle on roads?

_____ # hours on roads

Q: In the past 30 days, how many hours did you ride your motorcycle off roads?

_____ # hours off-roads

After talking to a few motorcycle riders, we learned that they do not keep track of the *hours* they ride their bikes on and off roads. They have a better recollection of *days* they ride on and off roads.

Improved Question:

Q: In the past 30 days, how many days did you ride your motorcycle on roads?

_____ Days I rode on roads

Q: In the past 30 days, how many days did you ride your motorcycle off roads?

_____ Days I rode off roads

This example asks respondents for information they can recall.

The key is to make sure you are asking questions people can answer. Often you can make unanswerable questions answerable by thinking about what information you really need and asking for it in a way that matches how people think about the subject matter. Instead of asking doctors what their patients are doing, ask what doctors recommend. Instead of asking when someone got their first cold sore, ask when they remember getting their first cold sore. And think about the metric that makes sense to respondents. These bike riders could not report hours, but they could report days.

Qualitative interviews and pretesting will reveal what people can actually answer as well as how to ask the question.

Answerable #4: Screen Respondents to Make Sure Each Question Applies to Them

Here is an example of a skip pattern. In this case, we assume this will be a survey that is programmed into a computer. The questionnaire writer would use parentheses to indicate where there is a situation where question 1b is for females only (a skip instruction). In this case, the programmer would make sure that question 1b would only be asked of females. Males would be skipped over that question.

> *Skip Instructions:* Instructions that direct respondents to questions they qualify for and skip respondents over questions they do not qualify for. If a respondent does not qualify for a question, then we say we "skip" that respondent to a later question. Many people refer to all of these possible "skips" in a questionnaire as the skip pattern.

1. Are you…?
   ☐ Male
   ☐ Female

1b. (IF FEMALE) Have you yourself given birth to any children?
   ☐ Yes
   ☐ No

2. Do you have any children that you have adopted?
   ☐ Yes
   ☐ No

If this question were to be printed and administered on a piece of paper, the question might look like this. In this case, a bold and clear arrow would point females to the second question. The questionnaire writer would have written the question like the example above, but the person who does the print layout would create the arrow and possibly the indentation:

1. Are you … ?
   ☐ Male
   ☐ Female
   ↓
   1b. **IF FEMALE:** Have you yourself given birth to any children?
      ☐ Yes
      ☐ No

2. Do you have any children that you have adopted?
   ☐ Yes
   ☐ No

The previous guideline advises against asking for information that *none* of the respondents could possibly have (Answerable #3). But what if you need information that some, but not all, respondents can provide? This is where you use a screening or qualifying question to find out whether a given respondent qualifies for the next question or set of questions. This allows you to skip some respondents over questions that are not appropriate for them.

Consider a question on a questionnaire card that was given to hotel guests as they checked out of the hotel:

How Are We Doing?
Thank you for choosing our hotel.
To help provide better service in the future, we would appreciate your feedback.
Please rate the following questions from 1 to 5.
(1 poor — 3 average — 5 excellent)

Food quality	1	2	3	4	5
Cleanliness of room	1	2	3	4	5
Bed comfort	1	2	3	4	5
Bathroom cleanliness	1	2	3	4	5
Service at the front desk	1	2	3	4	5
Parking	1	2	3	4	5
Overall experience	1	2	3	4	5

Adam:
I don't know what to say for food quality. I didn't eat here. I don't want anyone to get in trouble, so I'll give it a 5.

Tony:
I didn't use parking. I'll give it a middle score like 3.

The problem with this question is that not all respondents can rate all the listed items. We can try to fix this question by adding NA (Not Applicable).

Improved Question A:

How Are We Doing?
Thank you for choosing our hotel.
To help provide better service in the future, we would appreciate your feedback.
Please rate our performance on the following scale:
(1 poor — 3 average — 5 excellent)
(Choose NA if rating an item is Not Applicable to your stay.)

Food quality	1	2	3	4	5	NA
Cleanliness of room	1	2	3	4	5	NA
Bed comfort	1	2	3	4	5	NA
Bathroom cleanliness	1	2	3	4	5	NA
Service at the front desk	1	2	3	4	5	NA
Parking	1	2	3	4	5	NA
Overall experience	1	2	3	4	5	NA

Adding NA allows people to indicate that the item is not applicable to them and avoids forcing them to make up answers. We also defined NA in the question. This is important because some people do not know what the acronym stands for.

Note that the questions about parking and food quality require two pieces of information. One, did you have experience with it? Two, if you did have experience with it, what is your rating of it? In this version of the question, we are essentially combining two questions into one.

We can make this question a little bit better by using screening questions. That way we do not have to use "Not Applicable," and we can avoid lumping two questions into one. Frequent use of "Not Applicable" conveys to the respondents that the questionnaire is not appropriate for them or that it was poorly written. By using screening questions, you can greatly limit the need for "Not Applicable."

Recall that this questionnaire will be given to hotel guests as they check out of the hotel. We know they will have had experience with the cleanliness of the room, bed comfort, bathroom cleanliness, and service at the front desk. However, they may *not* have had experience with the restaurant or parking.

In the next version of the question, we added two additional screener questions about whether they used the restaurant and the parking. This allows us to remove NA as an answer choice. We can skip people over the question if they have no experience with the restaurant or parking.

Improved Question B:
How Are We Doing?
Thank you for choosing our hotel.
To help provide better service in the future, we would appreciate your feedback.
Please rate our performance on the following scale:

(1 poor — 3 average — 5 excellent)

Overall experience	1 2 3 4 5
Cleanliness of room	1 2 3 4 5
Bed comfort	1 2 3 4 5
Bathroom cleanliness	1 2 3 4 5
Service at the front desk	1 2 3 4 5

I used hotel parking.
Yes ☐ No ☐
　　　IF YES, my rating of parking:　　1 2 3 4 5

I ate in the hotel.
Yes ☐ No ☐
　　　IF YES, my rating of food quality:　1 2 3 4 5

You can easily avoid using "Not Applicable" with Internet administration of questionnaires or with telephone interviews where a computer is used to determine which questions to ask. With paper questionnaires, you can use formatting to direct people away from questions that do not apply to them.

Related Guidelines

Answerable #3	Answerable #4
Don't ask people for information they simply don't have.	Screen respondents to make sure that each question applies to them.

Answerable #3 reminds us that there are limits to the information that survey respondents can provide. Doctors can't necessarily tell us what their patients are actually doing. People only have certain types and amounts of information.

Answerable #4 counsels that only a subgroup of respondents may have the information you are after. Therefore, screen people into the question based on whether they qualify for that question. For a survey of hotel guests, it is perfectly fine to ask people about the restaurant if they ate at the restaurant! But first screen them into this question so that those who did not eat at the restaurant are not forced to make up an answer.

Answerable #5: Make "Don't Know" an Answer Choice If Some Respondents Simply Don't Know the Answer to Your Question

Consider a question that might appear in a questionnaire about skin-care products:

Q: Please indicate whether each statement describes each brand by circling "Yes" or "No."

	Brand A		Brand B	
Has a pleasant scent	Yes	No	Yes	No
Contains aloe vera	Yes	No	Yes	No
Contains SPF	Yes	No	Yes	No
Is doctor-recommended	Yes	No	Yes	No
Comes in a pump	Yes	No	Yes	No
Is hypoallergenic	Yes	No	Yes	No

Thinking through all the possible answer choices a respondent can give reveals the problem with this question. What if the respondent simply *does not know* whether a statement describes one of the brands? For example, what would respondents say if they do not know whether Brand A contains aloe vera? Some might circle "Yes" because they think it *might* contain aloe vera. Others might say "No" because they simply don't know if it contains aloe vera. The point is that without the legitimate answer choice of "Don't Know," they have to make up an answer.

Here is an improved version of the question:

Q: Please indicate whether each statement describes each brand by circling "Yes" or "No." If you don't know, please circle "Don't know."

	Brand A			Brand B		
Has a pleasant scent	Yes	No	Don't know	Yes	No	Don't know
Contains aloe vera	Yes	No	Don't know	Yes	No	Don't know
Contains SPF	Yes	No	Don't know	Yes	No	Don't know
Is doctor-recommended	Yes	No	Don't know	Yes	No	Don't know
Comes in a pump	Yes	No	Don't know	Yes	No	Don't know
Is hypoallergenic	Yes	No	Don't know	Yes	No	Don't know

For this situation, "Don't Know" is a legitimate response for some people. Without "Don't Know" as an answer choice, they are forced to make up an answer. That substantially reduces the quality of the data.

It is important to also realize that "Don't Know" is often very useful information to collect. In this case, if people do not know something about your brand that you want them to know, then some sort of change in the marketing effort may be warranted.

Some questionnaire writers avoid adding "Don't Know" as a response option. There is the feeling that it allows respondents to opt out of answering questions. This makes sense in situations where you want to measure attitudes and you know that respondents lean in one direction or another, such as in the following example:

Q: How strongly do you favor or oppose the death penalty?
Strongly oppose   1   2   3   4   5   6   Strongly favor

Adding "Don't Know" to this question would indeed give those who are on the fence the option to avoid making the difficult choice about which way they lean, which would reduce the usefulness of their response.

However, in many situations, "Don't Know" is a legitimate response that should be available for respondents to select. Otherwise your data will be flawed.

The Differences between Applications of "Not Applicable" and "Don't Know"

Many questionnaires include as possible answer choices both NA for "Not Applicable" and DK for "Don't Know." Both are often used inappropriately.

First of all, do not assume that respondents understand the acronyms. When you use them, spell them out:

- Not Applicable
- Don't Know

Understand the difference between the two possible response options. "Not Applicable" al- lows respondents to indicate that the question does not apply to them. In other words, they are not an appropriate audience for the question. If you do *not* own a car and a question asks you about the make and year of your car, then the question does not apply to you.

If you follow Answerable #4 (screen respondents to make sure each question applies to them), there will be few situations where it makes sense to use "Not Applicable." Screening respondents into and out of questions that apply to them works much better.

The "Don't Know" response option is used for situations where the respondent qualifies for the question but simply does not know the answer—and not knowing matches the frame of reference of respondents. In other words, the question is appropriate for them, but they just don't have the answer.

To illustrate, suppose we asked a group of men and women, "Are you pregnant?" For men, "Not Applicable" would be a legitimate response, since there is no opportunity for a man to be pregnant. For women, "Don't Know" might be a legitimate response for those who might be pregnant but don't know for sure.

CHAPTER 8

Make Questions Easy

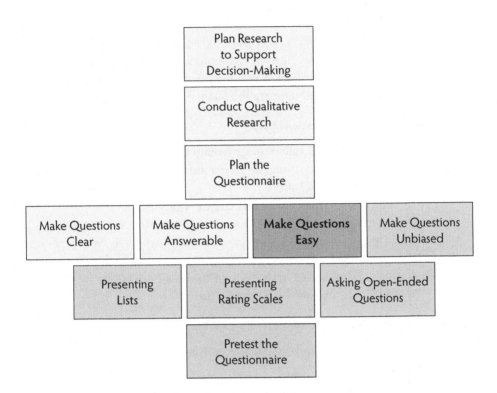

In chapter 6 we discussed how to make questions clear. Making questions clear involves ensuring all respondents understand each question by removing vagueness and ambiguity. It is about conveying meaning accurately. In chapter 7 we talked about making sure we ask questions respondents can answer.

Once we have made the question clear and answerable, our task is to make the question as easy as possible to answer. Remember, respondents are only going to expend so much energy and effort to answer your questionnaire. The easier you make the questions, the better the data you will get.

Krosnick (1991) reminds us that answering questions is much harder than it may seem. To answer a question, respondents have to go through four steps:

1. Interpret the meaning of the question
2. Recall all relevant facts related to the question
3. Summarize those facts
4. Report summary judgment accurately

He shows that respondents take shortcuts to make answering questionnaires easier. He uses the term *satisficing*, which refers to respondents taking shortcuts to come up with a satisfactory rather than an optimal answer. An example of satisficing would be when respondents are asked to select from a list all the food items they have consumed in the past 24 hours, and they select some items but do not go through the entire list to select all the items they have consumed. In their minds, they have provided a satisfactory, though not optimal, response to the question.

Given that you want to use the energy of respondents wisely and not wear them out—in other words, you want to reduce satisficing—you need to do all you can to make answering your questions as easy as possible.

In this chapter, we present seven guidelines that will help make questions easy, which in turn will improve the quality of data you collect.

Seven Guidelines for Making Questions Easy

1. Keep the question stem under twenty-five words. (Easy #1)
2. When writing questions, say the question out loud as if you were talking to someone. (Easy #2)
3. Limit the length of the questionnaire. (Easy #3)
4. Don't ask for more detail than you really need. (Easy #4)
5. Soften questions with phrases such as *approximately, your best estimate,* or *as best you can remember.* (Easy #5)
6. Don't ask questions in the form of complex grids. (Easy #6)
7. Add labels to answer categories. (Easy #7)

Easy #1: Keep the Question Stem under Twenty-Five Words

Consider this 40-word question stem from a consumer survey:

Q: How much of the household shopping, if any, do you, yourself, usually do? By household shopping, we mean all of the food, cleaning, paper, personal care (like health products, cosmetics, etc.), pet products, and other household products you usually buy. *(Select one.)*
☐ All
☐ More than half
☐ About half
☐ Less than half
☐ None

This question is somewhat long and cumbersome. When a question is too long, most respondents have to read it two or three times to understand it. Respondents are only going to expend so much energy to answer your questions. You might as well make the questions easier by making them short and to the point. We offer three primary ways to keep the question stem short. The first way is to tighten the wording in the question stem.

Let's get the question stem down to under twenty-five words.

Improved Question:

Q: How much of the household shopping do you, yourself, do for products such as food, toiletries, cleaning items, health products, and cosmetics? (*Select one.*)
☐ All
☐ More than half
☐ About half
☐ Less than half
☐ None

The improved question is easier to read and it gets the needed information.

Note that in the improved question, we took out the concept of *usually*. Words like *usually* and *typically* are not clearly defined. (Recall Clear #3.)

The second method for keeping questions shorter is to make the question stem brief and to move some of the information you need into the answer choices.

> *Tip:* Use Microsoft Word to count the words in your question stem. Highlight the question, and then from the toolbar at the top of your screen select Tools, then Word Count. In Word 2007, select Review, then Word Count.

Here is a question about washing machines in the home:

Q: Have you ever used a front-loading washer? By that we mean a washer for which you load the clothes in through the front and it has a revolving tub, which is different from a top-loading washer for which you load the clothes from the top and there is an agitator in the center of the tub that turns to wash the clothes.
☐ Yes
☐ No

This sixty-two-word question stem is cumbersome. The improved question stem below uses only fifteen words:

Improved Question:

Q: Have you ever personally used the types of washing machines listed below to wash clothes?
A washing machine you load through a DOOR YOU OPEN IN THE FRONT of the machine
☐ Yes
☐ No

A washing machine you load through a LID YOU OPEN IN THE TOP of the machine
☐ Yes
☐ No

By pointing the respondent to the answer choices, we can keep the question stem short and to the point. Respondents understand the question and then look to the answer choices for their response.

As an aside, we also took out the term *front-loading washer* and instead described the washing machine as one that "you load through a DOOR YOU OPEN IN THE FRONT of the washing machine." This is an example of using precise words and phrases (Clear #3) and avoiding industry jargon (Clear #2).

The third way to keep the question stem short involves terms that need to be defined. In this case, consider making the question stem short and placing concepts that need definition after the question as instructions. Italicize these instructions so the respondent knows that the information is meant to clarify the question.

Here is an example from the American Community Survey from the U.S. Census Bureau. In this question, the concept of "separate rooms" needed to be defined:

> **Q:** How many separate rooms are in this house, apartment, or mobile home?
> *Rooms must be separated by built-in archways or walls that extend out at least 6 inches and go from floor to ceiling.*
> *INCLUDE* bedrooms, kitchens, etc.
> *EXCLUDE* bathrooms, porches, balconies, foyers, halls, or unfinished basements.
> ___ Number of rooms

The question stem is concise and clear. It is only twelve words long.

Making the question stem short is best for the vast majority of questions. Note that we are saying that the question stem (the initial question statement) needs to be fewer than twenty-five words. There are other places in the question, such as in the instructions, where more information can be provided.

You may, for example, use a transition statement such as the one below (Questionnaire Planning #8) to introduce the next question or set of questions:

> Now we are going to ask you some questions about medicines you personally may or may not have taken over the past 30 days.

Or you might use an introductory statement to encourage elaboration on an open-ended question (Open-Ended #6):

> We want to understand why you chose to leave the university so we can make changes to improve student retention.

Transition statements and introductory statements prepare respondents for the next question or set of questions. They are not considered part of the question stem.

You may also include product profiles or scenarios that you ask respondents to read to prepare them for a set of questions. Again, these are not part of the question stem.

In most cases, the question stem can be written in fewer than twenty-five words. You should make that your goal. If you have trouble keeping the question stem short, try saying it out loud, as if you were talking to someone. Or ask someone to read the question and say it back to you in his or her own words (see Easy #2).

There are, of course, exceptions to the rule. You may be writing a questionnaire for a professional audience where the question stem cannot be shortened to fewer than twenty-five words but respondents understand the question in one reading. This is more common in surveys of professionals than in surveys of the general population.

Shorter Is Not Always Better

We struggled with how to phrase this principle. We thought about saying "make questions as short as possible," but that is not always best. Below is an example of a question that we made longer in order to make it a little easier on respondents:

Q: How many e-mails did you receive in the past 24 hours?

___ # e-mails received in the past 24 hours

Here is an improved version of the question that acknowledges that a best guess is good enough:

Improved Question:

Q: As best you can remember, about how many e-mails did you receive in the past 24 hours?

___ # e-mails received in the past 24 hours

Easy #2: When Writing Questions, Say the Question Out Loud as if You Were Talking to Someone

Here is a question that is rather complicated:

Q: When thinking about Company X, do you believe the word *innovative* describes the company "very well" or do you believe it describes the company "not very well"? On a scale of 1 to 5, with 1 being "a poor description of Company X" and 5 being "a very good description of Company X," how would you rank Company X in terms of being innovative?

The question is far more convoluted than necessary. If you were talking to someone, you would probably ask, "How well does the word *innovative* describe Company X?" Or you might say, "How innovative is Company X?" So ask it this way:

Improved Question:

Q: How innovative is Company X? *Please use the scale below, where 1 = not at all innovative and 5 = very innovative.*

Not at all innovative				Very innovative
1	2	3	4	5
○	○	○	○	○

One method of identifying the best way to write a question is to say the question out loud as if you were talking to someone. Find a colleague and read questions to each other. By asking the question as if you were in a conversation, you often find phrasings that are clearer and easier for respondents to answer.

We recently saw a CBS News Poll with the following question:

Q: How interested are you in the wedding of Prince William and Kate Middleton?
☐ A lot
☐ Some
☐ Not much
☐ Not at all

What we liked about this question is that the labels for the points along the scale seem to match how people think about the issue. If you were talking to someone and asked about their interest in the wedding, they would use phrases like "some," "not at all," etc.

Short, conversational questions often work best. If you are having trouble figuring out how to write the question, try saying it out loud as if you were talking to someone.

Easy #3: Limit the Length of the Questionnaire

Your questionnaire will get a limited amount of energy and attention from each respondent, so don't waste too much of it on unnecessary information. An overlong questionnaire reduces data quality because respondents give less attention to questions that really matter and may even drop out of the survey. As best you can, include only the questions that will give you the information needed for decision-making, as determined during Questionnaire Planning. This is hard, but having it as a goal will help.

Questionnaire length includes both the number of questions and the number of answer choices. The number of questions is easy; they are numbered and we can see how many we have. But each question may ask for one or more responses. For example, a single question may ask someone to rate ten items on a scale of 1 to 5, which means that one question has asked for ten responses. Be sure to consider both the number of questions and the number of answer choices when measuring the length of your questionnaire.

It is hard to come up with good rules of thumb for questionnaire length because the appropriate length will depend on the respondent group, the topic, and whether or not you are paying respondents to take the survey. For surveys where respondents are being compensated, try to keep the questionnaire under thirty questions and one hundred responses. Fewer questions is always better, so if you can tighten the questionnaire further, all the better.

For surveys where there is little to no compensation, you are better off keeping the questionnaire under fifteen questions and twenty-five responses. We have seen very effective questionnaires that ask under ten questions with fewer than twenty responses. If you know what you want and you write your questionnaire well, you can get solid data.

Questionnaire length can also be measured in terms of time. When you pretest your questionnaire, both with colleagues and with the population of interest, record how many minutes it takes each person to complete the questionnaire. By limiting your questions to those that really matter, you will limit the length of the questionnaire and improve the quality of the data you collect.

Easy #4: Don't Ask for More Detail Than You Really Need

Here is a question from a survey of physicians:

Q: In the past 30 days, how many patients did you see for hypertension?

_____ # patients seen for hypertension

Physicians want to answer the question correctly, but they can't. They simply don't know how many hypertension patients they saw in the past 30 days. Furthermore, this may not be how they think about their work. Doctors do not sit around adding up how many hypertension patients they see per month just so they can answer surveys correctly!

Since they are going to give an estimate anyway, provide categories for their responses to make the question easier to answer.

Improved Question A:

Q: In the past 30 days, how many patients did you see for hypertension?

☐ 1–10   ☐ 56–60
☐ 11–15   ☐ 61–65
☐ 16–20   ☐ 66–70
☐ 21–25   ☐ 71–75
☐ 26–30   ☐ 76–80
☐ 31–35   ☐ 81–85
☐ 36–40   ☐ 86–90
☐ 41–45   ☐ 91–95
☐ 46–50   ☐ 96–99
☐ 51–55   ☐ 100+

Unfortunately, this version of the question is not much better. It still asks for more precision than is really needed.

Offering fewer, broader answer choices will simplify the question further and make it easier for respondents to answer. In this case, let's assume that the people who designed the questionnaire needed only a rough estimate of the number of hypertension patients seen per month.

Improved Question B:

Q: In the past 30 days, about how many patients did you see for hypertension?

☐ 1–25
☐ 26–50
☐ 51–75
☐ 76–100
☐ 101+

Asking respondents to check a category, rather than provide a precise number, is one of the most common ways to make questions easier. Just make sure the categories are broad enough, and that the range from the lowest category to the highest category represents the distribution of possible answers from your respondent group.

Another way questionnaire writers ask for more detail than is really needed is with rating scales. Consider the question below:

Q: On a scale of 1 to 10, where "1" means *not at all likely* and "10" means *extremely likely*, please tell us how likely you are to stay at the following hotels in the next 6 months.

	1	2	3	4	5	6	7	8	9	10
Courtyard Marriott	○	○	○	○	○	○	○	○	○	○
Days Inn	○	○	○	○	○	○	○	○	○	○

	1	2	3	4	5	6	7	8	9	10
Embassy Suites	○	○	○	○	○	○	○	○	○	○
Sheraton	○	○	○	○	○	○	○	○	○	○
Wyndham	○	○	○	○	○	○	○	○	○	○
Ritz Carleton	○	○	○	○	○	○	○	○	○	○
Four Seasons	○	○	○	○	○	○	○	○	○	○
Holiday Inn	○	○	○	○	○	○	○	○	○	○
Best Western	○	○	○	○	○	○	○	○	○	○
Hampton Inn	○	○	○	○	○	○	○	○	○	○
Renaissance Inn	○	○	○	○	○	○	○	○	○	○
Homewood Suites	○	○	○	○	○	○	○	○	○	○
Hilton	○	○	○	○	○	○	○	○	○	○
La Quinta	○	○	○	○	○	○	○	○	○	○
Ramada Inn	○	○	○	○	○	○	○	○	○	○
Fairfield Inn	○	○	○	○	○	○	○	○	○	○
Holiday Inn Express	○	○	○	○	○	○	○	○	○	○

There are two problems with this question. First, a rating scale of 1 to 10 is probably overkill. Delivering this level of detail is very difficult for respondents. Do customers of hotels actually have ten different levels of *likelihood to stay* at a hotel? Think about it. When you ask respondents to rate something from 1 to 10, you are asking them to make a distinction between 1 and 2, 2 and 3, 3 and 4, 4 and 5, and so on. It is more difficult than using a shorter scale. As we will point out in chapter 11, "Presenting Rating Scales," lengthy scales often introduce other problems, such as respondents not really using the entire scale.

Second, does the questionnaire writer really need ratings of respondents' likelihood to stay at all sixteen hotels? If this is an initial round of research, there may be a sound reason for asking about all of these hotels. But it is more likely that data on all of these hotels is unnecessary.

We will assume, for purposes of illustration, that they need information for only a subset of these hotels, either hotels that compete with each other or hotels that respondents have already indicated they would consider.

Improved Question:

Q: How likely are you to stay at each of the hotels in the next 6 months, where 1 = not at all likely and 5 = very likely?

	1	2	3	4	5
Courtyard Marriott	○	○	○	○	○
Fairfield Inn	○	○	○	○	○
Hampton Inn	○	○	○	○	○
Holiday Inn Express	○	○	○	○	○
La Quinta	○	○	○	○	○

Keep your questions as simple as possible. Going for too much information and too much detail has a negative effect on the quality of your data.

Related Guidelines Note the similarity between these two guidelines:

Easy #3	Easy #4
Limit the length of the questionnaire.	Don't ask for more detail than you really need.

The goal of both of these guidelines is to make the questionnaire easier to answer, which in turn ensures that you get a higher quality of information from the questions that really matter. Both guidelines originate in the underlying principle of organizing research to support decision-making. To decide what questions you need to ask and how much detail to ask for, the decision-making that the research will support has to be clear to everyone involved in the research project.

Easy #5: Soften Questions with Phrases Such as *Approximately, Your Best Estimate,* or *As Best You Can Remember*

Not many people would be able to give an exact answer to the following question:

Q: How many e-mails did you receive in the past 24 hours?

_____ # e-mails received in the past 24 hours

Most people like to follow directions and answer questions accurately, so many respondents will feel stressed when asked for an exact number that they do not have. Letting them know that an exact number is not necessarily needed can help. When a precise number is not required, add phrases such as *about how many, as best you can remember,* or *approximately.*

Here are two improved versions of the question that acknowledge that a best guess is good enough:

Improved Question A:

Q: As best you can remember, about how many e-mails did you receive in the past 24 hours?

_____ # e-mails received in the past 24 hours

If you knew the range of the possible number of e-mails your respondents receive in a 24-hour period, you could also provide categories from which to select. Let's assume you had already confirmed that each respondent had received at least one e-mail:

Improved Question B:

Q: As best you can remember, about how many e-mails did you receive in the past 24 hours?

☐ None
☐ 1–10
☐ 11–20
☐ 21–30
☐ 31–40
☐ 41–50
☐ 50+

Here is a question given to business owners about the number of customers they served:

Q: What is the number of customers you served last week, from Monday through Saturday?

_____ # of customers served

Improved Question:

Q: What is your best estimate of the number of customers you served last week, from Monday through Saturday?

_____ # of customers served

These modified ways of asking the question let respondents know that they are not expected to remember the exact number. You don't want them to feel like a high-school student taking a difficult test. Their efforts to answer your questions are helpful, and you certainly don't want to make them unnecessarily stressed.

Related Guidelines Note the relationship between these two guidelines:

Easy #4	Easy #5
Don't ask for more detail than you really need.	Soften questions with phrases such as *approximately, your best estimate,* or *as best you can remember.*

Both of these guidelines make answering the question easier for respondents. Easy #4 facilitates question answering by not asking for unnecessary detail. Sometimes categories are enough. Easy #5 facilitates question answering by telling the respondent that an approximate answer is fine. In both cases, we are settling for less detail to avoid frustrating respondents or wearing them out.

Easy #6: Don't Ask Questions in the Form of Complex Grids

Here is a question from a survey of physicians who treat men with urinary problems associated with an enlarged prostate:

Q: The next series of questions will list several treatment approaches you may use for your male patients with an enlarged prostate (EP)—including prescription and non-prescription products, watchful waiting, and surgery.

For the sake of this survey, we'll divide these patients into three groups:
1. Enlarged prostate with <u>no</u> urinary symptoms
2. Enlarged prostate with <u>moderate</u> urinary symptoms
3. Enlarged prostate with <u>severe</u> urinary symptoms

Q: For each of these types of patients that you've seen in the last 30 days, what percent were treated in the following ways?

	Enlarged prostate with <u>no</u> urinary symptoms	Enlarged prostate with <u>moderate</u> urinary symptoms	Enlarged prostate with <u>severe</u> urinary symptoms
No treatment / watchful waiting	____ %	____ %	____ %
OTC therapy only	____ %	____ %	____ %
Rx therapy only	____ %	____ %	____ %
Rx and OTC Therapies	____ %	____ %	____ %
Surgery	____ %	____ %	____ %
Other (please specify____)	____ %	____ %	____ %
	100 %	**100 %**	**100 %**

Dr. Glenn:
The grid doesn't say which direction the percentages go. I reread the thing three times, and I still don't know.

Dr. Vanderhoof:
Every time I see one of these big tables, I get dizzy. I'll just make up some answers.

The grid is confusing. Dr. Glenn wants to answer it correctly but can't figure out whether the percentages are to go across the rows or down the columns. Dr. Vanderhoof has seen these grids before and decided a long time ago not to stress over them.

Grids (also known as tables or matrices) require respondents to read the question and then read both the column and row titles to determine how to answer the question. This is usually harder than it needs to be.

Breaking the original grid into separate questions for each patient type makes it easier for respondents to understand the question. It will also make them less likely to calculate the percentages across the rows when we want them to calculate the percentages down the columns.

In this case, we are going to ask three separate questions—one for each column. Note that this is also like following Clear #6 (Make sure the question is really asking only one question). The grid is lumping three questions into one.

Improved Question Sequence:

Q1: Of the patients you saw in the past 30 days with enlarged prostate with <u>no</u> urinary symptoms, what percent were treated in the following ways?

No treatment / watchful waiting	____%
OTC therapy only	____%
Rx therapy only	____%
Rx and OTC therapies	____%
Surgery	____%
Other (please specify _____)	____%
	100%

Q2: Of the patients you saw in the past 30 days with enlarged prostate with <u>moderate</u> urinary symptoms, what percent were treated in the following ways?

No treatment / watchful waiting	____%
OTC therapy only	____%
Rx therapy only	____%
Rx and OTC therapies	____%
Surgery	____%
Other (please specify _____)	____%
	100%

Q3: Of the patients you saw in the past 30 days with enlarged prostate with <u>severe</u> urinary symptoms, what percent were treated in the following ways?

No treatment / watchful waiting	____%
OTC therapy only	____%
Rx therapy only	____%
Rx and OTC therapies	____%
Surgery	____%
Other (please specify _____)	____%
	100%

Asking each question separately makes it a lot easier for respondents because they do not have to read the row and column titles to understand the grid. We have made the question easier by asking about one column, or one question, at a time. We also eliminate the potential for respondents to sum the data incorrectly—summing across rows when we want them to sum by columns or vice versa.

Grids can make answering the questionnaire especially difficult in other ways as well.

Here is a question from a survey of people with migraine headaches:

For Columns B, C, D, and E, for Each Non-Drug Treatment, Please Do the Following:

Q1: In column B, indicate if you have ever used this non-drug treatment for your migraine headaches.

Q2: In column C, indicate if you are currently using this non-drug treatment for your migraine headaches.

Q3: In column D, indicate how satisfied you are with this non-drug treatment.

Q4: When you are finished responding for each non-drug treatment, go to column E and indicate which of the non-drug treatments you are currently using is the 1st non-drug treatment you are likely to use for your next migraine headache.

Non-Drug Treatments	B Ever Use for Migraine Headache		C Currently Using for Migraine Headache		D How satisfied are you with those non-drug treatments you are currently using for your migraine headaches?					E I am most likely to use for my next migraine headache
			Yes ↓ Continue	No ↓ (Go to Next Treat-ment)	Extremely Dissatisfied	Dissatisfied	Neither Satisfied Nor Dissatisfied	Satisfied	Extremely Satisfied	
Acupuncture	Y	N	Y	N	○	○	○	○	○	
Aroma Therapy	Y	N	Y	N	○	○	○	○	○	
Chiropractic Care	Y	N	Y	N	○	○	○	○	○	
Diet	Y	N	Y	N	○	○	○	○	○	
Herbal Remedies	Y	N	Y	N	○	○	○	○	○	
Ice Packs	Y	N	Y	N	○	○	○	○	○	
Massage	Y	N	Y	N	○	○	○	○	○	
Yoga	Y	N	Y	N	○	○	○	○	○	

It should be obvious that this is a difficult set of questions to answer in a grid or table format. No respondent should have to go back and forth between the questions and the grid to figure out what we are asking them to do.

Asking the questions one at a time with no grid will make them much easier to answer. First ask what non-drug treatments they have ever used. Then find out which treatments they have been using over a more recent time frame. Then ask for their satisfaction with only those treatments they have used over the more recent time frame. Finally ask about their intention to use treatments over some future time frame, such as the next 12 months.

Grids are difficult for most respondent groups and result in both poor data and people dropping out of the survey. Make the questions easier by avoiding the use of grids. As with all guidelines, there are exceptions. You may find that professional groups prefer to answer some information requests in a grid for-mat. If you stumble across such situations, make sure the column and row head-ings are clear, and pretest the questions well to ensure that they are easy to answer and not open to misinterpretation.

Rating Items Relative to Each Other Can Be Accomplished without a Grid

Sometimes we need to present a list of items that we want respondents to rate, and it is necessary to present all the items together because we want respondents to consider each in relation to the others.

> **Q:** How likely are you to rent a car from the following car rental companies in the next six months, where 1 = not at all likely and 5 = very likely.

Enterprise	1	2	3	4	5
National	1	2	3	4	5
Avis	1	2	3	4	5

Alamo	1	2	3	4	5
Hertz	1	2	3	4	5
Thrifty	1	2	3	4	5

In this situation, we want respondents to see and consider all the listed car rental companies together rather consider one company at a time.

We do not consider this a grid question because there are no rows and columns to interpret. It is basically one question with a list of items to rate on the scale provided.

Easy #7: Add Labels to Answer Categories

Here is a typical question:

> **Q:** How many years have you been married? _____

Many surveys provide only a blank line for respondents to fill in, as in this example. Most respondents will answer the question correctly, but why not make the information needed even more explicit by providing an answer label, as in the example below?

Improved Question A:

> **Q:** How many years have you been married?
>
> _____ Number of years married

There is another reason to provide an answer label. When confronted with a blank line, respondents will not know whether you want a numerical or text response. Most respondents will give a number, but some will write in a text response, like "ten" or "ten years."

Sure, you got the information you needed, but its format will cause all sorts of difficulties when you're analyzing the data. Imagine having data from one thousand respondents, sixty-five of whom wrote a text response. You would have to either go through the entire data set to change the text to numbers or write a program that does it for you so you can analyze the data. Not fun, trust us!

You should also consider using a guideline we present later in chapter 12 on asking open-ended questions. Open-Ended #1 tells us to format and label answer boxes to help respondents understand the response task.

Improved Question B:

> **Q:** How many years have you been married?
>
> [___]   Number of years married

Adding labels to the answer box and formatting the answer box help make the response task easier, both for respondents and for whoever has to analyze the data.

In this example, we use the symbol for a number:

Q: How many days were you on the cruise ship?

[   ] # of days on cruise ship

This guideline also applies to questions where you *do* want a text response, as in this example:

Q: In what county do you currently live?

_____ Name of county

In this case, be sure the answer space is large enough for respondents to write in the name of their county.

Adding labels to response categories makes it easier for respondents to see exactly what you want and to provide their answer in the right format.

CHAPTER 9

Make Questions Unbiased

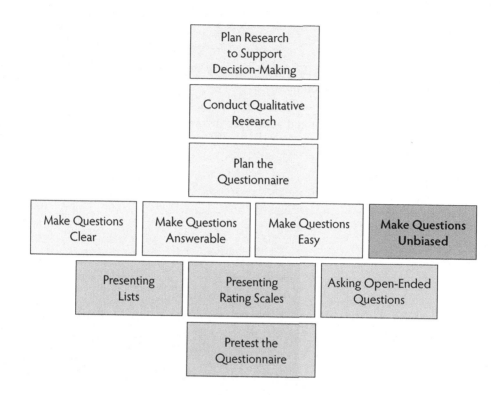

In part 2, "Plan the Questionnaire," we talked about how to avoid bias *between* questions. Specifically, Questionnaire Planning #6 tells us to order the questions throughout the questionnaire to account for the potential for order bias. A respondent's answer to one question may influence their answers to subsequent questions.

This chapter addresses how to avoid introducing bias *within* a question. The five guidelines presented here help us to avoid the most common ways bias gets inadvertently introduced into questions. Using these guidelines will help you get more accurate data.

These five guidelines directly reduce bias within a question, yet most of the other guidelines have an indirect effect on bias as well. Questions that are unanswerable, unclear, and not easy invariably lead to guessing and higher dropout rates. Such results will introduce either bias or random error into your data.

Five Guidelines to Make Questions Unbiased

1. Do not introduce ideas or opinions that will influence responses. (Unbiased #1)

2. Make sure that no one answer choice is more loaded than any other. (Unbiased #2)

3. Make clear that either a positive or a negative answer is equally acceptable. (Unbiased #3)

4. Randomize answer choices if there is a possibility of order bias. (Unbiased #4)

5. To get sensitive information, consider disguising the question, shifting the focus away from the respondent, softening the question, or collecting correlated data. (Unbiased #5)

Unbiased #1: Do Not Introduce Ideas or Opinions That Will Influence Responses

It is easy to influence responses—intentionally or unintentionally—through the wording of a question. What do you think of this question?

Q: Considering the extremely high price of gasoline, for your next vacation are you most likely to: (choose one)
☐ Fly
☐ Drive
☐ Take a train
☐ Take a bus
☐ Other

Here is what two respondents thought:

Jack:	Jules:
Wow, I think they are right. Gas is likely to be through the roof this summer. If we go anywhere, we might try the bus.	*I wonder how the price of gas is going to affect all of these forms of transportation. I think airlines are going to be hit hard. In spite of the high price of gas, for our family of four it may be cheaper to drive rather than fly as we usually would.*

You can see the impact of the question's wording on these respondents. They answered in reaction to the biasing phrase "Considering the extremely high price of gasoline" instead of simply responding to the question about their most likely method of travel on their next vacation.

Let's use this principle to clean up this question by removing the idea about the extremely high price of gas.

Improved Question:

Q: For your next vacation, are you most likely to: (choose one)
☐ Fly
☐ Drive
☐ Take a train
☐ Take a bus
☐ Other

We saw the following question in a survey from a nationally recognized restaurant chain.

Q: Thinking about your last visit to the restaurant, how would you describe your satisfaction with your greeting by a friendly associate.
☐ Very satisfied
☐ Satisfied
☐ Neither satisfied nor dissatisfied
☐ Dissatisfied
☐ Very dissatisfied

The question certainly encourages respondents to say they are satisfied, since it describes the associate as friendly!

The question can be improved in a couple of ways, depending on the information the restaurant wants to collect.

Improved Question A:

Q: Thinking about your last visit to the restaurant, how dissatisfied or satisfied were you with the staff?
☐ Very satisfied
☐ Satisfied
☐ Neither satisfied nor dissatisfied
☐ Dissatisfied
☐ Very dissatisfied

Improved Question B:

Q: Thinking about your last visit to the restaurant, how unfriendly or friendly was the staff?
☐ Very friendly
☐ Friendly
☐ Neither friendly nor unfriendly
☐ Unfriendly
☐ Very unfriendly

In summary, be careful not to introduce into the question ideas or opinions that will cause respondents to answer the question in a positive or negative way.

Planning Research for Decision-Making: The Restaurant Example

Let's make the connection between how we ask questions and the primary thesis presented in chapter 1, "Plan Research to Support Decision-Making." When organizations invest the time and money to conduct surveys with their customers, they are planning to take some sort of corrective action based on the results. For example, this company might decide that if less than 75 percent of customers indicate that they are satisfied or very satisfied with the staff, they will look more carefully into how a store is being managed. Or this company might decide that if less than 75 percent of customers indicate that the staff was friendly or very friendly, they will investigate the store and take corrective action. Hey, it might even decide to celebrate with the employees if the scores stay very good or go up!

If the restaurant chain is not careful to write questions that avoid bias, its data will be flawed, and it will not have the information it needs to make such decisions. Getting questions right can make all the difference when it comes to managing an organization.

Unbiased #2: Make Sure No One Answer Choice Is More Loaded Than Any Other

Read this question and see what you think about it.

> Q: Which of the following do you consider to be most responsible for obesity in America: *(choose one)*
> ☐ Poor diet
> ☐ Exercise

> *Loaded:* having attitudes or ideas embedded in a question or answer choices that bias responses.

The question stem is fine. The problem lies in the answer choices. "Poor diet" is more loaded than "Exercise."

Improved Question:

> Q: Which of the following do you consider to be most responsible for obesity in America: *(choose one)*
> ☐ Poor diet
> ☐ Lack of exercise

Here is an excerpt from a survey about political issues that was administered shortly after the 2008 presidential election.

> Q: Please rank your top 3 priorities in order of personal importance to you. *(1 = most important, 2 = second most important, 3 = third most important)*
> __ Lifting the economy out of the Bush recession
> __ Helping families avoid home foreclosure
> __ Expanding access to affordable health care
> __ Ensuring equal rights for all
> __ Protecting America against terrorism
> __ Bringing U.S. troops home from Iraq
> __ Stabilizing Afghanistan
> __ Improving educational opportunities
> __ Taking action to stop global warming

The most obvious problem with this question is that the first answer choice is more loaded than the others. Referring to the recession as the "Bush recession" introduces connotations that may bias responses. Democrats might select that item more often, whereas Republicans might *not* select the item—even when the recession is their top priority—because they believe that the Democrats share the blame for the recession.

The way to fix it is pretty simple. We would just remove the reference to former president George W. Bush in that item.

Improved Question:

> Q: Please rank your top 3 priorities in order of personal importance to you. *(1 = most important, 2 = second most important, 3 = third most important)*
> __ Lifting the economy out of the recession
> __ Helping families avoid home foreclosure
> __ Expanding access to affordable health care
> __ Ensuring equal rights for all
> __ Protecting America against terrorism

___ Bringing U.S. troops home from Iraq
___ Stabilizing Afghanistan
___ Improving educational opportunities
___ Taking action to stop global warming

When we ask respondents to answer questions, we need to have as little influence as possible on their answers.

Related Guidelines

Unbiased #1	Unbiased #2
Do not introduce ideas or opinions that will influence responses.	Make sure that no one answer choice is more loaded than any other.

There is a subtle difference between Unbiased #1 and Unbiased #2. Unbiased #1 tells us to make sure the question stem does not contain anything that might influence responses. Unbiased #2 tells us to make sure the answer choices are equal and do not contain anything that might influence responses.

Unbiased #3: Make Clear That Either a Positive or a Negative Answer Is Equally Acceptable

Consider this question:

Q: Are you aware of the advertising of products that allow you to dry clean your clothes in your home washing machine?
☐ Yes
☐ No

Acquiescence: the tendency of respondents to offer agreeable or positive answers to survey questions

Jean:	Sheza:
I guess I should be. I'll say yes.	*I am now, so I'll say yes!*

Both respondents were led to say that they have heard of the advertising—a positive response. In fact, the question itself raises awareness of products for dry cleaning. Respondents become aware of the issue by reading the question!

Simply using the word *aware* can be troublesome because it sounds like a challenge to some people. Asking "are you aware…" may create a bias toward a Yes answer. ("What do you mean? Of course I'm aware!")

Many people are naturally inclined to offer agreeable or positive answers, so it's important to make clear that both positive and negative responses are equally acceptable. Here are a few ways to repair this question.

Improved Question A:

Q: Have you, yourself, seen or heard any advertising about products that allow you to dry clean your clothes in your home washing machine, or not?
☐ Yes
☐ No

This question shifts the focus from whether or not they are *aware* of to whether or not they have *seen or heard* of advertising for these products. This

new version is less likely to influence respondents to say yes when the true answer is no.

Second, the question ends with the phrase *or not*. This simple phrase helps
give respondents permission to say no. It is a technique questionnaire writers
use to help convey that a negative answer is acceptable.

Let's also give respondents the option to say they are not sure.

Improved Question B:

> **Q:** Have you, yourself, seen or heard any advertising about products that allow
> you to dry clean your clothes in your home washing machine, or not?
> ☐ Yes
> ☐ No
> ☐ I am not sure

Providing this option helps deal with the situation where respondents are just
not sure. Rather than forcing them to say yes or no, why not offer "I am not sure"
as an answer choice? We could have phrased this response as "Don't know," but
"I am not sure" may fit the situation a little better.

Here is an example from a question about favoring or opposing a tax increase:

> **Q:** Do you favor a tax increase for people making over $250,000 per year?
> ☐ Yes
> ☐ No

Improved Question:

> **Q:** Do you favor or oppose a tax increase for people making over $250,000 per
> year?
> ☐ Favor
> ☐ Oppose

In the next example, respondents are asked to represent their satisfaction or
dissatisfaction on a scale:

> **Q:** How satisfied were you with your most recent stay at our hotel?
> Very dissatisfied   1   2   3   4   5   6   7   Very satisfied

Improved Question:

> **Q:** How satisfied or dissatisfied were you with your most recent stay at our hotel?
> Very dissatisfied   1   2   3   4   5   6   7   Very satisfied

In each of these examples, including both positive and negative answers in
the question stem makes it clear that both answers are equally acceptable and
avoids biasing respondents toward a positive response.

There are other ways we inadvertently influence respondents to give a positive answer. These include questions where we are asking about what people
have done, or intend to do, over some time frame.

Here is a sample question about what people intend to do from a survey about
health-care issues:

Q: When do you expect to see your doctor about your headaches?
☐ Within a month
☐ Within 3 months
☐ Within 6 months
☐ Within a year
☐ Never

This question stem implies or assumes that respondents will see their doctor. The fact that *never* is an option does not adequately solve the problem.

Improved Question:

Q: Do you expect to see your doctor in the next 12 months about your headaches, or not?
☐ Yes
☐ No

(IF YES) When do you expect to see your doctor about your headaches?
☐ Within a month
☐ Within 3 months
☐ Within 6 months
☐ Within a year

This question about past behavior comes from a company that markets products for car maintenance:

Q: In the past 6 months, how many times have you personally had the oil changed in your car?
☐ None
☐ Once
☐ Twice
☐ Three or more times

Despite offering 0 as an option, this question contains a bias because it assumes that respondents have changed their oil in the past 6 months.

Let's look at a couple of ways to improve this question:

Improved Question A:

Q: In the past 6 months, have you personally had the oil changed in your car, or not?
☐ I have had the oil changed in my car in the past 6 months.
☐ I have <u>not</u> had the oil changed in my car in the past 6 months.

(IF YES) In the past 6 months, how many times have you personally had the oil changed in your car?
☐ Once
☐ Twice
☐ Three or more times

Here is another version of the same question that provides an introduction to help make clear that no is an acceptable answer:

Improved Question B:

Q: You personally may or may not have had the oil changed in your car in the past 6 months. Please select the item below that reflects whether or not you personally had the oil in your car changed in the past 6 months.

☐ I have had the oil changed in my car in the past 6 months.

☐ I have <u>not</u> had the oil changed in my car in the past 6 months.

(IF YES) In the past 6 months, how many times have you personally had the oil changed in your car?

☐ Once

☐ Twice

☐ Three or more times

This second way of asking the question makes some respondents feel more comfortable indicating that they have not had the oil changed in the past 6 months. The opening statement tells respondents that plenty of other people answering this survey have not had their oil changed in the past 6 months! Sending this sort of message makes it more acceptable to give a negative answer.

These techniques will help you avoid steering respondents to give a positive response. As with any questionnaire, you will find out in pretesting if any additional modifications are necessary. Pretesting will be discussed in part 4.

The Length of a Question

Chapter 8 focuses on ways to make questions easy to answer. One way to make questions easy is to make them shorter. Easy #1 reminds us to keep the question stem under twenty-five words.

However, there are also situations where it is desirable to add a statement prior to the question stem that makes the overall question a little longer, as we did in this chapter with the following introductory statement and question stem:

Q: You may or may not have had the oil changed in your car in the past 6 months. Please select the item below that reflects whether or not you had the oil in your car changed in the past 6 months.

___ I personally have had the oil changed in my car in the past 6 months.

___ I personally have <u>not</u> had the oil changed in my car in the past 6 months.

In this case, we are actually making the question longer to ensure unbiased responses.

There are few rules that have no exceptions. We have to balance the benefits of making the question stem short with the need to encourage unbiased responses. In this case, adding the introductory sentence to facilitate an unbiased response is probably worth it.

Unbiased #4: Randomize Answer Choices If There Is a Possibility of Order Bias

As we'll discuss in chapters 10 and 11, two of the tasks we often ask of respondents are selecting items from a list and rating a list of items on a scale. For selecting items from a list, we may ask respondents to select one item or all items that apply, or we may force them to indicate yes or no to each item. For rating items on a scale, we usually present several items and ask respondents to provide a rating on satisfaction, interest, performance, and so on.

The obvious potential bias comes from which items are toward the top and which are toward the bottom. Placement has an effect on which ones get chosen, especially if the list is long. On a paper or computer-administered questionnaire, items at the top may get more attention than items lower down. On the other hand, if the questionnaire is read to respondents over the phone or in person, the items at the end of the list are easier for respondents to remember.

If there is no natural order to the items on the list, then randomize the order of items to minimize possible bias. With computer-administered questionnaires, randomizing the items is easy.

Here is a question that asks respondents to select yes or no from a list of items:

Q: Which of the following mouthwash brands have you ever heard of? *Please circle yes or no.*

Listerine	yes	no
Lavoris	yes	no
Targon	yes	no
Tom's of Maine	yes	no
Salivart	yes	no
Biotene	yes	no
Plax	yes	no
Viodent	yes	no
Cepacol	yes	no
Dentyl pH	yes	no

Because this list is long, the order in which brands are presented will most likely have an effect on responses. You are better off randomizing the list so that the order of items is different from respondent to respondent.

Here is a question with a list of items for respondents to rate on a scale:

Q: How well does each of the following statements describe you? *Use the scale below, where 1 = Does not describe me at all and 5 = Describes me very well.*

	1	2	3	4	5
I dress better than most people.	○	○	○	○	○
I like to watch sports on TV.	○	○	○	○	○
I like to watch movies at home.	○	○	○	○	○
I like to watch movies at the theater.	○	○	○	○	○
I like to go to the gym.	○	○	○	○	○
I enjoy mowing the lawn.	○	○	○	○	○
I get enough sleep on weekdays.	○	○	○	○	○
I get enough sleep on weekends.	○	○	○	○	○
I try to eat a healthy diet.	○	○	○	○	○
I enjoy cooking at home.	○	○	○	○	○

Again, you need to randomize the list of items to ensure that none of these statements has a systematic advantage or disadvantage.

However, this list has two sets of items that should be randomized together. "I like to watch movies at home" and "I like to watch movies at the theater" are best kept together in the randomization to help respondents see that they are being asked to make the distinction between the two venues for movies. If respondents just saw "I like to watch movies in the theater" early in the list, they might lump some of their interest in seeing movies at home into their answer to that item. Pairing in randomization helps avoid that possibility. We suggest pairing "I get enough sleep on weekdays" and "I get enough sleep on weekends" for the same reason.

The increasing use of computers in survey administration—either in person, online, or on the telephone—makes it easy to present the list items in random order for each respondent. It is also easy to keep two or more items together in the randomization process. Always ask whoever is programming your questionnaire to randomize the list and keep particular items paired if necessary.

Randomizing response items does not completely eliminate bias. Whatever order each respondent sees has an order bias for him or her individually. The purpose of randomization is to ensure that no one item is systematically put in the first or last position. In other words, no one item is subject to more opportunity for bias than any other.

Related Guidelines

Questionnaire Planning #6	Unbiased #4
Organize the order of questions to avoid order bias.	Randomize answer choices if there is a possibility of order bias.

Both of these guidelines help reduce bias. Questionnaire Planning #6 addresses the order of questions. Bias #4 addresses the order of answer choices *within* a question.

Rating Scales Have a Natural Order

Do not confuse lists of items from which to select with rating scales. Scales, such as the purchase-intention scale listed below, need to have their answer choices listed as a continuum in a set order.

Q: How likely are you personally to purchase Product X in the next 30 days?

☐ Definitely will buy
☐ Probably will buy
☐ May or may not buy
☐ Probably will not buy
☐ Definitely will not buy

Unbiased #5: To Get Sensitive Information, Consider Disguising the Question, Shifting the Focus Away from the Respondent, Softening the Question, or Collecting Correlated Data

Consider this question:

Q: Have you, yourself, used a laxative in the past 30 days?
☐ Yes
☐ No

Jill:	Addison:
I kinda don't want to say anything about that.	*Why do they need to know about my private life?*

There are many topics that some people feel are private or that they might be embarrassed to address in a questionnaire. Although use of a laxative may seem like no big deal, some people do not like to share information related to bowel movements. Other topics that people often consider sensitive include income, sex, religion, racism, sexism, and attitudes toward their place of employment. Questions that respondents consider private, confidential, none of your business, or threatening may result in false answers or termination of the survey. Both of these outcomes contribute to bias in the data.

Disguise the Question

One way to deal with this issue is to disguise the question. Instead of asking a question exclusively about the use of a laxative, ask about a variety of household products. Embedding the real question in a list makes it easier for some people to check that item, probably because their attention is shared among a number of items.

Improved Question:

Q: Which, if any, of the following commonly used products have you, yourself, used in the past 30 days? *Please check all that apply to you.*
☐ Eye drops
☐ Tooth whitener
☐ Foot powder
☐ Laxative
☐ Fluoride rinse for your teeth
☐ Hair coloring product

It might be better to use a forced-choice format instead of check all that apply:

Q: Have you, yourself, used the following commonly used products in the past 30 days? *Please check yes or no.*

	Yes	No
Eye drops	☐	☐
Tooth whitener	☐	☐
Foot powder	☐	☐
Laxative	☐	☐
Fluoride rinse for your teeth	☐	☐
Hair coloring product	☐	☐

This format forces respondents to say yes or no to the laxative item rather than simply skipping it. It might be a little easier for some people to simply not check the item than to actually say no when the answer is really yes.

Shift the Focus

Another method is to shift the focus of the question. Here is a question that was asked of project team leaders at a manufacturing facility:

Q: Will you finish your project on budget?
   ☐ Yes
   ☐ No

You will not be surprised to hear that 100 percent of the team leaders answered yes. The president of the company did not believe their answers. We explained that this was because many people feel that responding "no" to such a question might put them at risk.

We rewrote this question and sent it out a month later.

Improved Question:

Q: Do you foresee any circumstances that might prevent you from finishing your project on budget?
   ☐ Yes
   ☐ No

(IF YES) Would you describe in the box below those circumstances and suggest how we might help you overcome them.

```



```

Shifting the focus of the question away from the respondent to the *circumstances* that might prevent the project from being finished on budget removed the pressure to give a positive answer.

The revised question worked better; 8 of 10 team leaders saw circumstances that might prevent them from completing their project on budget. The shift in the question was subtle but effective. The company needed accurate information on what might interfere with the completion of these projects on budget so they could do something about it.

When asking about demographics, consider shifting the focus of the question away from the personal nature of the information to the research requirements of the study.

Instead of asking:

Q: Would you please tell me your age?

You might ask:

Q: For statistical purposes only, would you please tell us your age?

Or you might ask:

Q: To ensure we have a representative sample, would you please tell us your age?

Another way to shift the focus away from age is to ask for year of birth:

Q: In what year were you born?

Some people are more willing to share their year of birth than they are their age.

Soften the Question

You might also soften this age question by listing categories. Some people would rather admit to an age range than to a specific number.

Improved Question:

Q: To ensure we have a representative sample, would you please tell me which age group you belong to?
☐ 19 or younger
☐ 20 to 29
☐ 30 to 39
☐ 40 to 49
☐ 50 to 59
☐ 60 to 69
☐ 70 or older

Let's look at another example. A local political group was attempting to assess awareness of the name of their district's U.S. congressional representative. Here is the question from their survey:

Q: Do you know the name of your congressional representative?
☐ Yes
☐ No

Not knowing the answer to this question is embarrassing to many respondents. Let's soften the question and put both the question and the answer in a less threatening tone.

Improved Question:

Q: Do you happen to remember the name of the U.S. congressional representative from your district?
☐ Yes, the name as best I remember it is _____.
☐ I can't recall it right now.

This way of asking the question is a little softer. The focus has also shifted to remembering the name of the congressional representative rather than knowing it. For some people, it is less embarrassing and more acceptable to say they can't remember right now than to say they do not know.

Correlated Data

Another way to get information that people may be unwilling to provide is to ask for correlated data. This approach is common in business-to-business research.

Let's say you are interested in how many lawn mowers a company produces in a given time period. They may be unwilling to share this information. However, you might know of something that correlates very well with the number of lawn mowers produced. For example, maybe you can get information about the number of a certain part that they order to manufacture the lawn mowers.

Try asking about the number of orders for that particular part. You could also present ranges of orders for that part to make the question more acceptable to answer.

Secondary Data

There are some topics, however, that people are unwilling to answer, no matter how you craft the question. Suppose you want to know whether a person has been diagnosed with HIV or genital herpes. Or suppose you want to know whether a person has ever cheated on his or her spouse. How many people are willing to tell a research organization the number of times they have hit their child in the face, slept with a prostitute, or driven under the influence of alcohol? Even though answers to these questions may be extremely important to the researchers, many people will not answer honestly.

When you are unable to get accurate data on certain topics, you may need to find secondary data or get estimates from sources other than your survey. For example, the Centers for Disease Control and Prevention (CDC) have data for the epidemiology of HIV, genital herpes, and many other diseases that may help you with your project. They won't be able to tell you about individuals, but they will have national estimates as well as estimates by sub-group populations. However, for other questions, such as infidelity or drunk driving, you may not even find good secondary data sources.

Getting sensitive information is one of the most challenging tasks in survey research. You can disguise the question, shift the focus, soften the question, or ask for correlated data, but it still may be difficult or impossible to get unbiased answers. Depending on the topic, there may be subject-matter experts who have worked for a long time on how to get the kind of information you need. For example, if you need information about domestic violence, there are surely many professionals who have worked on this topic and could provide some advice.

Using the techniques presented here will help you reduce bias in responses. Don't underestimate the range of topics that some people consider sensitive or none of your business. And realize that no matter how crafty you are in writing the questions, there are some topics that people will not answer truthfully in a questionnaire.

CHAPTER 10

Presenting Lists

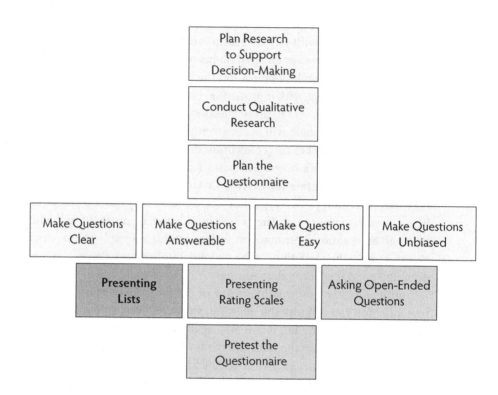

Two common tasks asked of respondents are selecting items from a list and rating items on a scale. Each of these tasks presents questionnaire writers with its own set of challenges. Therefore, we have created separate chapters for each of these tasks. You will see, however, that the guidelines for lists and for scales are in fact special cases of making questions clear, answerable, easy, and unbiased.

When we ask respondents to select from a list, we often ask them to tell us which of a list of categories or statements applies to them. Each item on the list has no numeric relationship to any other item on the list. We might ask people which issues are most important in an upcoming election. In such cases, we can ask respondents either to select one response or to give an affirmative or negative response to every item on the list.

We also use lists to organize numeric categories to make answering the question easier for respondents or to make the question more acceptable to answer. We might ask respondents which of the following income categories best describes their total household income, since some respondents do not want to tell us their exact income. Or we might ask how many hours per week respondents watch television and present a list with ranges of time frames (e.g., 0 hours, more than 0 but less than 1 hour, 1 to less than 5, 5 to less than 10, 10 to less than 15, 15 or more hours), which is an easier task than reporting an exact amount of time. In these cases each item on the list has a numeric relationship to the other items on the list.

Asking respondents to select from a list presents a host of challenges for the questionnaire writer. Some of these challenges are not so obvious, as you will see when you review the five guidelines presented in this chapter.

Five Guidelines for Asking Respondents to Select from a List

1. Make sure the list includes all possible answer choices. (Lists #1)
2. Make sure numeric categories are as broad and detailed as needed. (Lists #2)
3. Make sure items on the list do not overlap. (Lists #3)
4. Consider using forced choice instead of "check all that apply." (Lists #4)
5. Use the question to direct respondents to the list. (Lists #5)

Lists #1: Make Sure the List Includes All Possible Answer Choices

A common error in questionnaire writing is failing to include all possible answer choices when asking respondents to select from a list.

Take the following example. My mother decided to change banks. When the bank found out she was leaving, they sent her a survey asking her to select the item that was her primary reason for leaving the bank. The problem with the question was that her one and only reason for leaving the bank was not on the list of possible responses. There was also no option to select "other" and write in her reason. She left that bank because she could not get anyone on the phone at her local branch to talk to her. While answering this question, she had to decide whether to select one of the items on the list that was *not* her primary reason for leaving the bank or to just skip the question. She is looking forward to this book being published, and hopefully used, so that the questionnaires she receives will match how she sees the world!

Let's explore this topic further. Consider this question from a survey of homeowners from a home-building development company:

Q: Which one would you prefer for your <u>living space</u>? *(Check <u>ONE</u> only.)*
☐ A living room and a family room of equal size
☐ A smaller living room and a larger family room
☐ One large great room (living room and family room combined)

Here is what two homeowners thought when they read the question.

Al:	Joan:
I like a large living room and a smaller family room. I wonder why that isn't on the list?	*They have certainly limited the choices. I guess these are all they want to offer, so they want to know which we will pick even if we really don't like any.*

When we consulted with the people from the home-building development company who wrote the survey, we found that they needed to decide on home floor plans for a new development. They wanted to know the relative preferences for different sizes of living rooms, family rooms, and great rooms to help them determine which floor plans to put into the new development.

The problem with this question is that they left out the option for a larger living room and smaller family room. They said they left it out because they were not planning to build it. But even if they were not planning to build this option, they needed to include it on the list because some people answering this survey might be looking for this option. Some respondents might be irritated when their preference is not on the list. In addition, forcing people who prefer a larger living room and smaller family room to choose another option will result in biased data. The data collected from this survey will have inflated preferences for the options listed because people who preferred an option not listed were forced to choose another option.

Improved Question:

Q: Which one would you prefer for your living space? (Check ONE only.)
- ☐ Equal-sized living room and family room
- ☐ Larger living room and smaller family room
- ☐ Smaller living room and larger family room
- ☐ A great room combining the living room and family room into one

The improved question provides a list that matches respondents' frame of reference, so the data will be more accurate.

There is also the possibility that we cannot think of all the items respondents might select. Even when we do qualitative research before writing the survey and pretest afterward, we still may not capture all possible responses. Allowing respondents to select "other" and to write in their answer is a good idea.

Q: Which one would you prefer for your living space? (Check ONE only.)
- ☐ Equal-sized living room and family room
- ☐ Larger living room and smaller family room
- ☐ Smaller living room and larger family room
- ☐ A great room combining the living room and family room into one
- ☐ Other—please specify: _____

Qualitative research lets you explore the subject matter to ensure you know what items to put on the list and how respondents describe these items. For the banking example, a dozen or so interviews would probably capture the possible reasons why people left the bank. Pretesting is another opportunity to find out whether the list of items matches how respondents see the world.

Of course, there is no way to be sure you have *all* the possible answer choices. Having an answer choice that gives respondents the chance to list another option will ensure you don't force respondents to give inaccurate answers.

Lists #2: Make Sure Numeric Categories Are as Broad and Detailed as Needed

Consider this question about income:

Q: What was your total household income for 2013 before taxes?
☐ Less than $50,000
☐ $50,000 to $74,999
☐ $75,000 to $99,999
☐ $100,000 to $149,999
☐ $150,000 or more

This question might be fine if you do not need more precise information about household income. However, depending on your needs, there could be a couple of problems.

The first problem could be the *range* of income categories offered. In the United States in 2013, over half of adults have household incomes under $50,000. If this question is given to a representative sample of adults, over half the respondents would select the lowest income category offered. If you need to see the relationship between household income and anything else (e.g., interest in a new product, drug and alcohol usage, political views, etc.), you would not have enough detail for about half of the respondents. These categories are simply not broad enough.

Here is an improved version of the question with more categories on both the low and high ends of the income scale:

Q: What was your total household income for 2013 before taxes?
☐ Less than $20,000
☐ $20,000 to $34,999
☐ $35,000 to $49,999
☐ $50,000 to $74,999
☐ $75,000 to $99,999
☐ $100,000 to $149,999
☐ $150,000 to $199,999
☐ $200,000 to $249,999
☐ $250,000 or more

You also need to consider how much detail you want when presenting numeric categories. Let's assume that this study applies only to people who have a household income between $50,000 and $150,000. The original question offered only three categories between $50,000 and $149,000. This would not be detailed enough for what many surveys are attempting to measure and analyze. Providing more detailed categories would work better:

Q: What was your total household income for 2013 before taxes?
☐ Less than $50,000
☐ $50,000 to $59,999
☐ $60,000 to $69,999
☐ $70,000 to $79,999
☐ $80,000 to $89,999
☐ $90,000 to $99,999
☐ $100,000 to $109,999
☐ $110,000 to $119,999

☐ $120,000 to $129,999
☐ $130,000 to $139,999
☐ $140,000 to $149,999
☐ $150,000 or more

When you offer respondents numeric categories, you are making the question easier and more acceptable to answer since some respondents think something like their exact household income is none of your business. Make sure your categories are both broad and detailed enough so that when you analyze the data, you have enough information to make the necessary decisions.

There is another issue to consider when offering numeric categories. Smyth, Dillman, and Christian (2007, 2009) have found that the categories offered to respondents can have an effect on the responses themselves. In experiments asking students about the number of hours per day they study, watch TV, or spend time on the computer, the answers were surprisingly different depending on the answer categories offered.

As an example, Rockwood, Sangster, and Dillman (1997) asked students how many hours they studied per day. One group was asked to select from a low range of answer choices while another group was asked to select from a high range of answer choices.

Low Range of Answer Choices	High Range of Answer Choices
Less than .5 hours per day	Less than 2.5 hours
.5–1 hour	2.5–3 hours
1–1.5 hours	3–3.5 hours
1–2 hours	3.5–4 hours
2–2.5 hours	4–4.5 hours
More than 2.5 hours	More than 4.5 hours

When students saw the low range of answer choices, only 23 percent indicated that they studied more than 2.5 hours per day. When students were asked to select from the high range of answer choices, 69 percent indicated they studied 2.5 hours or more per day. The answer choices offered clearly influenced the responses.

These researchers speculate that people assume the range of categories offered represents what most people do. Respondents then calibrate their answers to adjust for their sense of how much they engage in the activity relative to their peers. Respondents may also not like to be in one of the extreme categories, which suggests that when you offer category options, it is best to make the range of numeric categories wide.

This research on how the numeric categories offered affect responses involves asking respondents for information they have to estimate. The average number of hours per day one spends studying is more difficult to estimate than numbers that are static such as age, household income, number of children, and so on. If you are concerned about getting the right estimates, you certainly want to make sure that the range of categories offered is broad enough to represent the entire range of possible answers.

To avoid the effect of numeric categories on responses, you might also consider replacing the categories with an answer box, as displayed in the question below.

Q: How many hours did you study in the past 24 hours?

_____ Number of hours

Or, if you just want to get an impression, you might ask:

Q: Thinking about the past 5 days, what is the average number of hours you studied each day?

_____ Average number of hours studied each day in past 5 days

Lists #3: Make Sure Items on the List Do Not Overlap

Consider the following question:

Q: Where have you seen or heard information about how to improve your credit score? *Please check all that apply.*
- ☐ Website
- ☐ Magazine
- ☐ Television
- ☐ Radio
- ☐ Newspaper
- ☐ News
- ☐ Other (Please describe _____)

The problem with this question is that "News" overlaps with other items on the list. You can receive news from websites, magazines, television, radio, and newspapers. Some respondents who saw a news story in a magazine, for example, might check magazine but not news, or vice versa. Some respondents will believe they have already given a sufficient answer to the question. As a result, the data you get back from questions with overlapping categories is flawed.

Below is an improved version of the question. Removing "News" eliminates overlapping categories.

Improved Question:

Q: Where have you seen or heard information about how to improve your credit score? *Please check all that apply.*
- ☐ Website
- ☐ Magazine
- ☐ Television
- ☐ Radio
- ☐ Newspaper
- ☐ Another person (friends, coworkers, or family members)
- ☐ Other (Please describe _____)

We also wondered whether the original list included all possible answer choices (Lists #1). Some respondents might have heard about how to improve their credit score from other people, so we added "Another person (friends, co-workers, or family members)" as an option.

The challenge for questionnaire writers is to come up with a comprehensive list of answer choices that do not overlap. This is why we suggest doing qualitative research first and recommend pretesting all surveys to further refine the categories and vocabulary of respondents.

Here is another example of a question with overlapping answer categories:

Q: Which of the following income categories best describes your total household income before taxes?
- ☐ $30,000 or less
- ☐ $30,000 to less than $40,000
- ☐ $40,000 to less than $50,000
- ☐ $50,000 to less than $60,000
- ☐ $60,000 to less than $70,000
- ☐ $70,000 to less than $80,000
- ☐ $80,000 or more

The problem with this question is that the first two categories overlap. If you make $30,000 before taxes, you actually fall into both of the first two categories. This question also requires a little more work for respondents than is necessary because each number (e.g., $40,000, $50,000, etc.) is used in two categories.

Improved Question:

Q: Which of the following income categories best describes your total household income before taxes?
- ☐ Less than $30,000
- ☐ $30,000 to $39,999
- ☐ $40,000 to $49,999
- ☐ $50,000 to $59,999
- ☐ $60,000 to $69,999
- ☐ $70,000 to $79,999
- ☐ $80,000 or more

Here is another question whose answer choices aren't as simple as they might seem:

Q: Are you:
- ☐ Married
- ☐ Single
- ☐ Divorced
- ☐ Separated
- ☐ Widowed

These may seem like independent categories, but they really aren't. People who are divorced are also single.

Improved Question:

Q: Have you ever been married?
- ☐ Yes
- ☐ No

[IF YES]

Q: Are you currently...?
- ☐ Married
- ☐ Separated
- ☐ Divorced
- ☐ Widowed

When asking respondents to select from a list, make sure the answer options do not overlap. This will help ensure that the data you get back from the survey is accurate.

Lists #4: Consider Using Forced Choice Instead of "Check All That Apply"

We often present respondents with a list of items and want to know which ones are true for them. One way is to ask respondents to check all that apply. Another way is to force respondents to indicate yes or no to each item on the list.

> *Forced choice:* an approach wherein you require respondents to answer yes or no to each item on the list.

In telephone-administered surveys, you almost always have to use the forced-choice approach. Respondents simply can't remember all the items on the list. But with paper or computer-administered surveys, you have to decide which approach is best.

Figure 10.1 is a side-by-side display of these two options from a study conducted at Washington State University (Smyth et al., 2005).

Figure 10.1

Check All That Apply	Forced Choice		
Which of the following items were reasons why you chose to leave the university? *Please check all that apply.*	**Please look at each item below and let us know if it was a reason why you chose to leave the university?**		
		Yes	**No**
	The social environment	☐	☐
☐ The social environment	Courses not available	☐	☐
☐ Courses not available	Lost financial aid	☐	☐
☐ Lost financial aid	Other financial pressures	☐	☐
☐ Other financial pressures	I became physically ill	☐	☐
☐ I became physically ill	I developed emotional problems (depression, anxiety, etc.)	☐	☐
☐ I developed emotional problems (depression, anxiety, etc.)	A family member became ill or died	☐	☐
☐ A family member became ill or died	Received a job offer	☐	☐
☐ Received a job offer	Conflict with a faculty member	☐	☐
☐ Conflict with a faculty member	☐ Other (Please specify _____)		
☐ Other (Please specify _____)			

The difference between these approaches is subtle. The "check all that apply" approach asks respondents to look at the list and check only those items that are true for them. Not checking an item is how they say no. The forced-choice format requires respondents to consider every item on the list and to explicitly indicate either yes or no.

Experts in questionnaire design have thought about which of these two approaches is best. Most of the research shows that forced choice delivers more accurate answers. Respondents take more time and answer affirmatively more often in the forced-choice format. One hypothesis is that the "check all that apply" format lends itself to a less rigorous review of each item. It is a little easier to just check enough items and move on to the next question. Another way to think about it is that forced choice requires respondents to say yes or no to each item, so naturally each item will get more attention than if it were embedded in a list and respondents were asked to simply find items on the list that apply to them.

To further explore the issue, let's look at another example. Here is a question from a survey of high school teachers:

Q: In the past 12 months, which of the following have you done? *Please check all that apply:*
- ☐ Taught any in-service workshops in science or science teaching
- ☐ Mentored another teacher as part of a formal program
- ☐ Received any local, state, or national grants for science teaching
- ☐ Served on a school or district science curriculum committee
- ☐ Served on a school or district science textbook selection committee

You can see how respondents might look at this list and not read every item carefully. They might think that answering a few questions accurately is good enough.

We can encourage better attention to each item by using the forced-choice approach. Since each response is, in effect, a separate question, we are essentially treating each item as an individual question with its own answer categories of yes or no.

Improved Question:

Q: In the past 12 months, have you:
- a. Taught any in-service workshops in science or science teaching? Yes ☐ No ☐
- b. Mentored another teacher as part of a formal program?   Yes ☐ No ☐
- c. Received any local, state, or national grants for science teaching? Yes ☐ No ☐
- d. Served on a school or district science curriculum committee?   Yes ☐ No ☐
- e. Served on a school or district science textbook selection committee?
                                                                    Yes ☐ No ☐

Forced choice is a better way to ensure that respondents think more carefully about each item. There has been enough research on this topic to lead us to recommend this approach in most circumstances.

There are, however, exceptions to the rule. Forced choice does require more time and effort from respondents. If the list of items is short, simple, and easy for respondents to answer, you may get equally good data from a "check all that apply" approach.

Here is a question for women who have stretch marks:

Q: Where on your body do you have stretch marks? *Please check all that apply.*
- ☐ Abdomen
- ☐ Breasts
- ☐ Thighs
- ☐ Arms
- ☐ Hips
- ☐ Lower legs
- ☐ Buttocks
- ☐ Other (Please specify _____)

In this case, the number of items is 7 (not counting Other). We suspect that women know where their stretch marks are and that it would be easy to look at this list and check the correct items. Asking them to check yes or no for each item would probably be onerous.

As a rule of thumb, we suggest using forced choice in most circumstances. Limit the exceptions to this rule to cases where the number of items is fewer than 10 and where the answer does not require much thought.

Lists #5: Use the Question to Direct Respondents to the List

Consider the following question and then read what two respondents thought when they first read the question:

Q: How would you describe the home in which you currently live? (*Select only one.*)
- ☐ Single-family home that I own
- ☐ Single-family home that I rent or lease
- ☐ Condominium or landominium
- ☐ Apartment
- ☐ Other (please tell us what it is _____)

Josh:
When I saw "how would you describe the home in which you currently live?" the first thing I thought about was "brick with wood trim," and that clearly wasn't what they wanted.

Dan:
When I saw "describe," the first thing I thought of was "too expensive!"

When people are asked something like "How would you describe the home in which you currently live?" they immediately form mental associations that may have nothing to do with the question. This may not seem like a big deal— not worthy perhaps of a formal guideline for questionnaire design to solve it. And it would be no big deal if the questionnaire had only 5 or 10 questions, but questionnaires usually ask for lots of information. The more respondents have to work, the more fatigued they become and the less they will attend to questions and give thoughtful answers.

Sometimes subtly adjusting questions makes them clearer and easier to answer. Let's apply the guideline and have the question direct respondents to the list, avoiding any premature associations.

Improved Question:

Q: Which one of the following descriptions best describes the home in which you currently live? *Select only one:*
☐ Single-family home that I own
☐ Single-family home that I rent or lease
☐ Condominium or landominium
☐ Apartment
☐ Other (please tell us what it is _____)

Directing respondents to the list makes the question more straightforward and a little easier to understand quickly.

Here is a question that was given to doctors:

Q: Is your practice solo, group (all one specialty), or group (multiple specialties)? *Choose only one answer.*
☐ Solo
☐ Group (all one specialty)
☐ Group (multiple specialties)

This question is somewhat cumbersome because the answer choices are stated in both the question stem and the list of possible answers.

Let's fix this question by using the question stem to direct respondents to the list:

Improved Question:

Q: Which one of the following best describes your practice? *Choose only one answer:*
☐ Solo
☐ Group, all one specialty
☐ Group, multiple specialties

This version of the question is a little easier to read and understand.

Other Applications of Having the Question and the Answer Choices Work Together

We learned in Clear #1 to state the unit of measurement in the question. While this is usually good practice, we can sometimes shorten the question and direct respondents to the list instead, as the following examples demonstrate.

Q: Are you . . . ?
☐ Under 20
☐ 20–29
☐ 30–39
☐ 40–49
☐ 50–59
☐ 60–69
☐ 70 or older

Q: Are you . . . ?
☐ Male
☐ Female

Directing respondents to the list in order to understand the question is a useful way to make questions easier to understand. In some situations, it is also a way to make the question clearer by avoiding any extra associations in the question stem. This simple technique improves the clarity of questions and helps reserve the energy of respondents for the rest of the questionnaire.

CHAPTER 11

Presenting Rating Scales

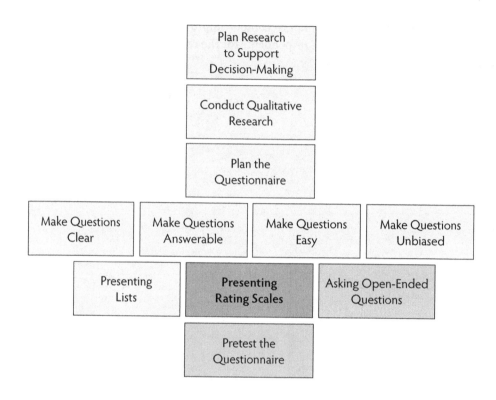

Like the guidelines for lists, these guidelines for rating items on a scale are in fact special cases of making questions clear, answerable, easy, and unbiased.

Rating scales are extremely useful in survey research because they allow us to measure the strength of a response along a continuum. Instead of simply asking respondents whether they are satisfied or dissatisfied, we use a scale to ask them to rate their *level* of satisfaction or dissatisfaction. Instead of asking respondents whether a list of issues is important to them in the upcoming election, we can find out *how important* each of these issues is by providing an importance scale.

We can illustrate the benefit of using rating scales with an example of two approaches to asking a question: the dichotomy approach and the rating-scale approach. Consider the following example about respondents' likelihood of purchasing a product:

Select from Categories We Provide:

Q: Are you likely or unlikely to purchase this product?
- ☐ Likely
- ☐ Unlikely

Provide a Rating on a Scale We Provide:

Q: How likely or unlikely are you to purchase this product?

☐ Very likely
☐ Somewhat likely
☐ Neither likely or unlikely
☐ Somewhat unlikely
☐ Very unlikely

We get more specific information by asking people to give us a rating of their likelihood to purchase the product on the scale we provided. We get the strength of their commitment.

Further, the rating scale provides answer choices that better reflect how people think about issues. The levels along the continuum of the scale are, in fact, answer choices. When it comes to satisfaction or dissatisfaction, with only two choices—satisfied or dissatisfied—some respondents will not feel able to accurately identify their point of view. Giving people several answer choices along a continuum helps them find a answer that reflects their views.

Some of the most frequently used rating scales include:

1. Satisfaction (Please rate your satisfaction . . .)
2. Likelihood (How likely are you to . . .)
3. Importance (How important is . . .)
4. Interest (How interested are you in . . .)
5. Performance (Please rate the performance of . . .)
6. Favor/Oppose (To what extent do you favor or oppose . . .)
7. Agree/Disagree (Please rate the extent to which you agree or disagree . . .)

There are many other less common scales that you can use, depending on the topics you are researching.

Think carefully about the scale you provide and what you want respondents to rate. What information do you really need for the decisions you intend to make? Do you want to measure *interest* in your new product or *likelihood to purchase* your new product? Do you want to know whether customers agree or disagree with a statement about the cleanliness of the bathroom, or do you want to know their rating of the cleanliness of the bathroom? Determining the right scale—one that matches how respondents think about the topic *and* gives you the information you need—is critical.

This chapter on scales requires a brief discussion of terminology. Consider the following two ways of asking about interest in learning more about questionnaire design.

Ordered Categories	Numeric Scales

How interested are you in learning more about questionnaire design?
☐ Extremely interested
☐ Very interested
☐ Interested
☐ Somewhat interested
☐ Not at all interested
	How interested are you in learning more about questionnaire design?
	
	Not at all interested Very Interested
	  1 2 3 4 5
	  ○ ○ ○ ○ ○

When all the response options are labeled and have an order, they are often referred to as ordered categories. Numbers are rarely attached to such categories. Owing to this lack of numbers, some people do not think of ordered categories as true scales, but it suits our purposes to present ordered categories in the chapter on scales because they are a natural alternative to a numbered scale, as the example above shows.

The guidelines on scaling that we provide in this chapter are best considered and applied together. They affect each other. For example, you need to think about the number of items you ask respondents to scale and the length of the scale together. If you are asking respondents to rate a lot of items, lean toward shorter scales. If you are asking respondents to rate only a few items, you can use a longer scale. However, make sure you are not asking respondents to provide their view on a scale with more levels than they have in their heads. Asking people to rate their likelihood to recommend a product that doesn't matter much to them on a scale of 1 to 10 is asking too much.

Scale Toolbox

It is helpful for questionnaire writers to have a toolbox of key issues to consider when constructing rating scales. Here is a toolbox:

- What do you want to measure (e.g., likelihood, interest, satisfaction)? Consider how people think about the topic of interest and what information you really need.
- Should you use a unipolar or bipolar scale? Think about whether the dimension you are scaling has a natural opposite and whether you need to capture information from the opposite end of the spectrum.
- What will be the length of the scale (e.g., 5 points, 7 points, or some other length)? Think about how many levels people actually have in their heads, how many items you are asking respondents to rate, and how much effort you can expect respondents to invest.
- Will you label only the endpoints or also all of the midpoints along the scale? Think about practical issues, such as how the survey will be administered and the amount of space available on paper or screen. Also consider whether respondents will understand a numbered scale without labels for the midpoint.
- What will you call the endpoints (e.g., very satisfied and very dissatisfied, or extremely satisfied and extremely dissatisfied)?
- If you have a bipolar scale, should you provide a midpoint? Does it make sense to force respondents toward one side of the scale or the other?

Twelve Guidelines for Rating Scales

1. Make the scale match how people think about the topic. (Scales #1)
2. Ask the question before describing the scale. (Scales #2)
3. Consider using bipolar scales, unless what you are measuring does not have a clear opposite. (Scales #3)
4. For bipolar scales, decide whether you want a midpoint and what to call it. (Scales #4)
5. Whether to label the middle points is usually a practical decision. (Scales #5)
6. Limit the number of times you ask respondents to rate things. (Scales #6)
7. Make the scale length reasonable—shorter is usually better. (Scales #7)
8. Don't make the endpoints too extreme. (Scales #8)
9. Make sure bipolar scales are balanced. (Scales #9)
10. Replace agree/disagree scales with direct questions about what you really want to measure. (Scales #10)
11. If you are naming only the endpoints, present the scale horizontally with the positive endpoint and higher numbers to the right. (Scales #11)
12. When naming all the points on the scale, put the more positive labels at the top when displayed vertically or to the right when displayed horizontally. (Scales #12)

Scales #1: Make the Scale Match How People Think about the Topic

Here is an example from a questionnaire given at a nationally recognized restaurant chain:

Q: How satisfied were you with your coffee?
- ☐ Very satisfied
- ☐ Satisfied
- ☐ Neither satisfied nor dissatisfied
- ☐ Dissatisfied
- ☐ Very dissatisfied

One of us actually took this survey after having lunch at this restaurant. I indicated that I was satisfied with the coffee, but afterward I wondered why I gave that answer. Truthfully, I thought their coffee was mediocre.

The issue here is subtle but important. How do people actually think about the coffee at a restaurant chain? Do they think about coffee in terms of *satisfaction*? Is that their vocabulary—their internal scale for coffee at a place where they go for lunch? To make questions clear, the rating scale you provide needs to match how respondents think about the topic.

One way to determine how people think about the topic would be to imagine how you would naturally ask someone about it. In this case, you might say, "Did you like the coffee?" or "How good was the coffee at the restaurant?"

Maybe the better way to ask the question—if we consider how people actually think about coffee—would be like this:

Improved Question:

Q: Please let us know how much you liked or disliked the coffee you had at your most recent visit to our restaurant.

I did NOT like the coffee at all	1	2	3	4	5	I LIKED the coffee very much

Do you see how the improved question may be a better match with the scale people have in their heads—their way of thinking about coffee at a place where they go for lunch?

It has become almost reflexive for questionnaire writers to provide satisfaction scales when in fact the scale people have in their heads may be something else. Satisfaction measures are appropriate for many types of issues but not all. It all depends on how respondents think about the topic. For example, they might think of their hotel stay in terms of satisfaction but measure coffee or food on a different dimension such as likability, taste, or some other measure. The key is to do qualitative research first to find out how respondents think and to make sure that what you are measuring is indeed what you need for decision-making.

When we go back to the basics—organizing research to support decision-making—we suspect that the restaurant chain is asking about their coffee to determine whether they need to make any changes to its quality. Their chances of getting an accurate answer will improve if the scale they provide matches how respondents think about coffee. They'll have less bias and less acquiescence.

Here is another question from a survey of people who recently shopped at a major grocery-store chain:

Q: How would you rate the value provided by the produce department?

Poor value	1	2	3	4	5	Excellent value

Do you think people who shop at grocery stores think about the *value* provided by the produce department? For the purposes of illustration, let's assume grocery-store shoppers actually think about freshness, prices, availability of fruits and vegetables, and so on.

Assuming the questionnaire writers screen people into the next set of questions based on their having shopped for produce, they might ask about freshness:

Improved Question:

Q: Thinking about your most recent shopping trip, how would you rate the overall freshness of the produce?

Not at all fresh	1	2	3	4	5	Very fresh

They might also ask whether they found all the items they were looking for, and if not, what items they were not able to find. This would be a yes/no question with a follow-up open-ended question or a select-from-list question.

Another way to gauge how people view your product or service is to ask if they would recommend it. Here is another question from a restaurant's survey about their coffee:

Q: How likely are you to recommend our coffee to friends or family?
- ☐ Very likely
- ☐ Likely
- ☐ Neither likely nor unlikely
- ☐ Unlikely
- ☐ Very unlikely

I said that I was likely to recommend the coffee. But when I thought about my answer, it occurred to me that I do not go around recommending coffee to people. I took the survey over a year ago, and I have yet to recommend the coffee to anyone!

Does the "likelihood to recommend" scale fit how people think about coffee? Maybe yes, if the setting is a coffeehouse or if the restaurant features coffee. But probably not if coffee is not the central focus of the restaurant.

Improved Question:

Q: In the past 30 days, have you recommended our coffee to friends or family?
- ☐ Yes
- ☐ No

Here is another question from a survey we received from a marketing research company we worked with:

Q: How would you rate the quality of performance of our company on the most recent project?
- ☐ Very good
- ☐ Good
- ☐ Slightly good
- ☐ Neither good nor poor
- ☐ Slightly poor
- ☐ Poor
- ☐ Very poor

The first problem lies with the question stem. It is a subtle problem, and you might consider it a little picky. Do you think the question would better match how people think about the topic if it simply asked about *performance* rather than *quality of* performance? We thought about their performance as either good or bad on a series of different dimensions such as responsiveness, sophistication with recruiting, flexibility, and so on.

Let's change the question stem to ask about performance. We will also show two versions of the scale: one that labels each item and one that labels only the endpoints:

Improved Question A:

Q: How would you rate the overall performance of our company on the most recent project?

☐ Very good
☐ Good
☐ Slightly good
☐ Neither good nor poor
☐ Slightly poor
☐ Poor
☐ Very poor

Improved Question B:

Q: How would you rate the overall performance of our company on the most recent project?

Very poor   1   2   3   4   5   6   7   Very good

Another reason to remove the idea of quality from the question stem is that it might add a positive bias. (Recall Unbiased #1: Do not introduce ideas or opinions in questions that will influence responses.)

We see a lot of questions whose rating scale reflects the views of the organization doing the survey, not the views of respondents. Some of these measurements come from whatever is popular in management. If the popular measure is "exceeding expectations," then we see questionnaires that ask people whether their expectations were exceeded. If the popular measure is "quality," then we'll see questions that ask about quality.

In qualitative research and later in pretesting, make sure the rating scales you construct reflect the rating scales respondents have in their heads. Using their rating scales and their vocabulary will make the questions clearer, and you will get more accurate data.

Related Guidelines

Scales #1	Clear #2	Clear #5
Make the scale match how people think about the topic.	Use the vocabulary of respondents.	Make sure the question is really asking only one question.

Scales #1 is a special case of making questions clear. Making the scale match how people think about the topic is like using the vocabulary of respondents (Clear #2).

Additionally, when we ask respondents to rate something on a scale that they do not use, we are actually asking them to do two things. If we ask someone to rate their *satisfaction* with the coffee, yet they naturally think about whether they *liked* the coffee, they have to translate their assessment of how much they liked the coffee into a rating of their satisfaction with it. This is a special case of Clear #5 (make sure the question is really asking only one question).

Scales #2: Ask the Question before Describing the Scale

Consider this question, which describes the scale first, and then read what two respondents thought.

Q: On a scale of 1 to 7, where 1 means poor and 7 means excellent, how would you rate the quality of the hotel?

Poor   1   2   3   4   5   6   7   Excellent

Charles:	Jennifer:
When I read the scale, I thought they were going to ask me about the restaurant. I had to rethink my answer when I saw the real question.	*I had to read this question twice. When I thought about the overall quality of the hotel, I then had to go back to see what the 1 and the 7 meant.*

The problem is that respondents are asked to think about the rating scale before they know what they are rating. One respondent had automatic associations that veered away from what the question was intending to measure. The other had forgotten the scale by the time she got to the question.

It is easier for respondents to encounter the question before you describe the scale.

Improved Question:

Q: How would you rate the quality of the hotel, where 1 means poor and 7 means excellent?

Poor   1   2   3   4   5   6   7   Excellent

Here is a question from a survey about a new perfume:

Q: On a scale of 1 to 6, where 1 is very unfavorable and 6 is very favorable, what is your opinion of the scent of the perfume you just tried?

Very unfavorable   1   2   3   4   5   6   Very favorable

As in the previous question, we need to ask the question before describing the scale. Because this question is a little longer, we will use a second sentence to describe the scale.

Improved Question:

Q: What was your opinion of the scent of the perfume you tried? Use the scale below, where 1 is very unfavorable and 6 is very favorable.

Very unfavorable   1   2   3   4   5   6   Very favorable

The improved question is better because it makes the actual question about the scent clear and precise before respondents are presented with the scale.

Here is a question from a survey of people who called their managed-care company about a health-care claim.

Q: On a scale of 1 to 5, where 1 means not at all helpful and 5 means very helpful, how helpful or unhelpful was the representative the last time you spoke to our representative about your claim?

Not at all helpful   1   2   3   4   5   Very helpful

Here is what two respondents thought when we asked them how they answered the question during pretesting.

Allegra:	Alesya:
When I read the scale, I thought they were going to ask about how helpful the pamphlet was that goes with the form I had to fill out.	*I had to read this question twice. I thought they were going to ask about the helpfulness of the nursing staff at the hospital.*

These respondents had immediate associations with other topics when they read the scale. When they saw the question, they had to replace those automatic associations with the new topic. One of them had to reread the question.

In the improved version of the question below, we first ask respondents to think about the event (talking to our representative about your claim) and then ask about the helpfulness of the representative. But instead of describing the scale in the question stem, we let the scale describe itself.

Improved Question:

Q: Thinking about the last time you talked with our representative about your claim, how helpful or unhelpful was the representative?

Not at all helpful   1   2   3   4   5   Very helpful

The question stem starts with what you want the respondent to think about and follows with how to scale their response, using the scale itself to define the meaning of the endpoints.

This technique of asking respondents to think about a specific event (the last time they talked to our representative) and then asking something about that event (the helpfulness of the representative) helps make what you are asking about crystal clear. Assuming your question stem and scale match (as they should!), pointing respondents to the scale is an efficient way to ask the question.

We said earlier that these guidelines on scaling are special cases of making questions clear, answerable, easy, and unbiased. Asking the question before describing the scale makes it easier for respondents. As we said in the introduction to chapter 6, "Make Questions Clear," when respondents read your question, they should be able to say, "I know what they want from me."

Scales #3: Consider Using Bipolar Scales, Unless What You Are Measuring Does Not Have a Clear Opposite

A unipolar scale measures the presence or absence of an attribute. One end of the scale represents the absence of the attribute, while the other end of the scale represents an abundance of the attribute. A bipolar scale measures an attribute and its polar opposite on the same scale. It has two endpoints that represent clear opposites.

Bipolar scales measure both the negative and positive sides of an attribute along the same continuum. They allow respondents to place themselves along a continuum from positive to negative, high to low, large to small, or any other paired opposites. For example, if you are using positive and negative, the left side of the scale measures strength of negative, while the right side of the scale measures strength of positive. This makes sense when respondents think about the positive and negative aspects of the subject matter along the same continuum.

As an example, people who stay at a hotel think about their satisfaction or dissatisfaction with their stay in the same breath. It makes sense to provide a scale that offers all of their possible responses to their stay.

Below are examples of unipolar and bipolar scales.

A unipolar scale measures the presence or absence of an attribute.

Unipolar Scale Question:

Q: How much do you favor or not favor the proposed new school tax?

Do not favor at all   1   2   3   4   5   Strongly favor

A bipolar scale measures an attribute and its polar opposite on the same scale.

Bipolar Scale Question:

Q: How much do you favor or oppose the proposed new school tax?

Strongly oppose		Neither favor nor oppose		Strongly favor
1	2	3	4	5
○	○	○	○	○

While the unipolar scale measures the strength of favoring the proposed new school tax, it does not measure respondents' opposition. The bipolar scale captures both the strength of favoring and the strength of opposing the tax.

Many of the issues we want respondents to rate—favorability, satisfaction, approval, likelihood to purchase, and so on—can be presented as unipolar or bipolar scales. However, not all issues we want to scale have natural opposites. We will discuss that later. For now, we are going to show that when an issue has a natural opposite, a bipolar scale captures more information than a unipolar scale does.

Read the following question that has a unipolar scale, and then read what two respondents thought when they answered it.

Q: How satisfied were you with the car you rented?

Not at all satisfied   1   2   3   4   5   Very satisfied

Bob:
I wasn't really dissatisfied, but I can't say that I was satisfied, so I guess that means a 1.

Fred:
The car was terrible! I'll give it a 1, but I should probably give it a negative 10!

The problem with this question is that the full range of responses is not represented in the scale. Bob was not satisfied or dissatisfied, so he gave a 1. Fred hated the car, but the worst score he could give was a 1.

Using a bipolar scale improves the question.

The Importance of Understanding What Low Scores Mean

When you give respondents a unipolar scale for something that has a natural opposite, like satisfaction in the car-rental example, you simply cannot know what respondents meant when they gave low scores. All you can know is that they were not satisfied.

Let's assume you are in charge of marketing research for one of the large rental car companies. You are presenting the results of a study you commissioned with over five hundred customers. The company spent a lot of money to understand factors that lead to satisfaction and dissatisfaction. Your question asked respondents to rate their satisfaction on a unipolar scale, where 1 equals "not at all satisfied" and 5 equals "very satisfied."

As you present the results, the vice president of the division asks you, "What about those people who answered that question with 1s and 2s? Are they dissatisfied, or are they just not satisfied?" Your answer with the unipolar scale could only be, "I don't know." With the bipolar scale, you would be able to answer the question.

Improved Question:

Q: How satisfied or dissatisfied were you with the car you rented?

Very dissatisfied   1   2   3   4   5   Very satisfied

This version of the question has two endpoints that are clear opposites, which is the definition of a bipolar scale. It allows respondents to find their full range of possible responses to the question. A bipolar scale allows someone like Fred who was very dissatisfied to give a rating that accurately reflects his opinion—a 1. Someone like Bob can give a rating that is closer to the middle of the scale: not satisfied, but not necessarily dissatisfied—a 3.

The benefit of a bipolar scale is that it allows you as a researcher to more accurately measure and interpret responses. In the original version of the ques-

Figure 11.1

Unipolar:	Bipolar:
How satisfied or not satisfied are you with the car you rented? Not satisfied 1 2 3 4 5 Very satisfied	**How dissatisfied or satisfied are you with the car you rented?** Very dissatisfied 1 2 3 4 5 Very satisfied
How strongly do you favor or not favor the tax on cigarettes? Do not favor at all 1 2 3 4 5 Strongly favor	**How strongly do you favor or oppose the tax on cigarettes?** Strongly oppose 1 2 3 4 5 Strongly favor
How likely or not likely are you to purchase the product? ☐ Extremely likely ☐ Very likely ☐ Likely ☐ Somewhat likely ☐ Not at all likely	**How likely or unlikely are you to purchase the product?** ☐ Very likely ☐ Likely ☐ Neither likely nor unlikely ☐ Unlikely ☐ Very unlikely

tion, a rating of 1 could mean not satisfied, or it could mean extremely dissatisfied. You simply don't know.

Figure 11.1 shows a few side-by-side examples of scales that can be presented to respondents as either unipolar or bipolar.

When the positive and negative sides of the issue appear along the same continuum and can be clearly described with labels, the bipolar scale gives the full spectrum of choices for respondents to consider.

What about situations where what you want people to rate does not have a natural and clear opposite?

Consider the following example from a dental survey:

Q: How painful was the root canal?

Not at all painful   1   2   3   4   5   6   7   8   9   10   Extremely painful

There is really not a natural opposite of pain for this situation. We suppose that there are situations where the opposite of pain would be pleasure, but not for a root canal! The best you can hope for is a pain-free, or nearly pain-free, experience.

Suppose you want respondents to rate their interest in something. The natural opposite is probably no interest:

Not at all interested   1   2   3   4   5   Very interested

Sure, you could argue that the opposite of interest is disinterest, but for many topics the scale that respondents have in their minds goes from a lack of interest to a lot of interest.

The scale is also inherently unipolar when we ask respondents how well a list of statements describes something. In this example the question is asking about how well each statement describes the respondent:

Q: Please rate how well each statement describes you. *Use the following scale, where 1 = does not describe me at all and 5 = describes me very well.*

| | Does Not Describe Me at All | | | | Describes Me Very Well |
	1	2	3	4	5
Statement 1	○	○	○	○	○
Statement 2	○	○	○	○	○
Statement 3	○	○	○	○	○

The statements either describe the respondent or they don't. It would be somewhat awkward to construct a clear opposite. The unipolar scale makes sense and will collect accurate information.

There will be times when you have to choose between using a unipolar scale and a bipolar scale. Let's look at an example that presents the desirability of attributes of a skin-care product on a unipolar scale:

Q: Below is a list of characteristics of skin-care products that may or may not be desirable to you. Please rate how not at all desirable or desirable each item is to you using the rating scale below.

	Not at all desirable				Very desirable
	1	2	3	4	5
Is greaseless	○	○	○	○	○
Is colorless	○	○	○	○	○
Contains no scent	○	○	○	○	○
Contains aloe vera	○	○	○	○	○

Yet for the desirability of attributes of skin-care products, there may be a natural opposite: undesirable. We could present the question with a bipolar scale.

Q: Below is a list of characteristics of skin-care products that may or may not be desirable to you. Please rate how undesirable or desirable each item is to you using the rating scale below.

	Very undesirable				Very desirable
	1	2	3	4	5
Is greaseless	○	○	○	○	○
Is colorless	○	○	○	○	○
Contains no scent	○	○	○	○	○
Contains aloe vera	○	○	○	○	○

We would have to think long and hard about which scale would provide better information. The argument for the unipolar scale is that it is easier for respondents to use. If all we needed to know is which attributes were most desirable, we might choose the unipolar scale. However, if we need to know which of these attributes were particularly undesirable, we would need to use the bipolar scale.

Here is an example from a survey about the effectiveness of a lotion for treating the pain associated with sunburn:

Q: How effective was the lotion for treating the pain associated with your sunburn?

Not at all effective   1 2 3 4 5   Very effective

When rating the effectiveness of a treatment, there really is no natural opposite. It either provided some level of effectiveness or none at all.

However, what if you had reason to believe that the lotion could make the pain worse? You might have to change how you label the endpoints because there is not a clear word or phrase that is the natural opposite of effectiveness. Here we made the scale bipolar by replacing "effectiveness" on the positive side of the scale with "made the pain much better," making it easy to find the words for a natural opposite:

Q: Did the lotion for your sunburn make the pain better or worse? Please check the box below to indicate the effect of the lotion on your sunburn pain.

Made the pain much worse		Made the pain neither worse nor better		Made the pain much better
1	2	3	4	5
○	○	○	○	○

In summary, think about the underlying nature of what you are measuring. Does it have a natural opposite? If so, then a bipolar scale is often preferable. It is usually better to make available all the answer choices that respondents might have, even if they are negative. It helps reduce bias and collects better information because people who have negative responses will not be forced to give neutral responses simply because no negative answer choices were offered.

Keep in mind that just because a natural opposite exists in your mind does not necessarily mean it exists for respondents. Check out your views with respondents in qualitative research and during pretesting.

Related Guidelines

Scales #3	Unbiased #3	Lists #1
Consider using bipolar scales, unless what you are measuring does not have a clear opposite.	Make clear that either a positive or a negative answer is equally acceptable.	Make sure the list includes all possible answer choices.

Scales #3 is a special case of making questions unbiased. By giving respondents both the positive and negative side of the scale, you are helping to convey that either a positive or a negative response is equally acceptable. In failing to give the negative side of the scale, you are biasing responses (Unbiased #3).

Also note the similarity between Scales #3 and Lists #1, which says when giving respondents a list from which to select, make sure the list contains all possible choices. For rating scales, the list of possible choices is each point along the scale. If the scale has a natural opposite and respondents might have that view, you need to give them the negative option.

Scales #4: For Bipolar Scales, Decide Whether You Want a Midpoint and What to Call It

When creating a bipolar scale, you need to decide whether to offer respondents a midpoint between the positive and negative sides of the scale. The midpoint usually represents neither a positive nor negative response to the question. If some respondents truly do not have a positive or negative response to the question, it makes sense to offer them a midpoint. Otherwise they would have to give a positive or negative response—even though that would not represent their perspective—in order to move on to the next question.

If you do offer a midpoint to the bipolar scale, make sure you name it even if you do not name all the points along the scale. You need to make sure respondents know what the midpoint means.

In other situations, you may know with certainty that respondents will have either a positive or negative response to the question. In these cases, you may want to remove the option of giving a neutral response, which is sometimes the easiest response, and force respondents to one side of the scale or the other. In these cases, forcing respondents to reveal which way they lean may give you better data.

Consider a question that asks respondents whether they favor or oppose a new school tax.

Q: How much do you favor or oppose the proposed new school tax?

Let's say that you are offering a bipolar scale from "strongly oppose" to "strongly favor." Here are two versions of the scale, one with and one without a midpoint.

With Midpoint:

Strongly oppose		Neither favor nor oppose		Strongly favor
1	2	3	4	5
○	○	○	○	○

Without Midpoint:

Strongly oppose				Strongly favor
1	2	3	4	5
○	○	○	○	○

If you were giving this survey to the entire voting population, it is possible that some people might not care about the topic; others might not know anything about it. In other words, some people will neither favor nor oppose the new school tax. In this case, you need to provide a midpoint to indicate that point of view. Otherwise you will be forcing respondents to give responses that do not reflect their point of view, and the data you collect will be flawed.

Now suppose you are testing a political advertisement supporting or opposing the new school tax with a sample of people. Your job is to estimate the extent to which the advertisement is persuading voters. In this case, you might want to force respondents to reveal whether they lean in one direction or the other after seeing the advertisement. Surely they all have a point of view because they all saw the advertisement.

The key to deciding whether to have a midpoint begins with deciding whether the positive and negative sides of the scale will offer all respondents the chance to answer honestly. We don't want to force people to choose a positive or negative value if they really don't have a positive or negative point of view. Yet in cases where you know that all respondents have had enough experience to form an opinion (e.g., they saw the political advertisement, they stayed in the hotel, they rented a car, etc.), you may want to force respondents to reveal whether they lean to the positive or negative side of the scale, even if their leaning is slight.

When you decide to offer a midpoint, give it a label. To illustrate why, let's revisit the previous bipolar scale, this time without a label for the midpoint:

Q: How much do you favor or oppose the proposed new school tax?

Strongly oppose   1   2   3   4   5   Strongly favor

The problem with not labeling the midpoint is that some respondents will not know what a 3 really means. Some may think a 3 represents a slight level of favorability; others might think it represents a slight level of opposition. Not all respondents read every scale carefully. Someone going through the survey quickly could easily misinterpret this scale as unipolar scale, in which a 3 would represent some level of favorability.

If you want to be sure respondents understand what the midpoint means, provide a label.

Labeling the midpoint is even more important with longer scales. Suppose you presented this question with a 7-point scale to give respondents 3 levels of "oppose" and 3 levels of "favor."

Here are two versions of the question—with and without the midpoint labeled:

Q: How much do you favor or oppose the proposed new school tax?

Midpoint Not Labeled:

Strongly oppose						Strongly favor
1	2	3	4	5	6	7
○	○	○	○	○	○	○

Midpoint Labeled:

Strongly oppose			Neither favor nor oppose			Strongly favor
1	2	3	4	5	6	7
○	○	○	○	○	○	○

The 7-point scale without the midpoint label requires respondents to figure out where the midpoint lies and determine what it means. Remember to make questions easy for respondents for answer! There is no need to require them to figure these things out.

Labeling the midpoint also makes the scale easier to understand because it draws a line between the positive and negative sides of the scale. It also helps respondents see more clearly that each side of the scale has three levels. Again, you want to avoid the circumstance where some respondents have different interpretations of the meaning of the midpoint than you intended.

Let's consider the meaning of the midpoint and what to label it. Most survey researchers have adopted the convention of having the midpoint in a bipolar scale mean *neither the positive nor the negative side of the scale*. In the case of the scale presented earlier, you would label the midpoint "Neither favor nor oppose," as shown below:

Q: How much do you favor or oppose the proposed new school tax?

Strongly oppose		Neither favor nor oppose		Strongly favor
1	2	3	4	5
○	○	○	○	○

Here are a few examples of questions with bipolar scales whose midpoints are labeled:

Q: Please rate your satisfaction with your most recent stay at the hotel.

Very unsatisfied		Neither satisfied nor dissatisfied		Very satisfied
1	2	3	4	5
○	○	○	○	○

Q: How likely are you to visit this national park in the next 12 months?

Very unlikely		Neither likely nor unlikely		Very likely
1	2	3	4	5
○	○	○	○	○

Q: How likely are you to purchase this product in the next 4 weeks?
- ☐ Definitely will purchase
- ☐ Might purchase
- ☐ May or may not purchase
- ☐ Might not purchase
- ☐ Definitely will not purchase

Note that the scale on purchasing is a slight variation on the wording from the other scales. Its meaning is still the same, indicating neither the positive nor negative sides of the scale.

"Just Right" Bipolar Scales

Most bipolar scales contain the positive and negative sides of the spectrum and a midpoint that represents neither the positive nor the negative side. Another kind of scale, which we call the "just right" scale, is structured a little differently. This form of a bipolar scale is often used in testing products.

Look at this example from product testing for a new snack food:

Please rate the snack food on the following characteristics. You may use any number from 1 to 5 to represent your opinion.

Not salty enough		The right amount of salty		Too salty
1	2	3	4	5
○	○	○	○	○

Not sweet enough		The right amount of sweet		Too sweet
1	2	3	4	5
○	○	○	○	○

Figure 11.2

Unipolar Scale: Midpoint not labeled				
Do not favor at all				Strongly favor
1	2	3	4	5
○	○	○	○	○

Bipolar Scale: Midpoint labeled				
Very unsatisfied		Neither satisfied nor dissatisfied		Very satisfied
1	2	3	4	5
○	○	○	○	○

What is different about these scales is that the left and the right side both represent negative values. The midpoint is the positive point on the scale. The midpoint needs to be labeled differently than it would be in the other scales presented in this chapter. "Neither not salty enough nor too salty" would be technically accurate, but awkward.

Think carefully about whether it makes sense to provide a midpoint. You do not want to force people to give a positive or negative response if they do not have one. Yet there are situations where you know respondents have some leaning toward the positive or negative side of the scale. In these cases, it may make sense to require respondents to indicate which way they lean.

As we said before, whenever you have a midpoint, provide a label. There is no need to leave each respondent to interpret the midpoint. Clearly labeling the midpoint in bipolar scales will improve the quality of your data.

Scales #5: Whether to Label the Middle Points Is Usually a Practical Decision

In Scales #4 we discussed whether to provide a midpoint for a bipolar scale and recommended naming it if you decide to have one. Here we are addressing a different concept: *middle points*. By middle points we mean *all the points* between the endpoints for both unipolar and bipolar scales.

When you create a unipolar or bipolar scale, you obviously have to label the endpoints. But what about the *middle points* along the scale? For the bipolar scale, we said in Scales #4 that if you have a *midpoint* (the level that separates the positive and negative sides of the scale), you should provide a label for that one specific point to ensure that respondents recognize the dividing line between both ends of the scale and are clear about what it means. But what about the other middle points for the bipolar scale? And what about the middle points for a unipolar scale?

If you are conducting a survey with a group of people that will not understand the meaning of a numbered scale with only the endpoints labeled, you need to label the middle points. Keep in mind, that is the exception, not the rule.

Most people who answer surveys understand the concept of a numbered scale with only the endpoints labeled. So how do you know when to label the middle points as well?

The decision to label the middle points rests largely with practical issues. If the survey is going to be read over the phone, you might want to label the endpoints only, as hearing each label can be tiresome to respondents. Additionally, the most recently heard labels are the easiest to remember, so reading all the labels introduces an inherent bias.

If the questionnaire is on paper, you might want to conserve space and not label the middle points.

Suppose you plan on reporting the data in publications. You might elect to have labels for middle points so you can provide a table with summary results next to each label in the scale, as displayed in Figure 11.3. It would be awkward to report these results if the scale had only the endpoints and the midpoint labeled.

Figure 11.3: Results from Survey on the Proposed New School Tax

25% Strongly favor
21% Favor
12% Neither favor nor oppose
23% Oppose
19% Strongly oppose
Question: How much do you favor or oppose the proposed new school tax?

Since in most cases you will have a choice as to whether to label the middle points, let's walk through a few examples and discuss some issues to consider.

Here are two versions of a question with a unipolar interest scale—one with the middle points labeled and one with the middle points not labeled.

Middle Points Labeled	Middle Points Not Labeled
How interested are you in learning more about climate change? ☐ Very interested ☐ Interested ☐ Somewhat interested ☐ Slightly interested ☐ Not at all interested	**How interested are you in learning more about climate change?** Not at all interested Very interested 1 2 3 4 5

For this unipolar scale, both options would elicit useful information. It is hard to argue that one is that much better than the other.

There is no obvious right or wrong answer, with one exception. If you pretest the scale and find that your respondents find one version unclear or harder to answer, use the other one.

Here are two versions of a question with a bipolar scale asking respondents to rate the extent to which they favor or oppose a cigarette tax:

Middle Points Labeled	Middle Points Not Labeled
How strongly do you favor or oppose the new cigarette tax? ☐ Strongly favor ☐ Favor ☐ Neither favor nor oppose ☐ Oppose ☐ Strongly oppose	**How strongly do you favor or oppose the new cigarette tax?** Strongly oppose Neither favor nor oppose Strongly favor 1 2 3 4 5 ○ ○ ○ ○ ○

Both of these methods of presenting the scale would elicit accurate information from respondents. Again, you may have practical reasons associated with the method of administration, the available space on a piece of paper or computer screen, or data reporting needs that make you lean in one direction or the other. As always, pretest the questionnaire to find out whether the scale is working for your target group of respondents.

There is, however, some debate over whether to label the middle points beyond what we have described here. Those who argue for labeling middle points say that associating a label with the level allows you to know what respondents meant when they selected that category. For example, with regard to the question presented earlier on interest in learning more about climate change, they would say that if you don't label the middle points—in this case, 2, 3, and 4—respondents won't necessarily know what 2, 3, or 4 actually mean. Likewise, when you get the results back from the question, you will not know what respondents meant. By replacing these numbers with category labels—in this case, "slightly interested," "somewhat interested," and "interested"—you will ensure that respondents know what these three middle points mean, and you will know what respondents mean when they select them.

This is a reasonable argument, but it's not airtight. Selecting "slightly interested," "somewhat interested," or "interested" does not mean the respondent agrees entirely with the label. A respondent might think, "Well, I am sort of interested and I don't know if that means I am *slightly* interested or *somewhat* interested, but since I would definitely not go out of my way to learn anything about this topic I'll select slightly interested." The label allows you to say that the respondent chose it, but it does not guarantee that there is a perfect fit between their level of interest and the label you provided.

Some people argue in favor of not labeling the middle points. One argument for this approach is that most respondent groups understand that the numbers along the scale represent levels between the endpoints. The interest scale with unlabeled middle points represents levels along the scale from not interested to very interested. Adding our own category labels may only clutter the situation. It might also require respondents to think about the category labels for each level instead of just giving their answer.

Another subtle issue has to do with the implied distance between the points.

One could argue, for example, that leaving the interest-scale middle points un-labeled implies that the points along the scale are equidistant from one another, much like inches along a ruler. It may also be easier for respondents to map their level of interest on the scale when all they have to do is interpret the endpoints and then find a spot on the ruler that fits best.

Labeling the middle points certainly requires a little more work from respondents. They have to hear or read them all and then map their level of interest to the right category. There may also be less of a sense that the levels are equidistant from one another. In the case we just discussed, what is the difference between "slightly interested," "somewhat interested," and "interested"? Researchers like to think that our levels are equidistant from each other, but to respondents, they may not be. Some respondents may think that "slightly interested" is quite distant from "somewhat interested," while "somewhat interested" and "interested" are fairly close together.

In summary, there is no clear rule about whether to label the middle points in the scale. The decision is often determined by practical matters such as how the survey will be administered, the space available on a piece of paper, or whether the data needs to be reported with category labels. If you are struggling with which way to present the scale, pretest the question carefully with enough respondents to find out which way works best.

Scales #6: Limit the Number of Times You Ask Respondents to Rate Things

Rating items on a scale is more challenging to respondents than many questionnaire writers realize. It involves reading the question; determining what the question is asking, thinking about the right answer, often considering several factors that affect the answer; reading the categories on the scale; and then figuring out where their answer fits best on the scale.

To illustrate, consider two versions of the same seemingly simple question below. The version on the left has category labels for all levels of the scale, while the version on the right displays the endpoints along a numbered scale:

Both of these questions require more effort than meets the eye. Respondents have to think about their most recent stay at the hotel and then consider all

Category Labels	Endpoints and Midpoint Labeled along Numbered Scale		
How satisfied or dissatisfied were you with your most recent stay at the hotel? ☐ Very satisfied ☐ Satisfied ☐ Somewhat satisfied ☐ Neither satisfied nor dissatisfied ☐ Somewhat dissatisfied ☐ Dissatisfied ☐ Very dissatisfied	How satisfied or dissatisfied were you with your most recent stay at the hotel? Very dissatisfied Neither satisfied nor dissatisfied Very satisfied 1 2 3 4 5 6 7 ○ ○ ○ ○ ○ ○ ○		

the factors that go into their overall level of satisfaction or dissatisfaction—the room, the bed, Internet access, noise, smell, food, service at check-in, service at check-out, parking, and so on.

These various considerations may make the question less clear than it seems. For example, some respondents might struggle with whether to factor in the noise from the room next door. Was that really the hotel's fault? Others might have had wonderful experiences in the past but found this stay substandard. Even though the question is about the most recent stay, respondents often assume they know the intention of the survey and respond according to their more typical experience. Who would want to get that hotel manager in trouble for just one bad experience when all the others were great?

Once respondents have a sense of their answer, they have to decide where it fits best on the scale. What is the difference between "somewhat satisfied" and "satisfied"? Or, if they are looking at the scale with the endpoints labeled along the numbered scale, what is the difference between a 5 and a 6? It isn't clear. It takes mental energy to answer questions correctly.

We are spelling out the steps in rating something on a scale—in this case, satisfaction or dissatisfaction with a hotel stay—to draw attention to the challenge of the task. Surely many respondents will not take the time and effort to work through every detail and nuance of their answer. Most will give you a reflexive response or impression.

But on some level respondents realize that answering lots of rating-scale questions is difficult. Some rating-scale questions will require respondents to think hard about their answer. Asking respondents to answer only a few questions like this is not too challenging. The problem is when you ask respondents to rate a lot of things. Most people we know are annoyed by questionnaires that ask them to rate more than 15 or 20 items.

To get a better sense of how difficult it is for respondents to rate a lot of items, look at this question from a survey of physicians about products they use for a particular disease.

Q: Please rate how well each statement describes each brand using the scale below:

Does not describe at all   1 2 3 4 5 6 7 8 9 10   Describes very well

	Brand A	Brand B	Brand C	Brand D	Brand E	Brand F	Brand G
Fast onset of action							
Safe for children							
Safe for pregnant women							
Safe for people with diabetes							
Low GI side effects							

	Brand A	Brand B	Brand C	Brand D	Brand E	Brand F	Brand G
Low incidence of sexual dysfunction							
One-a-day dosing							
Safe for long-term usage							
Good for anxiety							
No muscle spasms							
Improves sleep							
Improves energy							
Good compliance among patients							
Low incidence of weight gain							
Low incidence of short-term agitation							
Easy to titrate to proper dose							
Good sales representatives							
From a good company							
Has convenient return policy							
Improves HDL							
Reduces LDL							
Positive effect on triglycerides							
Availability of samples							
Good reimbursement							
Has few drug-to-drug interactions							
Excellent patient support materials							
Ethical advertising to consumers							
Low incidence of nausea							
Low incidence of constipation							
Easy to use in combination with other products							

This question is quite arduous, as it asks respondents to choose a rating of 1 to 10 for each of 30 statements about 7 brands. This means respondents have to provide 210 ratings (30 statements x 7 brands)!

Improving this question begins with going back to the basics. What decisions will this survey address, and what information is needed to make those decisions? In our experience, it is quite rare that so many statements about the brand truly need to be measured. Some statements are central to upcoming decision-making, while others are not. We also find that some brands are much more important, while others are essentially irrelevant.

Here is an improved version of this question that includes only the statements and brands that really matter. We also reduced the length of the scale to make the task easier, or more reasonable, for respondents.

Improved Question:

Q: Please rate how well each statement describes each brand using the scale below:

Does not describe at all   1   2   3   4   5   Describes very well

	Brand A	Brand B	Brand C
Fast onset of action			
Safe for pregnant women			
Safe for people with diabetes			
Low incidence of sexual dysfunction			
Improves sleep			
Improves energy			
Good compliance among patients			
Low incidence of weight gain			
Has few drug-to-drug interactions			
Low incidence of nausea			

This improved question asks for only 30 ratings instead of 210. The data will be much better.

Think about the number of ratings you ask respondents to make, for individual questions as well as for the entire survey. If you have taken surveys that contained several questions with lots of items to rate, you know how hard it is. Many of us have quit surveys because we got to another set of items to rate after plowing through previous questions with lots of items to rate. There are limits to what respondents will do.

Remember that you are organizing research to support decision-making. In reality, most decision-making is based on a handful of pieces of information. By limiting the list of items to scale to those related to the decisions that need to be made, you will focus respondents on the important information and will improve the accuracy of the data that matters.

Next, we will discuss scale length. Limiting the number of times you ask respondents to rate things (Scales #6) and making the scale length reasonable (Scales #7) need to be thought about together. If you have a few items to rate, you can get away with longer scales. But if you have lots of items to rate, shorter scales make more sense.

Related Guidelines

Scales #6	Research Planning #1	Easy #4
Limit the number of times you ask respondents to rate things.	Plan research to support decision-making.	Don't ask for more detail than you really need.

Scales #6 is an application of designing research to support decision-making. When there are no limits on what you ask in a questionnaire, you could end up asking hundreds of questions. You are much better off being guided by the decisions the research will address and the information needed to make those decisions.

Scales #6 is also an application of making questions easy. To further ensure respondents are expending their energy on questions that really matter, don't ask for more detail than you really need.

Scales #7: Make the Scale Length Reasonable—Shorter Is Usually Better

Making the scale length reasonable means two things. First, it means making the number of levels you want respondents to consider *match how they think about the topic*. The scale needs to reflect the number of levels they actually have in their heads. In other words, don't ask people to rate the quality of the coffee, their likelihood to purchase, or the extent to which they favor or oppose some-

---

Split the Sample If You Have Too Many Rating Scales for Respondents

In most cases, you can limit the number of items you ask respondents to rate by asking only for information that is needed for decision-making.

However, there are situations that require you to get more information from individual respondents than is reasonable. This is sometimes the case in the early stages of research, when you are exploring issues or when you have many concepts and you want to screen some out to ensure you proceed with the best ones. In these cases, consider splitting the sample into two or more groups. This way you can ask one group of respondents one set of questions and the other group or groups of respondents another set of questions.

Suppose, in this particular example, that you really do need data on all seven brands. Assuming you have a large enough sample, you might split the sample into two groups. One group would provide ratings for Brands A, B, and C, while the other group would provide ratings for Brands D, E, F, and G. The rest of the questionnaire will be the same.

This approach assumes your sample is large enough to split into two groups that are themselves still large enough. You would also have to work with your analytical team, including a statistician, to make sure you can do what you need to do with the data. There are certain relationships between some of the variables that you won't be able to analyze. In other words, since some respondents rated only Brands A, B, and C and other respondents rated only Brands D, E, F, and G, you won't be able to see, for example, how people who rated Brand A also rated Brand G.

These are issues that can be addressed in the analysis-planning phase of developing the questionnaire.

thing on a 10-point scale if all they have in their heads is a few different levels to report. Giving respondents scales that are too long is a common mistake.

Second, making the scale reasonable means understanding that *longer scales are harder to answer than shorter ones*. So if you are going to ask respondents to rate a large number of items, make the scales shorter. Long scales wear out respondents, and as a result, reduce the quality of the data you collect.

As we discussed earlier, a unipolar scale has the presence of an attribute at one end of the scale and the absence of the attribute at the other end of the scale. Alternatively, a bipolar scale has the absence of an attribute in the middle of the scale, with the positive and negative ends of the continuum on either end. The unipolar scale measures one end of the spectrum (e.g., satisfaction), while the bipolar scale measures two ends of the spectrum (e.g., satisfaction and dissatisfaction).

We will discuss scale length separately for unipolar and bipolar scales. Although the guidelines are the same, there are subtle yet important differences.

Unipolar Scales

This first example comes from a company that develops and markets skin-care products to women. The question asks respondents to rate 10 items on a unipolar desirability scale of 1 to 10.

Q: Below is a list of characteristics of skin-care products that may or may not be desirable to you. Please rate how desirable or not desirable each item is to you using the rating scale below.

	Not at all desirable									Very desirable
	1	2	3	4	5	6	7	8	9	10
Is greaseless	○	○	○	○	○	○	○	○	○	○
Is colorless	○	○	○	○	○	○	○	○	○	○
Contains no scent	○	○	○	○	○	○	○	○	○	○
Contains aloe vera	○	○	○	○	○	○	○	○	○	○
Contains SPF	○	○	○	○	○	○	○	○	○	○
Has a pleasant scent	○	○	○	○	○	○	○	○	○	○
Doctor recommended	○	○	○	○	○	○	○	○	○	○
Comes in a pump	○	○	○	○	○	○	○	○	○	○
Comes in a tube	○	○	○	○	○	○	○	○	○	○
Is hypoallergenic	○	○	○	○	○	○	○	○	○	○

The issue to consider is whether respondents actually have 10 levels in their minds for the desirability of these product features. Do you think respondents have that many gradations of desirability for such issues as "comes in a pump" and "has a pleasant scent"? Most people do not.

Second, consider the challenge of actually understanding and using all 10 points in the scale. For example, take the first item, "Is greaseless." If that is a desirable characteristic of a skin-care product, respondents have to decide which of 9 gradations of desirability matches how they think about it. Chances are respondents who find it desirable find an *area* on the 10-point scale—like the low, middle, or high numbers—and just pick out a number so they can move on to the next task, without considering very deeply the difference between the meaning of a 6 versus a 7, a 7 versus an 8, or an 8 versus a 9. Even if they did have 10 gradations for desirability, determining these differences for a lot of items would be tough.

Here is an improved version of the question:

Improved Question:

Q: Below is a list of characteristics of skin-care products that may or may not be desirable to you. Please rate how desirable or not desirable each item is to you using the rating scale below.

	Not at all desirable				Very desirable
	1	2	3	4	5
Is greaseless	○	○	○	○	○
Is colorless	○	○	○	○	○
Contains no scent	○	○	○	○	○
Contains aloe vera	○	○	○	○	○
Contains SPF	○	○	○	○	○
Has a pleasant scent	○	○	○	○	○
Doctor recommended	○	○	○	○	○
Comes in a pump	○	○	○	○	○
Comes in a tube	○	○	○	○	○
Is hypoallergenic	○	○	○	○	○

We changed the scale length to 5 points, but we could argue that a 4- or 6-point scale would work well, too. At this point we are splitting hairs. The point is that asking respondents to rate these items on a 10-point scale is unreasonable because they do not have 10 levels for desirability in their heads. Asking for this many 10-point ratings is asking too much of respondents.

Consider using shorter unipolar scales. Below is an example of a 3-point unipolar scale in a study from the Cooperative Institutional Research Program (CIRP), *Freshman Survey* (2010), administered by the Higher Education Research Institute at the University of California at Los Angeles. Because the survey is quite long—43 questions that ask students for about 150 responses—a short scale makes sense. Also, this answer scale probably accurately reflects the scale people have in their heads.

Q: Below are some reasons that might have influenced your decision to attend this particular college. How important was each reason in your decision to come here? *(Circle one answer for each possible reason.)*

	Not important	Somewhat important	Very important
My parents wanted me to come here.	N	S	V
My relatives wanted me to come here.	N	S	V
My teacher advised me.	N	S	V
This college has a very good academic reputation.	N	S	V
This college has a good reputation for its social activities.	N	S	V
I was offered financial assistance.	N	S	V
The cost of attending this college.	N	S	V
High school advisor advised me.	N	S	V
Private college counselor advised me.	N	S	V
I wanted to live near home.	N	S	V
Not offered aid by first choice.	N	S	V
Could not afford first choice.	N	S	V
This college's graduates gain admission to top graduate/ professional schools.	N	S	V
This college's graduates get good jobs.	N	S	V
I was attracted by the religious affiliation/orientation of the college.	N	S	V
I wanted to go to a school about the size of this college.	N	S	V
Rankings in national magazines.	N	S	V
Information from a website.	N	S	V
I was admitted through an Early Decision program.	N	S	V
The athletic department recruited me.	N	S	V
A visit to the campus.	N	S	V
Ability to take online courses.	N	S	V

Don't hesitate to consider shorter unipolar scales. For many things that we ask respondents to scale, they really have only a few ratings. Longer scales are also harder to answer than shorter ones. Giving people more levels than they have in their minds and asking them to use long scales many times results in measurement error.

Bipolar Scales

Here is a question from a survey to test the characteristics of a new soap that is in development. Respondents use the soap and then rate the soap on a series of rating scales. This question uses a series of 10-point bipolar scales.

Q: Please rate this soap on the following characteristics. *You may circle any number from 1 to 10 to represent your opinion.*

Overall I disliked it very much	1 2 3 4 5 6 7 8 9 10	Overall I liked it very much
Too little lather	1 2 3 4 5 6 7 8 9 10	Too much lather
Too little fragrance	1 2 3 4 5 6 7 8 9 10	Too much fragrance
Bar was too small	1 2 3 4 5 6 7 8 9 10	Bar was too big
Bar was too soft	1 2 3 4 5 6 7 8 9 10	Bar was too hard
Bar was very unattractive	1 2 3 4 5 6 7 8 9 10	Bar was very attractive
Color I dislike very much	1 2 3 4 5 6 7 8 9 10	Color I like very much

The problem with this question is that the scale length is too long. Respondents are trying a new soap. They probably don't have five levels of positive ratings and five levels of negative ratings for such an exercise.

You may not have noticed, but a 10-point bipolar scale does not have a midpoint. This scale is forcing respondents to lean in one direction or the other. For most respondents, it is not clear where the dividing line between positive and negative lies, and they should not have to figure it out.

Here is an improved version of the question with a 6-point bipolar scale with no midpoint:

Improved Question:

Q: Please rate this soap on the following characteristics. *You may circle any number from 1 to 6 to represent your opinion.*

Overall I disliked it very much	1 2 3 4 5 6	Overall I liked it very much
Too little lather	1 2 3 4 5 6	Too much lather
Too little fragrance	1 2 3 4 5 6	Too much fragrance
Bar was too small	1 2 3 4 5 6	Bar was too big
Bar was too soft	1 2 3 4 5 6	Bar was too hard
Bar was very unattractive	1 2 3 4 5 6	Bar was very attractive
Color I dislike very much	1 2 3 4 5 6	Color I like very much

The scale length in this improved question is less daunting. Having six levels better matches how respondents testing the soap might think. With this bipolar scale, they can choose between three levels of positive responses and three levels of negative responses. This scale is easier for respondents to use because it does not ask them to work too hard to understand distinctions in the scale that are too fine. See figures 11.4 and 11.5.

For most issues you want respondents to rate, respondents have only a few levels to reveal. If you are asking about the importance of something, it may only be unimportant, somewhat important, or very important. If you are asking about satisfaction or dissatisfaction, they may only have a few gradations of

Figure 11.4

The 10-Point Scale

Longer scales do make sense in some situations. If you use a longer scale, consider the 10-point scale, as it has an almost universal appeal in our culture. If someone said, "On a scale of 1 to 10, how do I look?" most people know that the correct answer is 10! No one bothers to say what the endpoints mean, but we know that a 10 is at the top of the scale.

Q: When doctors ask patients to rate their pain, they often use the following scale.

How would you rate the pain right now, where 1 means not at all painful and 10 means extremely painful?

Not at all   Extremely
painful   1   2   3   4   5   6   7   8   9   10   painful

Keep in mind that while there are some situations where longer scales might be better, there aren't many. Also remember that respondents would probably not do a good job at answering too many long scales.

Figure 11.5

Try Naming All the Levels of the Scale

Whenever you find yourself wondering whether you have too many levels, try naming each level. For the 10-point unipolar desirability scale presented in this chapter, try this starting with 1 and proceeding upward:

1 = Not at all desirable
2 = Very slightly desirable
3 = Slightly desirable
4 = A little bit desirable
5 = Somewhat desirable
6 = Moderately desirable
7 = Desirable
8 = Very desirable
9 = Very to almost extremely desirable
10 = Extremely desirable

It gets quite difficult. When it is virtually impossible to come up with intelligible labels for each level, you probably have too many levels. If it is hard for you to come up with labels, it is probably hard for respondents to have a clear idea of what each of the points actually means. If that is the case, then the scale has too many points or levels and should be shortened.

Below are two versions of a bipolar satisfaction/dissatisfaction scale—one with 5 points and one with 7 points—where we labeled each level. Here's a 5-point version:

1 = Very dissatisfied
2 = Somewhat dissatisfied
3 = Neither satisfied or dissatisfied
4 = Somewhat satisfied
5 = Very satisfied

Now let's make this a 7-point scale:

1 = Very dissatisfied
2 = Dissatisfied
3 = Slightly dissatisfied
4 = Neither satisfied or dissatisfied
5 = Slightly satisfied
6 = Satisfied
7 = Very satisfied

These labels seem reasonable, suggesting that both scale lengths probably make sense to respondents.

---

each. On top of that, if you are asking respondents to rate a lot of items, long scales are more difficult to answer, and respondents do not give each item that much attention.

Generally speaking, for unipolar scales, a scale length of 3 to 6 is appropriate for most issues. For bipolar scales, scale lengths of 4 to 7 are best for most circumstances. With shorter scales, you are likely to retain the interest of the respondents longer and make their choice process easier. Everything you can do to retain the cooperation of the respondents will pay off with better data.

Scales #8: Don't Make the Endpoints Too Extreme

Let's look at a few questions and consider their use of endpoints.

Q: Please rate the carbonated beverage you just tried on the following characteristics. *Please circle any number from 1 to 5 to represent your opinion.*

Completely unsatisfying		Neither satisfying nor unsatisfying		Completely satisfying
1	2	3	4	5

Extremely bitter		Neither extremely bitter nor extremely sweet		Extremely sweet
1	2	3	4	5

The problem with these scales is that the endpoints of the rating scale are too extreme. The beverage being tested is probably not *completely* unsatisfying or *completely* satisfying or *extremely* bitter or *extremely* sweet. When the endpoints are too extreme, many respondents ignore them. In this case, these two 5-point bipolar scales become essentially 3-point bipolar scales. As a result, you will not get the level of detail you wanted.

Let's fix these two scales by making the endpoints less extreme.
Improved Question:

Q: Please rate the carbonated beverage you just tried on the following scale. *Please any number from 1 to 5 to represent your opinion.*

Very unsatisfying		Neither satisfying nor unsatisfying		Very satisfying
1	2	3	4	5

Very bitter		Neither bitter nor sweet		Very sweet
1	2	3	4	5

This improved version of the question is more likely to give you better data because respondents will be more likely to use the entire rating scale. They have two levels on each side of the bipolar scale that are reasonable.

Here is a question from a survey about a skin-care product:

Q: Please rate how well each statement describes each brand on a scale of 1 to 5, where 1 means "does not describe at all" and 5 means "describes completely."

	Does not describe at all 1	2	3	4	Describes completely 5
Does not irritate sensitive skin	○	○	○	○	○
Is hypoallergenic	○	○	○	○	○
Can purchase at grocery store	○	○	○	○	○
Has a pleasant scent	○	○	○	○	○
Has an ungreasy feel	○	○	○	○	○
Does not stain clothing	○	○	○	○	○
Good value for the money	○	○	○	○	○
Is recommended by doctors	○	○	○	○	○

The endpoint "describes completely" is a little too extreme. Can any statement describe a product completely?

Here is an improved version of the rating scale with a less dramatic endpoint. Improved Question:

Q: Please rate how well each statement describes each brand on a scale of 1 to 5, where 1 means "does not describe at all" and 5 means "describes very well."

	Does not describe at all 1	2	3	4	Describes very well 5
Does not irritate sensitive skin	○	○	○	○	○
Is hypoallergenic	○	○	○	○	○
Can purchase at grocery store	○	○	○	○	○
Has a pleasant scent	○	○	○	○	○
Has an ungreasy feel	○	○	○	○	○
Does not stain clothing	○	○	○	○	○
Good value for the money	○	○	○	○	○
Is recommended by doctors	○	○	○	○	○

Since the highest endpoint in this unipolar scale is more reasonable, respondents are more likely to use the entire range of levels offered.

There are, however, some situations where you need to make one or both of the endpoints extreme. Suppose you are asking respondents to rate the severity of their headaches. The answer choices need to reflect the possible experiences of respondents.

Q: How painful was your most recent headache?

Not at all painful   1 2 3 4 5   Extremely painful

The point is that the upper end of the scale needs to reflect the reality of respondents, and headaches can be quite extreme.

We recently saw a survey that asked college-bound students about the personal importance of a list of items:

Q: Please indicate the importance to you personally of each of the following: (*Mark one for each item.*)

	Not important	Somewhat important	Very important	Essential
Becoming accomplished in one of the performing arts (acting, dancing, etc.)	○	○	○	○
Becoming an authority in my field	○	○	○	○
Obtaining recognition from my colleagues for contributions to my special field	○	○	○	○
Influencing social values	○	○	○	○
Raising a family	○	○	○	○
Being very well off financially	○	○	○	○

The upper end of this unipolar scale, "essential," is an extreme endpoint. It seems appropriate for this circumstance. Many college-bound students have strong feelings about these issues, so the scale needs to give them the ability to reflect those feelings.

We debated what to name this guideline. We settled on "don't make the endpoints too extreme" because endpoints that are too extreme are the most common error we see. Yet there are situations where extreme endpoints make sense. The point is to make sure the endpoints match the reality of respondents.

Learn as much as you can in qualitative research about how people view the topic. What words do they use to describe their experience? If you have access to survey research that used the scales you are considering, look at the distribution of responses across the levels of the scale. If you find that few people are selecting the endpoints, they may be too extreme for the topic. On the other hand, if you find that many responses are at one of the endpoints, you may need to stretch out the scale and have a more extreme label for the endpoint.

The Poor-to-Excellent Scale

Use of the poor-to-excellent scale is so common in our culture that it works well in many situations. Although the endpoint "excellent" may seem extreme, it is how we talk about our positive experiences at restaurants, movies, hotels, and the like.

Here is an example:

Q: How would you rate your most recent stay at our hotel?

Poor 1 2 3 4 5 Excellent

For a hotel stay, having "excellent" as the positive endpoint makes sense because that is a common word people use to describe such an experience.

Scales #9: Make Sure Bipolar Scales Are Balanced

Consider what might be wrong with this question:

Q: Please rate your overall satisfaction with your stay at our hotel, using the scale below.
- ☐ Extremely satisfied
- ☐ Very satisfied
- ☐ Somewhat satisfied
- ☐ Neutral
- ☐ Somewhat dissatisfied
- ☐ Very dissatisfied

The problem with this question is that there are three options for satisfaction and only two options for dissatisfaction.

Here is an improved version of the question:

Q: Please rate your overall satisfaction with your stay at our hotel, using the scale below.
- ☐ Very satisfied
- ☐ Somewhat satisfied
- ☐ Neutral
- ☐ Somewhat dissatisfied
- ☐ Very dissatisfied

This improved version now has two levels for both satisfaction and dissatisfaction. We have also made sure that the levels are balanced by giving them the same modifiers (e.g., "somewhat" satisfied and dissatisfied and "very" satisfied and dissatisfied).

The Purchase-Intention Scale

One of the scales used most often in questionnaires is the purchase-intention scale. The scale below is appropriately balanced, with the same number of options for buying as for not buying.

Q: How likely are you to purchase Product X in the next 30 days?
- ☐ Definitely will buy
- ☐ Probably will buy
- ☐ May or may not buy
- ☐ Probably will not buy
- ☐ Definitely will not buy

See how this question is evenly balanced with two versions of buying and two versions of not buying? Note how the items are labeled similarly, too.

Companies use the purchase-intention scale to measure interest in new products and services. This scale is useful because it enables companies to track the relationship between what respondents say and how they actually behave—that is, whether or not they actually buy the product. Repeated use of the purchase-intention scale—and tracking the actual behavior of customers—gives companies more accurate information about interest in their products or services

What might be wrong with this question?

Q: How easy or difficult is shopping for headache treatments?
- ☐ Very easy
- ☐ Easy
- ☐ Somewhat easy
- ☐ Neither easy nor difficult
- ☐ Difficult
- ☐ Very difficult
- ☐ Extremely difficult

This question has the same number of positive and negative response options: three for easy and three for difficult. The problem is that the labels along the positive and negative ends of the scale are not parallel. The strongest positive response is "very easy," but the strongest negative response is "extremely difficult."

Here is an improved version of this question:

Q: How easy or difficult is shopping for headache treatments?
- ☐ Very easy
- ☐ Easy
- ☐ Somewhat easy
- ☐ Neither easy nor difficult
- ☐ Somewhat difficult
- ☐ Difficult
- ☐ Very difficult

If we did not label the middle points, the endpoints would need to be parallel, too. Here is an unbalanced version of the previous question followed by a balanced version.

Unbalanced:

Q: How easy or difficult is shopping for headache treatments?

Extremely difficult			Neither easy nor difficult			Very easy
1	2	3	4	5	6	7

Balanced:

Q: How easy or difficult is shopping for headache treatments?

Very difficult			Neither easy nor difficult			Very easy
1	2	3	4	5	6	7

Make sure your bipolar scales are balanced by having the same number of positive and negative response choices and by assigning these choices parallel labels.

Related Guidelines

Scales #9	Unbiased #2	Unbiased #3
Make sure bipolar scales are balanced.	Make sure that no one answer choice is more loaded than any other.	Make clear that either a positive or a negative answer is equally acceptable.

Scales #9 is a way to avoid bias. Note the similarity between this guideline and two of the guidelines for avoiding bias. It reminds us to make sure that neither side of the scale is more loaded than the other and that positive and negative answers are equally acceptable.

Scales #10: Replace Agree/Disagree Scales with Direct Questions about What You Really Want to Measure

Agree/disagree scales are used all too often in the world of survey research. They ask respondents to assess a statement and then indicate the extent to which they agree or disagree with that statement. There is nothing terribly wrong with using agree/disagree scales. It is just that when you think about the information you need, there is almost always a better way to get it.

Let's illustrate with a few examples. Here is an example from a survey given to employees of a large company:

Q: How much do you agree or disagree that the company has a clear business strategy?
☐ Strongly agree
☐ Agree
☐ Neutral
☐ Disagree
☐ Strongly disagree

The problem with this question is that it is really asking the respondent to do two things: assess whether the company has a clear business strategy and translate that assessment into a level of agreement or disagreement. We can make the question easier and clearer by making it more direct.

Let's assume we want to know *whether* respondents think the company has a clear business strategy. As is often the case with agree/disagree questions, this can easily be revised as a yes/no question:

Q: Do you believe the company has a clear business strategy, or not?
☐ The company has a clear business strategy
☐ The company does NOT have a clear business strategy
☐ Not sure

Or suppose we want to know *how clear* the business strategy is to employees. That's what we need to measure.

Q: How clear or unclear is the company's business strategy?
Very unclear   1   2   3   4   5   6   Very clear

Agree/disagree questions are often the result of a failure to think through what information is really needed and how to ask the question. It is better to measure concepts directly because agree/disagree statements have an inherent bias. They state the issue in either a positive or a negative way. In this example, the proposed concept was that the company has a clear business strategy, which has an inherent positive bias. Respondents have to disagree to give a negative response. To make questions truly unbiased, we must make clear that either a positive or a negative answer is equally acceptable (Unbiased #3). In the two improved versions of the question, we made the question less biased because respondents did not have to disagree with any statement.

The other common way agree/disagree questions are posed is as a list of statements with which respondents must indicate how much they agree or disagree. Here is an example:

Q: Please let us know how much you agree or disagree with the following statements.

	Strongly disagree	Disagree	Neither agree nor disagree	Agree	Strongly agree
	1	2	3	4	5
Our company values its people.	○	○	○	○	○
We have developed an excellent business management approach.	○	○	○	○	○
I am allowed to make and implement decisions that help the business.	○	○	○	○	○
I am optimistic about the company's future.	○	○	○	○	○
Policies, procedures, programs, and systems communicate very well what is expected and what is important.	○	○	○	○	○
I need more training in marketing.	○	○	○	○	○
I need more training in finance.	○	○	○	○	○
I need more training in supply chain management.	○	○	○	○	○

This question format is appealing because it is easy to generate a list of statements and ask respondents to agree or disagree with each of them. It does not require much thought about what you really want to measure or how to design the scale.

This format has the same problems we pointed out in the previous example. Many of the statements have an inherent bias because they are stated positively. You don't want to put respondents in the position of having to disagree with a positive statement.

Furthermore, asking respondents to do two things—assess each statement and then translate that statement into a level of agreement or disagreement—is not only more difficult than it needs to be but also lends itself to measurement error in several ways.

One kind of measurement error comes from whether respondents answer the question literally or make an assumption about the question's intention. Consider the statement, "We have developed an excellent business management approach." In this example, a literal interpretation of the question would lead those who thought the business management approach was "good" but not "excellent" to strongly disagree. Yet others who assumed the intention of the question was to *rate* the business management approach and considered it good but not excellent would probably agree with the statement. Identical opinions would yield different results depending on whether respondents answered the question literally or made an assumption about the question's intention.

Another kind of measurement error stems from differing interpretations of the statements. In the statement "We have developed an excellent business management approach," some respondents might focus on the concept *developed*. They could say the company had an excellent business management approach well before new management came in and took over a couple of years ago and therefore disagree. Others might focus solely on the business management approach and ignore the development issue, choosing to agree. The point is that the statement is subject to differing interpretations.

In this case, ask the question directly, and take out any clutter (e.g., "we have developed").

Improved Question:

Q: How would you rate the business management approach?

    Poor   1   2   3   4   5   Excellent

If you want information about the *development* of the business management approach, ask for it in a separate question.

Finally, many of the statements listed in agree/disagree statements include two or more concepts. The statement "I am allowed to make and implement decisions that help the business" is a classic example. Making decisions and implementing decisions are two different things. How is a respondent supposed to answer this question in terms of agreement or disagreement?

Instead of asking people to rate their level of agreement or disagreement with statements, figure out what you really want to know and ask the questions directly.

Think carefully about what information you really need and ask a direct question about it. By making sure your question is really only one question and that both positive and negative answers are equally acceptable, you will have made the question clear and unbiased.

Related Guidelines

Scales #10	Clear #5	Unbiased #3
Replace agree/disagree scales with direct questions about what you really want to measure.	Make sure the question is really asking only one question.	Make clear that either a positive or a negative answer is equally acceptable.

Scales #10 is a special case of making questions clear. Replacing agree/disagree statements with direct questions about what you really want to measure is another way of making sure you are asking only one question (Clear #5).

Scales #10 is also a special case of making questions unbiased. The agree/disagree question format has the inherent bias of making people disagree in order to choose the negative response, making it seem less acceptable. By asking direct questions about what you really want to measure, you avoid this inherent bias.

Scales #11: If You Are Naming Only the Endpoints, Present the Scale Horizontally with the Positive Endpoint and Higher Numbers to the Right

Every culture has a few basic standards for presenting rating scales. The standards presented here have become common practice among survey researchers in the United States. If you design quantitative surveys for other countries, you will need to talk with survey researchers who know the norms in those countries.

The first standard involves how you present rating scales when you are naming only the endpoints. When you label only the endpoints, present the scale horizontally with the more positive endpoint and larger numbers to the right. This standard comes from the fact that we read left to right and more often associate higher numbers with better outcomes, such as in sports, test scores, and so on. If you asked someone to rate you on a scale of 1 to 10—in terms of good looks, intelligence, sense of humor, and so on—most people would automatically assume that a 10 is better than a 1. It is also the way most scales are presented.

To illustrate, here are four options for presenting the same rating scale:
<u>Vertical Scale:</u>

Q: Please share your opinion of the ad you just saw.
The ad I just saw was:
  Very boring
  1
  2
  3
  4
  5
  Very entertaining

<u>Negative Endpoint on the Right:</u>

Q: Please share your opinion of the ad you just saw.
The ad I just saw was:
  Very entertaining   1   2   3   4   5   Very boring

<u>Lower Numbers on the Right:</u>

Q: Please share your opinion of the ad you just saw.
The ad I just saw was:
  Very boring   5   4   3   2   1   Very entertaining

<u>Higher Numbers on the Right:</u>

Q: Please share your opinion of the ad you just saw.
The ad I just saw was:

    Very boring   1   2   3   4   5   Very entertaining

The problem with presenting the scale vertically is that we tend to think of ratings along a horizontal scale, much like a ruler on its side. We also run the risk of introducing a slight bias with the vertical presentation of the scale, as respondents may not read down the scale.

The problem with placing the negative category on the right is that most questionnaires present the scale with positive values to the right. It makes more sense to present the scales in the direction respondents are used to seeing. Also, seeing higher numbers with negative values is a little odd in that we usually associate higher numbers with more positive outcomes.

The problem with placing lower numbers on the right along with the positive endpoint is that it creates a mismatch between the numbers and the endpoint. We usually think of higher numbers as indicating better values.

At some point, you might be tempted to use negative numbers in a scale:

Q: Please share your opinion of the ad you just saw:
The ad I just saw was:

    Very boring   –1   –2   0   1   2   Very entertaining

Don't use negative numbers, as people tend to skew their responses away from negative numbers. You run the risk of getting an upward bias in the data.

In summary, when you are naming only the endpoints, present the scale horizontally with the positive endpoint and larger numbers to the right. This is how rating scales are usually presented to respondents, and it matches our cultural norms of having higher numbers mean more positive things.

Scales #12: When Naming All the Points on the Scale, Put the More Positive Labels at the Top When Displayed Vertically or to the Right When Displayed Horizontally

When you label all the points along the scale, you are essentially asking respondents which category label applies to them best. Sometimes these are called "word scales."

Below is a common scale that people use to assess health:

	Poor	Fair	Good	Very good	Excellent
Overall, how would rate your health?	○	○	○	○	○

When you present this scale horizontally, arrange the category labels from negative to positive. It will make the questionnaire easier for respondents to answer, as all rating scales—the numbered scales and the word scales—will have the positive categories on the right.

When you label all the levels on the scale, you also have the option to present the scale vertically. Note that Scales #11 says when you label only the end-points, present the scale horizontally. When you label all the points on the scale, however, and create what is essentially a word scale, you can present the scale either vertically or horizontally, depending on practical issues such as the space available on the page or computer screen.

There are several issues to consider when presenting the categories vertically. For purposes of discussion, here are three versions of the same rating scale:

Numbers with the Categories	Positive Categories at the Bottom	Positive Categories at the Top
Overall, how would rate your health? ☐ 5 - Excellent ☐ 4 - Very good ☐ 3 - Good ☐ 2 - Fair ☐ 1 - Poor	**Overall, how would rate your health?** ☐ Poor ☐ Fair ☐ Good ☐ Very good ☐ Excellent	**Overall, how would rate your health?** ☐ Excellent ☐ Very good ☐ Good ☐ Fair ☐ Poor

In the first example, the numbers that accompany the categories serve no purpose. Numbers only distract from the category labels, so don't include them.

The second example has the negative categories at the top. We suggest using the approach displayed in the third example, with the more positive categories at the top. In our culture, we more often think of the positive, or better, values being at the top. And since more often than not, survey researchers order the categories with the more positive values at the top, it makes sense from the standpoint of consistency to follow suit.

One of the keys to getting quality data from rating scales is to be consistent throughout the questionnaire. Always order the horizontal scales with the negative category labels to the left and the positive category labels to the right. When you present word scales vertically, always put the positive values at the top. Most survey researchers already apply these standards to their questionnaires. It would only help the field of survey research if we all adopted these standards.

Figure 11.6 provides more details about interpreting data collected from rating scales.

Figure 11.6

Rating Scales Provide Ordinal Data

When we ask respondents to rate something on a scale, we are asking them to reflect their attitude or perception along a continuum from negative to positive. When we label the endpoints only, we are asking respondents to use the *endpoints and the numbers* as their measure of their viewpoint. When we label each point, we are asking respondents to use the *category labels* to reflect their viewpoint.

The data collected from rating scales are usually considered ordinal data because all we know is that the levels of the scale are *in order* from negative to positive. We do not know if the distance between the categories is the same from point to point.

For illustration, look at one of the most widely used scales in survey research, the purchase-intention scale, where each level is labeled:

Q: How likely or unlikely are you yourself to buy Product X in the next three months?

☐ Definitely will buy

☐ Probably will buy

☐ May or may not buy

☐ Probably will not buy

☐ Definitely will not buy

Researchers have studied the relationship between how people respond to the purchase-intention scale and whether they actually buy the product. For example, for products under five dollars that people buy every month or so, people who respond "Definitely will buy" are about four times more likely to buy than those people who respond "Probably will buy." Yet the difference between the purchase likelihoods of people who respond "Probably will buy" and people who respond "May or may not buy" is much smaller.

The point is that the data reflect an order but do not necessarily measure an exact magnitude of the difference between points. Even if you were to present the scale with numbers and label only the endpoints, you would not be able to assume that the distances between the numbers are the same:

Q: How likely or unlikely are you yourself to purchase Product X in the next three months?

Definitely will not buy				Definitely will buy
1	2	3	4	5
○	○	○	○	○

Mathematically, the distance between 3 and 4 is the same as the difference between 4 and 5, but the meaning of these differences to people who provide ratings is not the same.

To further illustrate this point, look at the following two scales:

Health Scale	Satisfaction Scale
How would you rate your health? ☐ Excellent ☐ Very good ☐ Good ☐ Fair ☐ Poor	**Please rate your satisfaction or dissatisfaction with your most recent stay at the hotel.** Very dissatisfied ... Very satisfied 1 2 3 4 5 6

For the health scale, we have no idea what leads someone to choose between "very good" and "excellent" versus "good" and "very good." The magnitude of the difference between these two points is impossible to know.

The same is true for the satisfaction scale. Satisfied customers see three levels on the scale—4, 5, and 6—and are told to reflect their level of satisfaction by choosing one of those numbers. What each number means to them is hard enough to know, much less the differences between these numbers.

We know that the information we collect from well-crafted rating scales reflects ordinal measurement. The meaning of the differences between the categories, whether we use numbers or category labels, is almost always unknown.

CHAPTER 12

Asking Open-Ended Questions

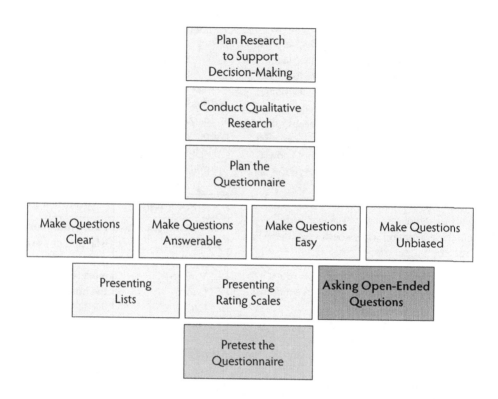

Open-ended questions serve an important role in survey research. They allow us to get answers that cannot be precoded, to explore thought processes, and in some cases to avoid biasing or leading our respondents. As Howard Shuman (2008) explains, open-ended questions "have limitations . . . but they do offer one way for investigators to minimize mistaking a mirror of their own minds for a window into the minds of others."

The simplest form of an open-ended question is the fill-in-the-blank answer box. This allows us to ask for information that cannot be precoded, such as zip codes or city of birth. We might also use a fill-in-the-blank answer box to avoid cluttering the page or when we think that a list might bias or otherwise influence responses.

Open-ended questions also allow respondents to supplement a list we present, as we discussed in Lists #1. Think of all the times we create a list of items from which respondents are to select and wonder if we have offered them all possible answer choices. We might ask, "Which of the following were reasons why you cancelled your cable service?" or "Which of the following statements best describes your reason for visiting the park today?" Since we can't think of every possible answer choice, we add an open-ended option to the end of the list, such as this:

Other. *Please specify*: _____

We can also use open-ended questions in *exploratory* ways. We might ask for information in a completely nonleading way, such as when we ask for unaided brand awareness:

Q: When you think of toilet paper, what brands come to mind? *Please list all the brands you can think of in the spaces below*:

Brand 1:	
Brand 2:	
Brand 3:	
Brand 4:	
Brand 5:	
Brand 6:	
Brand 7:	
Brand 8:	

We might also want to avoid influencing or leading respondents with a list of items from which to select. Instead, we can ask an exploratory open-ended question such as this:

Q: What are the top three issues for you personally in the upcoming election?
Issue 1: _____
Issue 2: _____
Issue 3: _____

Other applications of exploratory open-ended questions include asking respondents to clarify, elaborate on, or amplify a previous answer:

Q: How strongly do you favor or oppose the proposed state tax on cigarettes?
Strongly oppose 1 2 3 4 Strongly favor

Q: What is the primary reason why you favor or oppose the proposed state tax on cigarettes? *Please tell us in the box below*

Finally, we can ask completely open-ended questions, much as we do in qualitative research:

Q: Question one: What did you like MOST about your experience at Camp Jubilee?

```
┌─────────────────────────────────────────────────────────────┐
│                                                             │
│                                                             │
│                                                             │
│                                                             │
└─────────────────────────────────────────────────────────────┘
```

Q: Question two: What did you like LEAST about your experience at Camp Jubilee?

```
┌─────────────────────────────────────────────────────────────┐
│                                                             │
│                                                             │
│                                                             │
│                                                             │
└─────────────────────────────────────────────────────────────┘
```

As we have described, open-ended questions take several different forms, from fill-in-the-blank questions and questions that supplement a list to exploratory open-ended questions. We have developed six guidelines that will help you use open-ended questions effectively.

Six Guidelines for Open-Ended Questions

1. Format and label answer boxes to help respondents understand the response task. (Open-Ended #1)
2. Provide an appropriate space for answers. (Open-Ended #2)
3. Do not use exploratory open-ended questions as substitutes for qualitative research. (Open-Ended #3)
4. Recognize the limitations of exploratory open-ended questions. (Open-Ended #4)
5. Make exploratory open-ended questions specific. (Open-Ended #5)
6. Consider adding an introductory statement to improve the quality of responses. (Open-Ended #6)

Open-Ended #1: Format and Label Answer Boxes to Help Respondents Understand the Response Task

One of the formatting techniques you can use in surveys is providing information in the answer box to help respondents understand what is being asked of them.

Consider this question:

Q: In what year were you born? _____

In this version, you would get responses such as 1954, '54, nineteen fifty-four, and so on. To make clear to respondents how you want their answer to appear, format the answer box appropriately. The example below makes it clear that you want a four-digit date.

Q: In what year were you born?

When asking respondents to write their response, arrows can sometimes help, as in the 2010 American Community Survey conducted by the U.S. Census Bureau (see Figure 12.1).

Figure 12.1

6 **What is Person 1's race?** *Mark (X) one or more boxes.*

☐ White
☐ Black, African Am., or Negro
☐ American Indian or Alaska Native — *Print name of enrolled or principal tribe.* ↗

☐ Asian Indian   ☐ Japanese   ☐ Native Hawaiian
☐ Chinese   ☐ Korean   ☐ Guamanian or Chamorro
☐ Filipino   ☐ Vietnamese   ☐ Samoan
☐ Other Asian – *Print race,*   ☐ Other Pacific Islander –
  for example, Hmong,   *Print race, for example,*
  Laotian, Thai, Pakistani,   *Fijian, Tongan, and*
  Cambodian, and so on. ↗   *so on.* ↙

☐ Some other race – *Print race.* ↙

Arrows pointing to the answer boxes help respondents understand what to do.

As we said in chapter 8, one of the ways to make questions easy is to add labels to answer categories (Easy #7). In the question below, the answer box does not reinforce what is expected:

Q: What are the three most important reasons why you chose to leave the university?

In this revised version of the question, the answer box and the labels reinforce what is expected:

Improved Question:

Q: What are the three most important reasons why you chose to leave the university?

Reason 1:	
Reason 2:	
Reason 3:	

Using formatting and labels will help respondents understand each question's requirements and will improve the quality of their responses. Sometimes symbols such as arrows can also help respondents navigate the question.

Open-Ended #2: Provide an Appropriate Space for Answers

Respondents look at the entire question to understand how to answer it. The size of the answer space signals how much information to provide.

Compare this original question and the revised question.

Q: In the last visit by a sales representative, what issues were discussed?

Revised Question:

Q: In the last visit by a sales representative, what issues were discussed?

The original question clearly signals that less information is needed. In fact, there is no way to write in a lot of information! The revised question has an answer space that encourages the sharing of more information.

You can also use the size of the answer box to convey how you want information to be provided. Look at this example:

Q: Thinking of the last 7 days, how many of those days did you apply suntan lotion?

If you provide an answer box like this, you will get a variety of responses, such as "most days," "about 6," "all of them," and so on.

Here is an improved version of the same question. This version uses both the size of the answer box and a label to indicate that a number is required. It also provides the range of numbers to ensure that people think of an entire 7-day week instead of a 5-day work week or some other idiosyncratic interpretation of "week."

Improved Question:

Q: Thinking of the last 7 days, how many of those days did you apply suntan lotion?

The size of the answer box has a significant impact on how much information respondents think they are supposed to provide, as well as how much they *can* provide. Providing appropriately sized answer boxes, and labels when necessary, is a simple way to improve the quality of data collection.

Unaided Awareness as a Special Case of an Open-Ended Question

Marketers often want to capture awareness of a brand without prompting the respondent with a list of brands. This is called "unaided brand awareness." The question might take the following form:

Q: When thinking of brands of coffee, what brands come to mind?

The question is asked in an open-ended format without mention of brand names because the marketer is interested in which brands the person can recall as opposed to recognize.

Many marketers use recall as an indicator of advertising success.

After answering the open-ended question that measures recall, respondents are provided with a list of brands and asked which brands they recognize. Surely recall is a stronger indicator that the brand is in their heads than is recognition. Someone might automatically recall the name Starbucks but need prompting to recognize the name of more obscure brands of coffee.

Open-Ended #3: Do Not Use Exploratory Open-Ended Questions as Substitutes for Qualitative Research

We often see questionnaires that contain exploratory open-ended questions. This is no surprise, because when people are studying a topic, they want to know as much as possible about it. Below are examples of the types of exploratory open-ended questions we have seen many times:

"What did you like most about . . . ?"
"What did you like least about . . . ?"
"What would you like to see changed?"
"How did you make that decision?"
"Who has the most influence over making the decision about . . . ?"
"If you said YES, please explain why you said YES."
"If you said NO, please explain why you said NO."
"Please describe the major considerations that led you to . . . "
"Why are you considering . . . ?"

These questions are certainly important. The problem is that these are qualitative questions.

In part 1, "Plan Research," we talked about the importance of addressing qualitative issues with qualitative methods, such as focus groups and individual depth interviews. We also explained why you need to conduct qualitative research prior to writing a questionnaire, as many of the issues you need to explore can be addressed only with qualitative methods.

If you have questions like these, you will get much better information and insight by conducting qualitative research, where interviewers can interpret initial responses, follow up with probing questions, ask respondents for clarification, pose scenarios to help uncover deeper levels of thinking, and so on.

In general, avoid using exploratory open-ended questions as a substitute for qualitative research. There are, however, situations in which you may want or need to use exploratory open-ended questions. You don't always have the luxury of being able to explore topics qualitatively before conducting quantitative research.

The key is to have realistic expectations about what information you will get and to interpret the results accordingly. We will discuss this in the next guideline.

Open-Ended #4: Recognize the Limitations of Exploratory Open-Ended Questions

When you ask exploratory open-ended questions in a survey, keep in mind that writing is hard; most respondents expend limited effort in answering these sorts of questions. Without a trained qualitative interviewer, you also will not have the opportunity to rephrase questions, ask follow-up questions, and use other qualitative techniques to determine what respondents really meant by unclear written responses.

As an example, consider this exploratory open-ended question about a most recent hotel stay: "What did you like most about your stay at this hotel?" Let's say a male respondent wrote down, "Food." What was it about the food? Was it the fact that he could get food at any hour of the day, the quality of the service, the availability of vegetarian items, or what?

What if he said "food" simply because his favorite restaurant in the city is located within walking distance of that hotel? Sure, we could attempt to foresee such an issue and have follow-up quantitative questions to uncover the nature of the answer. But truthfully, many such answers to exploratory open-ended questions leave us hanging. Without a qualitative approach, these issues cannot be explored.

Now consider an exploratory open-ended question that asks why some action was taken. For example, suppose a survey asks, "Why did you decide to purchase this vehicle?" Questions that address *why* are almost always multifaceted. It might take some time and thought for a person to realize and articulate all the factors involved. In the case of the car, some of the deeper issues might include family considerations, expectations about the future, or self-image, as well as the more obvious factors such as cost, safety, reliability, repair records, and so on. The point is that what most respondents write down represents only a coarse snapshot of the full picture.

Without having an interviewer present to ensure that respondents understand the question, all sorts of interpretations can come into play. When asked, "Why did you decide to purchase this vehicle?" some respondents might write down why they purchased rather than leased the car; others might say why they purchased that car instead of another car they were considering; others might think you are asking why they decided to buy the car now instead of at some other time. Without addressing the question qualitatively, no one knows how respondents will interpret the question.

There is nothing wrong with using open-ended questions in surveys. We just want you to recognize that your ability to understand what the respondents meant by their responses is limited. Few respondents write well and take the time to craft an insightful response. Even if some write a thorough response, true understanding might require qualitative exploration.

Qualitative, Quantitative, and More Qualitative Research

It is always best to do qualitative research before quantitative research. Yet even the best-laid plans leave some questions unanswered.

You can always follow a survey with additional qualitative research. In fact, if you have the time and the budget, arrange to conduct additional qualitative research after the quantitative research is completed.

Many research projects we have been involved in have yielded some perplexing quantitative information. By going back and talking to the respondents whose answers we could not make sense of, we were able to develop a more complete understanding of the topics.

Open-Ended #5: Make Exploratory Open-Ended Questions Specific

Many of the exploratory open-ended questions we see in surveys are vague or ask for two or more pieces of information. When you write exploratory open-ended questions, think carefully about what information you need and ask a specific question.

Here is an example of an open-ended question at the end of a customer satisfaction survey given to people who had just had their heating-and-air-conditioning system repaired:

Q: Please share any additional comments or describe in your own words your overall experience.

This question is quite vague, and a lot of respondents would probably ignore it. In chapter 6, we stressed the importance of making sure that your question is really asking only one question (Clear #5). This question is asking respondents for additional comments, which is vague, and is also asking respondents to describe their overall experience, which could be a rather arduous task.

If we were consulting with this company, we would start by finding out what information they needed to make the decisions this research would support and then suggest a more specific question.

For example, let's assume they want information that would help them decide how to improve their service. How about this:

Improved Question A:

Q: What is the main thing we could have done to improve our service?

This more specific question is more likely to elicit useful information.

We might also add an introductory statement about the importance of their responses to encourage participation. This technique is discussed later in Open-Ended #6.

Improved Question B:

Q: We are very interested in any information you can provide to help us improve our company. Please help us by answering the following question:
What is the main thing we could we have done to improve our service?

Here is a question from a survey about a public school system:

Q: During the next five years, what do you consider to be the three most important issues, challenges, or concerns facing the system that the superintendent will likely have to face?

This is another example of a question that is really more than one, as it asks about "issues, challenges, or concerns" facing the system. Furthermore, it asks which of these issues, challenges, or concerns *the superintendent will likely have to face*, which is hard to predict, since the superintendent could elect not to face any number of issues, challenges, or concerns. What information does the questionnaire writer really want?

Here is an attempt to make the question specific:

Improved Question:

Q: During the next five years, what are the three most important issues you would like the superintendent to address?

Issue 1:	
Issue 2:	
Issue 3:	

Instead of asking about three things—issues, challenges, and concerns—the question focuses on the single theme of what the respondent wants the superintendent to address. And instead of asking what the superintendent is likely to face, which is impossible for respondents to know, the question asks respondents what they want the superintendent to address. By asking a more specific question, you are more likely to get specific answers.

Sometimes people use exploratory open-ended questions to better understand why respondents gave particular answers.

Here is an example:

Q1: How likely or unlikely would you be to buy this product if it were available where you shop?
☐ Definitely would buy
☐ Probably would buy
☐ Might or might not buy
☐ Probably would not buy
☐ Definitely would not buy

Q2: Why did you give the answer you just gave?

In this version of the follow-up question, many respondents will think, "Well, I gave the answer I gave because you asked me to give an answer!" What the questionnaire writer is looking for is not clear.

In the following revised version of the question, we assumed that the company who is paying for the survey wants to get some information about why someone would or would not want to buy the product. For the sake of brevity, we will assume that this is a computer- or voice-administered survey, and the computer or person reading the survey can insert each respondent's answer into the question:

Improved Question:

Q: What is the primary reason why you said you would [INSERT ANSWER] if it were available where you shop?

This frames the question much as you would ask it if you were talking to someone in person.

Exploratory open-ended questions have their place in survey research, even though the information they provide is limited. When you use them, be sure to follow the guidelines presented earlier, such as making the question really only one question, making questions short so that respondents understand them upon first reading, and avoiding unclear terms in the question. Making exploratory open-ended questions clear and easy to understand will encourage respondents to answer with the information you need.

Open-Ended #6: Consider Adding an Introductory Statement to Improve the Quality of Responses

One of the problems with open-ended questions is that respondents often give very short answers. Many responses to open-ended questions are one word or a brief phrase. You want better information.

One way to get better answers is to provide larger answer spaces and include instructions to encourage elaboration. You can also preface the question with an introductory statement. Consider the two questions in Figure 12.2:

Figure 12.2

No Introductory Statement	With an Introductory Statement
Please tell us why you chose to cancel your membership to the swim and tennis club.	We want to understand what we can do to improve the swim and tennis club, so your perspective is very important to us. Please tell us why you chose to cancel your membership to the swim and tennis club.

Providing an introductory statement has been shown to improve the quality of responses. Smyth, Dillman, Christian, and McBride (2009) conducted two experiments and found that adding an introductory statement resulted in more words, more themes, more elaboration on themes, and more time spent answering the question.

These authors suggest that the introductory statement increases respondents' motivation to answer the question. Other researchers have suggested that the introductory statement gives respondents a little more time to think about their responses (Sudman and Bradburn, 1982). It primes the mind. Whatever the reason, there has been enough research to suggest that an introductory statement often helps improve the quality of responses.

Another way to improve the quality of open-ended responses is worthy of mention. Miller and Cannell (1982) tested different methods for increasing the quality of open-ended responses in telephone surveys. Their research showed that response quality improved when respondents agreed to the statement that they would "think carefully about each question in order to give accurate information." This approach may work to increase the commitment of respondents as well as their motivation and effort to think about their answers.

Adding an introductory statement to exploratory open-ended questions can improve response quality. That said, we suggest using this approach judiciously. You would not want to make a questionnaire appear excessively long with too many open-ended questions with introductory statements. Use this approach on one, two, or maybe three questions that really matter.

PART 4. PRETEST AND REVISE THE QUESTIONNAIRE

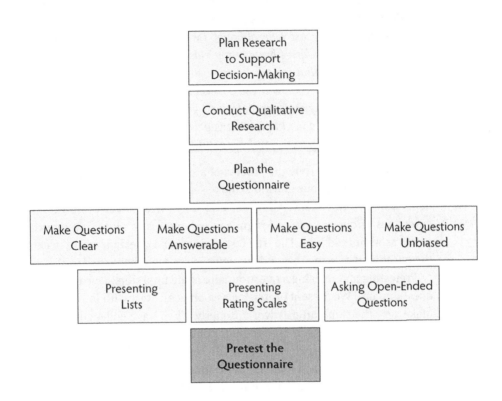

We began the research process by identifying the decisions that need to be made and the information needed to make those decisions. We started with qualitative research to better understand how our target audience thinks about the topic. To quantify the information needed, we ordered the information requests in the questionnaire and applied the guidelines for making questions clear, answerable, easy, and unbiased. We also applied these guidelines when presenting lists and rating scales and asking open-ended questions. After following these steps in logical order, you may think we have a pretty good questionnaire.

However, our job is not finished. Like any piece of writing, it needs to be tested to find out whether it really works. You wouldn't publish a book without first undergoing a serious editing process, nor should you implement a questionnaire without first pretesting and editing it.

Look at the following question from a survey and how a respondent thought about the question during a pretest:

Q: How many times have you talked to a doctor in the past 12 months?

Respondent: I guess that depends on what you mean when you say "talked." I talked to my neighbor, who is a doctor, but you probably don't mean that. I go to my doctor about once a year, for a general check-up, so I would count that one. I've also been to some type of specialist a couple of more times in the past year—once to get a bad knee diagnosed, and I also saw an ENT about a chronic coughing thing, which I am pretty sure was in the past year, although I wouldn't swear to it. I've also talked to doctors several times when I brought my kids to the pediatrician—I might assume that you don't want that included, although I really can't be sure. Also, I saw a chiropractor, but I don't know if you'd consider that to be a doctor in the sense you mean. So, what I'm saying, overall, is that I guess I'm not sure what number to give you, mostly because I don't know what you want. (Willis, Cognitive Interviewing, *2005. Reprinted with permission from publisher.)*

This respondent's thought process is a poignant example of how we really don't know whether our questions make sense and can be answered by respondents until we test them. All of our efforts to write effective questions, using guidelines of questionnaire design, can only get us so close to a question that works as we intend it to. The true test of whether a question works occurs when the question meets the respondent; you can see what happened in this case!

Pretesting and revising a questionnaire is the final step in writing an effective questionnaire. We present pretesting as a process. Start with internal pretesting. Make sure the skip patterns work properly. Then have colleagues with various skills review the questionnaire to find problems and make improvements.

After this internal review, pretest with respondents. Administer the questionnaire to a sample of each segment of respondents to find out whether each question is clear, answerable, easy, unbiased, and free of any problems that might affect the accuracy of the answers. Finally, conduct a soft launch as the final stage in quality control.

Properly pretesting your questionnaire brings immediate and clear rewards. In a short period of time you will uncover terms that are unclear, requests for information that people can't recall, lists that are missing legitimate responses, scales that do not represent how people think about the issues, and so on. Finding and fixing these problems yields a better questionnaire. Better questionnaires yield more accurate and less biased information upon which to develop your understanding of the issues upon which you will make decisions.

Unfortunately, pretesting is poorly practiced and not well understood. Many studies are not pretested at all. We often hear people say, "We don't have time for pretesting" or "We can skip pretesting, as most of these questions are straightforward." What a mistake! Far too many questionnaires are sent out to respondents with all sorts of errors that could easily have been fixed with just a day or two of pretesting. The idea that anyone can write a twenty- or thirty-minute questionnaire that will make sense to everyone taking the survey without pretesting it is preposterous. Remember what happened when a respondent was simply asked how many times he had talked with a doctor in the past 12 months.

A rich tradition of pretesting has evolved out of academic and government survey research. The discipline of pretesting, often referred to as cognitive interviewing, is common practice in many government agencies (e.g., Census Bureau, U.S. Bureau of Labor Statistics, National Center for Health Statistics, etc.).

Our colleague and friend, Gordon Willis, has written an excellent book on this topic called *Cognitive Interviewing: A Tool for Improving Questionnaire Design*. We will refer to it several times in this chapter. We recommend this book to anyone who is serious about the practice of pretesting questionnaires.

Six Guidelines for Pretesting

1. Make sure the skip patterns work properly. (Pretesting #1)
2. Examine the questionnaire with colleagues to find and fix flaws. (Pretesting #2)
3. Develop a plan for pretesting. (Pretesting #3)
4. Pretest the questionnaire in the mode in which it will be given to respondents. (Pretesting #4)
5. Pretest the questionnaire with 3 to 10 respondents per segment, and consider more than one round of pretesting. (Pretesting #5)
6. Conduct a soft launch of the questionnaire as a final step in quality control. (Pretesting #6)

Sending Out the Questionnaire and Getting Responses Is Not Pretesting

In the private sector, we have talked with many people who think pretesting amounts to sending out the questionnaire to a limited sample of respondents and seeing whether respondents answer all of the questions. This is not pretesting.

The core rationale for pretesting is making sure that each question performs as intended. Sure, sending the questionnaire out to a limited sample, often referred to as a soft launch, is helpful for seeing whether skip patterns worked, measuring the time it takes respondents to answer questions, and so forth. But a soft launch will not tell you how respondents interpreted the questions and came up with their answers.

We will discuss the purposes of a soft launch in chapter 14.

The most important step in pretesting involves going through the questionnaire with respondents to find out what each question meant to them, how they came up with their answers, and where they were confused or unsure. You have to talk with them to understand whether each question and the flow of questions are working.

CHAPTER 13

Internal Pretesting

Before pretesting with respondents, fix as many problems as you can. Pretesting with respondents requires time and money, so finding and fixing errors beforehand makes sense. Respondents will give you only so much of their time and energy. If the questionnaire is littered with problems you could have repaired beforehand, you won't detect more subtle problems when you pretest with respondents. Additionally, there are some questionnaire problems that only you and your colleagues will find, which makes this first step all the more important.

Internal pretesting is necessary for ensuring that the skip patterns work properly. Skip patterns can be complicated. Maybe you want to funnel people who purchased a product versus those who did not purchase a product into two different sets of questions. You might also want to funnel the purchasers into one question if they intend to purchase it again but into another question if they do not intend to purchase it again. The point is that you need to check the questionnaire carefully to make sure that these skip patterns work properly. This is the kind of error that you would detect more easily during internal pretesting.

Pretest the questionnaire with colleagues to clean it up as much as possible. Colleagues who are knowledgeable about the subject matter will help with how to write questions that make sense to respondents. They know how respondents think and can make sure the terms and phrases are the ones respondents use, not your jargon.

Colleagues who have questionnaire-design expertise can help with all the issues discussed in this book. You can't expect a respondent to find an unlabeled midpoint on a bipolar scale or to inquire about whether the information collected in question 11 is really going to help with the decision the research will support. You need a little help from your colleagues on such issues.

Internal pretesting is certainly no substitute for pretesting with respondents. It is simply a step in the quality-control or quality-enhancement process.

Pretesting #1: Make Sure the Skip Patterns Work Properly

The term *skip pattern* refers to funneling some respondents into some questions but not others. For example, you might ask respondents whether they have purchased a product in the past 30 days. Those who did might skip to one set of questions, while those who did not might skip to another set of questions.

Earlier in the book we presented Answerable #4, which instructs you to screen respondents to make sure each question applies to them. In this context, screening respondents refers to skip patterns. You would not ask someone who just told you they have no children about the ages and genders of their children. You would use a skip pattern to jump respondents over questions that do not apply to them.

Most questionnaires have skip patterns in them, and some have a lot of them. Make sure the skip patterns work properly by going through the questionnaire, question by question, to confirm that respondents are funneled into the questions you want them to answer and skipped over the questions you don't.

Here is an example of a series of questions with skip patterns:

1. Which of the following best describes the building where you live?
   ☐ A mobile home (IF YES THEN SKIP TO Q2)
   ☐ A one-family house detached from any other house
      (IF YES THEN SKIP TO Q2)
   ☐ A one-family house attached to one or more houses
      (IF YES THEN SKIP TO Q2)
   ☐ A building with 2 or more apartments (IF YES THEN SKIP TO Q3)
   ☐ A boat or recreational vehicle (IF YES THEN TERMINATE)
   ☐ Other (IF YES THEN TERMINATE)

2. About how many acres is your house or mobile home on?
   ☐ Less than 1 acre
   ☐ 1 to 4.9 acres
   ☐ 5 or more acres

3. About how many apartments are in your apartment building?
   ☐ less than 10
   ☐ 10-20
   ☐ 21-50
   ☐ 51 or more

4. (IF Q1 = A one-family house detached from any other house and Q2 = 5 or more acres) **Do you have a lake or pond on your property?**
   ☐ Yes
   ☐ No

This is just a small portion of a hypothetical questionnaire that involves a few skip patterns. You can see that some questions are meant for only some respondents.

If there was an error in the skip pattern and people who live in apartments were asked about the number of acres their house or mobile home is on, you would probably end up with erroneous data and with some respondents dropping out of the survey. The question about having a lake or pond on the property is meant for people with houses on 5 or more acres. You can imagine what would happen if people from apartment complexes were accidentally asked this question. Many apartment complexes have lakes or ponds, but some respondents who live in apartments might be confused by the term *your property*. The point is that ensuring skip patterns work properly gets you accurate data and avoids alienating respondents with questions that don't apply to them.

Make sure you check the skip patterns before and after the questionnaire has been set in the mode in which it will be administered. Checking before is always a good idea because finding errors early is always best. Checking skip patterns after the questionnaire has been programmed for, let's say, computer administration, is critical. The programmer might have made an error.

Checking skip patterns is tedious, but careful attention will avoid the awful circumstance of administering a study with errors in skip patterns. At their worst, skip-pattern errors mean that you spent all that time and money getting only some of the data you needed, and possibly invalidated even that data because too many respondents terminated the survey.

Pretesting #2: Examine the Questionnaire with Colleagues to Find and Fix Flaws

Have colleagues review the questionnaire for problems. Those who will be most useful include people with expertise in questionnaire design and people who are intimately familiar with the topics in the questionnaire.

People with Questionnaire Design Experience

Have a few people with expertise in questionnaire design review the questionnaire. Since they have not been staring at it for the past few weeks, they will almost always find problems that make the questionnaire writers wonder, "How the heck did I miss that?" Their distance from the project is beneficial because they can see the questionnaire with fresh eyes and without assumptions. They can raise questions that you might have overlooked about whether questions have bias, whether rating scales should be unipolar or bipolar, whether there are unclear terms and phrases, whether one question is actually two questions, and so on.

At this stage, it is not critical to have them review the questionnaire in the format in which it will be administered. Some may want to go through the questionnaire on paper so they can contemplate questionnaire design issues and think through any possible changes.

Also review the questionnaire by having one person read the questionnaire to another person. One or both of you may hear problems that you missed. Sometimes questions that looked fine on paper sound stilted or awkward when read aloud. It might make sense to reword the question to sound a little more conversational. You might also find that some questions have to be read to the other person twice for them to be comprehended. That would be a sure sign that the question needs to be simplified.

Another useful step is to ask your colleagues what information they think each question is intended to collect. Throughout the book we have emphasized the difference between the information needed and the way a question is asked. It is not unusual to find that a question is actually not getting at the information you really need or that you are asking for more detail than you really need or that you maybe don't need the question at all. Having colleagues tell you what information they think the question is intended to collect can reveal problems that need to be fixed.

People Familiar with the Topic

Ask colleagues who are intimately familiar with the topics in the survey to review the questionnaire. They may be drawn from your population of interest or from a group close to your population of interest, professionally or otherwise.

Suppose you are doing a survey among women who have recently given birth to a healthy baby. Finding a few women who have given birth to a healthy baby to review your questionnaire would help immensely. Finding a nurse midwife or lactation counselor would also be helpful. You might even venture outside of the office and ask someone else you know. Find a friend or family member who knows something about the topic and ask them how a question should be phrased.

Ask your colleagues and others familiar with the topic to consider these issues: Have you chosen the right words and phrases? Do the scales match how people from the population of interest actually think about the topic? Is some of the information sensitive? When you ask respondents to select from a list, have you left out legitimate responses? People who are close to the topics in the survey can help improve the questionnaire in ways that questionnaire design experts can't.

Most people who are intimately familiar with the topic do not have questionnaire design experience, so you will need to instruct them on how to review the questionnaire. It is usually best to work with them face-to-face or by phone. Go through the questionnaire, question by question, and ask them to rephrase each question in their own words to see whether the intention of the question is clear. Ask them what certain words and phrases mean to them. Ask them how they arrived at their answer, if it was easy or difficult, and why.

You can structure your review of the questionnaire with people who are familiar with the topic somewhat like a pretest with respondents. In the next chapter we will go into more detail about what kinds of questions to ask and when and how to probe for a better understanding of how people respond to questions.

A few years ago a colleague and I were reviewing a questionnaire for physicians. One of the questions was: "In the past 30 days, how many times have you been detailed by a sales representative about [drug X]?" Our colleague, who was not drenched in pharmaceutical industry jargon, asked, "What does it mean to be detailed?" In the pharmaceutical industry, the term *detailed* has come to mean a visit by a sales representative to talk about the products they are promoting. Our colleague's first association with the term *detailed* was cleaning a car!

After we explained what the term meant in the pharmaceutical industry, our colleague wondered whether every doctor would know what this term meant. The standard answer among people in the pharmaceutical industry is that they do, but we could not say for sure.

As we discussed ways to make the question clearer, we realized we had not thought through exactly what we wanted. Did we want to know whether the sales representative had visited the office, talked with the physician about something, or talked with the physician about drug X? Very often sales representatives visit the office to leave samples, talk with the office staff but not the physician, or talk with the physician about issues not associated with the drug. What information did we really want, and what does the term *detailed* really mean to physicians?

We wrestled with whether we needed to know whether a sales representative had visited the office or had discussed drug X with the doctor. These are two very different information requests, and therefore, different questions.

It is very helpful to have colleagues question your terms and phrases and help you think more deeply about what information you really need. Both questionnaire design experts and people familiar with the topic can help you iron out as many issues as possible before you begin pretesting with respondents.

CHAPTER 14

Pretesting with Respondents

Once you have checked skip patterns and pretested the questionnaire with colleagues, it is time to see how well it works with respondents. Make arrangements for a sample of people from your population of interest to take the questionnaire, and then interview them to find out how well the questionnaire worked. Your goal is to see whether the questions were clear, answerable, easy, and unbiased. Pretesting with respondents invariably yields a host of issues that need to be corrected.

The two primary methods for pretesting are think-aloud and verbal probing. Although think-aloud is not used nearly as often as verbal probing, it is intellectually interesting and might be preferable in some situations. We will review both along with other methods for finding and fixing problems with the questionnaire.

Think-Aloud

Think-aloud is one of the earliest developed methods of pretesting. Depending on how the questionnaire will be administered, either the interviewer or the respondent reads each question, and the respondent then verbalizes his or her thought process as he or she tries to answer.

In this example, the interviewer reads the question, and the respondent talks about the answering process:

Interviewer: How many cars do you currently own?

Respondent: We have three cars, in that I have a car, my wife has a car, and we have a car for our seventeen-year-old son. We only own one of them, though, and that would be the one that my son drives. The car that I drive is leased, so that probably doesn't count, and the one that my wife drives still has a year or so left on car payments, so we don't really own it. The title is with the credit union. And I am not sure if you mean us as a family, or me personally. Oh, and one other thing is that the car I drive is technically an SUV. I guess I would say two because I am not sure what you want, but that would probably be close enough.

Think-aloud is a useful method for peeking into mental processes. This example reveals several problems with the question. The concept of car ownership is ambiguous. This respondent appears to be wondering about the intention of the question and whether his answer should include a car that is not fully paid for. He also questions whether the concept of a car should include an SUV. The interviewer probably wonders how respondents who own a truck would reply. The word *you* is also ambiguous and needs to be more clearly defined in the question.

For think-aloud pretesting, the interviewer videotapes or records what respondents say and later goes back to these recordings and analyzes the results so that the questions can be modified as needed.

The problem with think-aloud is that some respondents do not do it well, even after instructions and practice. They have trouble verbalizing their thoughts, or they stray off task and talk about issues that are irrelevant. The interview then becomes more of a verbal probing exercise, which we describe later in this chapter.

Think-aloud also requires respondents to reveal what is going on in their heads. With verbal probing, the interviewer assumes more responsibility for directing the exploration to uncover problems with questions. In this example, suppose the respondent was not as adept at verbalizing his thoughts. Suppose he did not wonder out loud whether an SUV qualifies as a car. In verbal probing, the interviewer would come prepared with the probe, "What does the term *car* mean to you?" and would be trained to probe further if there were any hesitation in answering. Verbal probing is better at covering all the important bases.

Think-aloud is also a different task from taking the questionnaire in the field. The process itself may produce results that would not crop up when the questionnaire is actually administered. Might the process of verbalizing thoughts create thoughts that would not occur had the respondent just taken the questionnaire? How does verbalizing thoughts about one question affect how people respond to the next question?

For these reasons, think-aloud is not used nearly as much as verbal probing. However, it is a very insightful method for pretesting. You might want to use it in selected circumstances, such as in an early phase of a multiphase approach to pretesting or for selected questions or selected respondents.

Verbal Probing

Verbal probing is the most common method of pretesting questionnaires. Verbal probing involves asking respondents questions about how they responded to questions and components of questions in the questionnaire. The probing process is designed to uncover problems with comprehension, recall, willingness to answer, bias, and so on.

Figure 14.1 displays a list of common cognitive probes.

Figure 14.1: Common Cognitive Probes

Cognitive Probe	Example
Comprehension / Interpretation	What does the term *outpatient* mean to you?
Paraphrasing	Can you repeat the question in your own words?
Confidence Judgment	How sure are you that your health insurance covers drug and alcohol treatment?
Recall Probe	How do you remember that you went to the doctor five times in the past 12 months?
Specific Probe	Why do you think that cancer is the most serious health problem?
General Probes	How did you arrive at that answer? Was it easy or hard to answer? I noticed that you hesitated. Tell me what you were thinking.

Source: Gordon B. Willis, *Cognitive Interviewing: A Tool for Improving Questionnaire Design* (Thousand Oaks, CA: Sage Publications Inc., 2005). Reprinted with permission from the publisher.

This is merely a sample of common probes, not a complete list. In preparing for a pretest, you would create a list of probes designed to explore aspects of questions that you feel uncertain about, such as what questions mean to respondents, how they interpret certain words and phrases, whether they can recall time frames, and so on. You also need to be prepared to explore unexpected issues as they arise, as they almost always do in pretesting.

The benefit of verbal probing, as compared to think-aloud, is that it allows the interviewer to control the focus of the exploration. The interviewer can probe specific topics that seemed worthy of scrutiny while writing the questionnaire. It is also easier for respondents because they do not need to be trained, as they do with the think-aloud method, and almost anyone can answer the kinds of questions asked in pretesting. For these reasons, verbal probing has become the most widely used method of pretesting.

Proactive and Reactive Probing

Gordon B. Willis (2005) has developed a useful categorization of probing as either proactive or reactive. Proactive probes are questions designed to explore issues that the questionnaire writers deem important. From the process of writing the questionnaire and from internal review, you will identify words, phrases, time frames, lists, and so on that you are not sure respondents will understand or answer. Proactive probes are proactive because the questionnaire writing team generates them before interacting with pretest respondents.

Here are a few frequently used proactive probes:

• Can you repeat the question in your own words?
• What does the term _____ mean to you?
• How did you come up with that answer?

Reactive probes are questions the interviewer asks based on unanticipated issues that come up during the pretesting process. They are reactive because they are reactions to something observed or sensed in the respondent.

Look at the following question and note the need for the interviewer to come up with a reactive probe:

Interviewer: How would you rate your overall satisfaction with your experience at the airport?

Respondent: At the airport? Well, the whole experience was awful, but I have to say I wasn't particularly dissatisfied with the airport.

Interviewer's Reactive Probe: Tell me more about what you are thinking.

Respondent: Well, the airport is fine. The problem is that the flight was delayed several times and then cancelled. They put me on a flight the next day, and it took about two hours to shuttle us all over to the hotel. I am not sure who to blame for that—the airport or the airlines.

In this case the respondent said something at the beginning—"At the airport?"—that initially led the interviewer to suspect there was more to the story. So the interviewer came up with a reactive probe and asked an exploratory question about what the respondent was thinking.

As you can see, it was hard for this respondent to separate the experience with the airport from the experience with the airline. Assuming this is deemed to be a problem worth fixing, the next step would be to think carefully about what information is really needed and re-craft the question or set of questions to capture that information accurately.

Reactive probing requires skill, training, and judgment. If the respondent hesitates, you might ask, "I notice you hesitated. What were you thinking?" If the respondent blushes, you might follow up with "What are you feeling right now?" There are no absolute rules about when and how to throw in reactive probes. They require an astute and observant interviewer who is trained and skilled in exploring issues that are relevant to the questionnaire.

Concurrent and Retrospective Probing

Verbal probing can be done concurrently or retrospectively. In concurrent verbal probing, respondents read or hear each question, answer it, and then are interviewed about that question before proceeding to the next one. In retrospective verbal probing, respondents take the entire questionnaire as they would were the questionnaire being administered in the field. Then, the interviewer goes back through the questionnaire, one question at a time, and talks with respondents about each question and their answers.

Concurrent probing has the benefit of having each question fresh in the mind of respondents. Sometimes with retrospective pretesting, respondents don't remember what they were thinking when they answered some questions. A drawback is that answering probes about one question may affect how respondents answer the next question.

Retrospective probing has a couple of benefits. First, it better simulates the actual questionnaire process. When the questionnaire is administered in the field, respondents will not hear or read each question knowing they are about to get interviewed about it. This artificial situation could introduce a different quality of questionnaire taking by pretest respondents.

Retrospective probing also allows you to see how long it takes respondents to take the questionnaire. It offers the opportunity to verify that responses to questions are the same when you go through the questionnaire with respondents the second time as when they went through the questionnaire the first time. Where there is inconsistency, there is usually an opportunity to improve the question.

Figure 14.2

Partial Example of a Concurrent Verbal Probing Pretest

Below are instructions that you would give each respondent at the beginning of the pretest, followed by the first two questions with proactive probes and one possible reactive probe.

Instructions: Thank you for coming in today. Let me tell you about what we are going to do. We are testing a draft questionnaire that will eventually be given to people like you, after we improve it. We need to find out if the questions make sense and if people can answer them. I am going to ask you to read each question and answer it, just like a regular questionnaire. After you read each question and answer it, I am going to ask you a few questions. Our goal is to find ways to improve the questionnaire. Does that make sense?

Q1. In the past 12 months, how many times have you suffered a migraine headache?

___ # migraine headaches in past 12 months

Proactive Probes:

• In your own words, what do you think this question is asking?

• Tell me how you came up with your answer.

• Was it easy or hard to come up with this answer?

What does the phrase "suffered a migraine headache" mean to you? (PROBE on *suffered* or *migraine* if necessary)

Q2. In the past 12 months, how many times have you seen a doctor about your migraine headaches?

___ # times seen doctor about migraine headaches in past 12 months

Proactive Probes:

• Please rephrase this question in your own words.

• Tell me how you came up with your answer.

• How easy or hard was it?

Possible Reactive Probes:

• I noticed you laughed when you said "doctor." Why?

• You mentioned that you called your doctor about your most recent migraine but did not see him in person. What if the question asked "In the past 12 months, how many times have you talked to your doctor about your migraine headaches, either in person or by phone?" Would that be an adequate way of asking the question?

Both concurrent and retrospective probing have benefits. We can't argue that one method will be that much better than the other. If you have the time, consider using both. Conduct concurrent probing with a few respondents to explore each question while it is fresh in their minds, and conduct retrospective probing to look at the questionnaire from a slightly different perspective. This will also allow you to gauge the length of the questionnaire and to observe people taking the questionnaire without an interviewer by their side.

Hopefully, this brief example gives you a better idea of how a concurrent verbal probing pretest would be conducted. For retrospective verbal probing, respondents would simply answer the entire questionnaire before you take them through the probing process.

Planning for Pretesting

Pretesting requires planning. Here is a list of issues to consider:

- Recruiting. Recruit respondents to come to a professional facility for pretesting. In government work, there are cognitive laboratories, whereas in private industry we use focus-group facilities.
- Screening. To get people from the population of interest, you will need to develop a mini-questionnaire or screener that will be used to recruit people for pretesting.
- Scheduling. Schedule two to three times as much time as the questionnaire would take for the pretest. So for a 20-minute questionnaire, respondents can take 20 minutes to go through the questionnaire, and you will have another 20 to 40 minutes to talk with them about their answers.
- Recording. It can be useful to record pretests for further analysis. When the interview is recorded, you must get consent from the respondent.
- Rapport. It is important to establish good rapport with respondents. Be professional and courteous. Make good eye contact and use their name when talking to them. Let them know how much time you need from them. Tell them that you are working on improving the questionnaire and that you are going to interview them to figure out how to do so.
- Compensation. You usually need to pay people for their time and effort. How much you pay depends on who you are talking to and how much time you ask of them. You might pay some people as little as $25 for a pretest, while you might pay a professional, such as a doctor or a dentist, well over $100.

The people who run cognitive laboratories and focus-group facilities can help you with the details associated with planning pretests.

Limitations on Pretesting

Remember that the pretest situation is unavoidably different from how the questionnaire will be taken in the field. When respondents participate in pretesting, they go through the questionnaire with an interviewer who asks them many questions about their answers. This is certainly a different task from getting the questionnaire in the mail or receiving a questionnaire link on a computer and filling it out while managing household chores or making sure they get out of the house in time to pick up the kids.

The people who agree to spend an hour or so pretesting a questionnaire may also be different in subtle ways from the people who eventually take the survey. Despite all our efforts to recruit people for pretesting whose characteristics match those of our target population, we always wonder if these people who agree to pretest the questionnaire are more compliant, attentive, or agreeable, or different in some other way.

Pretesting is only a method for uncovering problems with the questionnaire. This is all the more important since the respondents who eventually take the survey may not be as tolerant of unclear questions, ambiguous requests, or questions that just don't make sense. The pretesting process may point us in a direction for fixing the problem, but it will not magically reveal the best way to do so. As a result of pretesting, we use our best judgment to revise questions. We often do not know whether the revised questions still have problems. Whenever possible, and certainly for questionnaires that are used to collect information for important decision-making, it is best to conduct more than one round of pretesting. By conducting two, three, or sometimes more rounds of pretesting with respondents, you will end up with a better questionnaire. Some studies, such as the American Community Survey conducted by the U.S. Census Bureau, undergo five or more rounds of pretesting to ensure the questions are getting the right data.

We hope this brief introduction to pretesting helps you become adept at using pretesting to find problems with questionnaires. You need to find these problems to create a better questionnaire.

Pretesting #3: Develop a Plan for Pretesting

The effectiveness of pretesting depends heavily on the experience and skill of the interviewer. Anyone can read predetermined probes, but many insights into problems with questions come from the interviewer sensing something from the respondent during pretesting and following up with probes they create on the spot.

Good pretesting comes from knowing the purposes of the study, having a good background in questionnaire design, possessing some knowledge of the subject matter being studied, and drawing on a lot of experience pretesting questionnaires. Knowing the purposes of the study helps the interviewer know what information each question needs to collect, and knowing something about questionnaire design lets the interviewer appreciate why certain questions are difficult. Knowing the subject matter can be crucial, too, especially if it is highly technical. If you are pretesting a questionnaire for oncologists about how various chemotherapeutic agents are administered, you certainly need to know something about the topic.

Below is a list of key issues for anyone who is pretesting a questionnaire:

1. Have a probing plan ready. Arrive at the pretest with a well-thought-out probing plan. Have proactive probes written down alongside each question. Make sure you have notes about specific terms or issues to explore.

2. Establish rapport. Be professional and courteous. Make good eye contact with respondents and use their name when talking to them. Let them know how much time you need from them. Tell them that you are working on improving the questionnaire and that you are going to interview them to figure out how to do so.

3. Be flexible. Be ready to adjust your line of questioning to how people respond to each question.

4. Talk rather than read. Even though your questions are written down, make sure your questions sound like you are just talking with respondents rather than reading them a series of questions. You want the experience to feel natural and conversational to help build rapport and to encourage respondents to reveal their thoughts.

5. Record the pretest. As we said at the beginning of this chapter, videotaping or audiotaping the pretest will make the analysis easier. Take notes or have someone take notes for you.

6. Maintain neutrality. Be careful not to lead respondents. Ask questions, listen to responses, and acknowledge that you understand their response without conveying value to their response. For example, it is better to say "Okay" than "Good." Pay attention to your facial expressions; avoid conveying that you like certain responses.

7. Observe carefully. Watch respondents carefully during the pretest. Pay attention to how long it takes them to answer questions. Watch their eyes. Are they going back and forth from the question to the answer choices? Listen to them too. Sometimes the sounds people make reveal that there is something going on in their heads that is worth exploring.

8. Follow your instincts. Many of the insights that arise in pretesting, and in qualitative research in general, come from an astute interviewer following instincts. As an interviewer, your sixth sense will sometimes be what leads you to probe down an avenue that reveals something important.

9. Make no assumptions. It is human nature to assume that some questions are straightforward and do not require exploration. We asked a teenager, "In your lifetime, how many bones have you broken?" His answer was four. It might seem like there was no need to explore further, but we asked him to say how he came up with his answer. He said, "Well, I broke my arm in two places rollerblading, then I broke my big toe, and I'm pretty sure I broke the goalie's nose when I played middle-school soccer."

To improve your pretesting skills, watch others pretest. Offer to take notes and write up commentary for them. Assuming you have videotaped some of your pretests, watch the videotape critically to find areas where you can improve your work. It is easy to inadvertently lead respondents, to rush respondents through questions, or not to follow a topic that might warrant additional probing.

Pretesting #4: Pretest the Questionnaire in the Mode in Which It Will Be Given to Respondents

Pretest the questionnaire in the same manner as respondents will take it. If respondents will respond to the questionnaire on the web, pretest with respondents on the web. If the questionnaire will be administered on paper, have respondents take the questionnaire on paper. If it is a telephone questionnaire, have them take the questionnaire with someone asking the questions over the telephone.

The key is to pretest in a setting that mimics as much as possible the setting in which the questionnaire will be officially administered. Some of the problems you need to find and fix are related to the mode of administration. For web questionnaires, you need to make sure that each screen is easy to understand and use. We conducted a pretest of a web survey and found that one question had only half of its response choices appear on the screen. Respondents had to scroll down to see about half of the response choices. Several respondents did not realize the additional choices were there at all. Had we tested this questionnaire in another mode, such as on paper, we would not have found that problem.

Navigational or visual problems are unique to the method of administration. Web surveys may not make it clear when and how to move to the next question. Paper questionnaires may have unclear skip patterns.

Voice-administered questionnaires often have problems with pronunciation. Respondents may also hear questions differently from how they would read questions. They might, for example, ask to hear the question twice in pretesting. This is a signal that the question might be too long or complicated for voice administration and needs to be revised. You might not detect such a problem if you pretested by having respondents read the questions on paper.

When a questionnaire is to be verbally administered, listen to some interviews administered by the people who will be administering the questionnaire in the field. This is an important step in the pretesting process. It allows you to test the questionnaire's quality of delivery by the person who will be administering it. Are they pronouncing words properly? Is there any tonal emphasis that might create a bias in the question? When someone reads the questionnaire to the respondent, you are basically pretesting both the questions and the delivery.

Although it is best to pretest in the mode in which the questionnaire will be administered, many situations warrant a multiphase approach to pretesting. For example, for a computer-administered questionnaire, you may want to pretest the questionnaire by phone or on paper with a few respondents while the questionnaire is being programmed. This will help you find and fix some of the problems quickly. Just be sure to also pretest in the mode in which the survey will be given to respondents.

Pretesting #5: Pretest the Questionnaire with 3 to 10 Respondents Per Segment, and Consider More than One Round of Pretesting

Think about the number of pretests in terms of the number of groups, or segments, that will eventually answer the questionnaire. If you are going to give a survey about attitudes toward public policy to a group of people who identify themselves as conservatives and to a group of people who identify themselves as liberals, you need to pretest with an equal number of conservatives and liberals. If you are also interested in the differences between the views of males and females within the conservative and liberal groups, you would then have four groups or segments with which to pretest.

Pretest with at least 3 to 10 respondents per segment. How many respondents you choose will depend on how accurate you want the data from the survey to be. If you are willing to accept some level of error in the data you collect, 3 per segment may be fine. If you want to be sure of finding and fixing more problems, pretest with up to 10 respondents per segment. Pretesting with more than 10 respondents will probably yield few new findings, at least for one round of pretesting.

For some questionnaires, particularly those wherein you are still learning about the topic or when the quality of the data collected is very important, you will need to conduct two or more rounds of pretesting. Recall that pretesting only identifies problems and points in the general direction of a solution. Once you rewrite the questions, you'll need to test them again. Conducting a second round of pretesting is often essential.

The complexity of the issues you will explore and the importance of the questionnaire will determine how many respondents per segment to pretest with and how many pretests to perform. For example, the American Community Survey from the U.S. Census Bureau was developed based on hundreds of pretests. But for most questionnaires, 3 to 10 pretests per segment will solve many problems. An additional round of pretesting to test the revised questions would be prudent.

Be prepared to adjust the questionnaire between pretests. Some problems will need to be fixed immediately. Suppose you forgot to state a time frame, have an obvious double-barreled question, or did not specify the referent of the term *you*. Correcting such problems as soon as you discover them allows you to use subsequent pretests to look for other problems with the questionnaire.

If the survey is important, getting it right is all the more important. A few days of pretesting for a questionnaire that may take two to three months to design and administer seems like a no-brainer. Remember that what you do with the data you collect may be with you for years. As they say, it is better to aim, and aim carefully, before you shoot.

Pretesting #6: Conduct a Soft Launch of the Questionnaire as a Final Step in Quality Control

After pretesting with colleagues and conducting pretests with respondents, there is one final step for finding errors that may have slipped through the cracks. In the industry, we call this step a soft launch. This means fielding the study with a limited sample of respondents to see if there is anything else lurking in the questionnaire that needs to be fixed.

There are no hard and fast rules about how many respondents to engage during a soft launch. Since each subgroup may respond differently to the questions, make sure you get responses from at least fifteen to twenty respondents per subgroup. More is better, depending on how important the questionnaire is to the decisions it will support.

A number of issues may surface during the soft launch as indicators of problems that need to be addressed. These are described below.

Time to Complete Questions

Examine the time a respondent needs to complete each question. If a question is taking too long to answer, there may be a problem with it. Compare response times by segment. A question may be easy for one group but not for another. For example, there may be a question that makes sense to women but not to men, or the other way around, depending on the topic.

You also need to check the time it takes to complete particular sections of the questionnaire. Again, take a look at your segments to see whether one group is having more trouble than others. Sometimes a particular section—not just a specific question—is hard or confusing to some respondents.

Skipped Questions and Drop-Outs

Take a look at skipped questions and areas of the questionnaire where respondents are dropping out. Is there a pattern? Questions that respondents skip usually have problems that need to be addressed. When respondents drop out of the survey, take a look at the last question they answered and the subsequent question that they did not answer. There may be a problem with one or both of these questions.

Questions that respondents skip or that result in terminations are often questions respondents can't answer or do not want to answer.

Respondent Requests for Clarification

In an interviewer-administered questionnaire, did respondents make requests for clarification? What do the clarification requests suggest is wrong with the question? In these situations, what respondents say will usually reveal where the problem lies.

Repetitive Non-Thinking Responses

Are there any questions to which respondents give repetitive non-thinking answers? A common place for this type of response would be questions that ask respondents to rate a number of items on a scale. Are there such questions where respondents are using one number on the scale too many times (e.g., repeatedly checking the number 7)? If so, there may be a problem with the question, the scale, or maybe the number of items you are asking them to rate.

Visual Examination of Data

Look at the answers. Make sure they make sense. For example, if you have a question that asks about how many days in a week respondents go to the grocery store, and you see responses like "23" or "mostly," you should look carefully at how the question is worded or how the answer box is constructed.

Read the open-ended responses. Do the answers suggest that respondents understood the question? Do the answers need to be more complete? Are some respondents skipping these questions? A careful look at the responses often reveals problems with the questionnaire.

Check Skip Patterns

During a soft launch, check the skip patterns by running cross-tabulations. In the survey-research industry, cross-tabulations allow you to examine responses of specific subgroups or segments of respondents. For example, cross-tabulations would allow you to see how males and females responded to each question. If males were supposed to be skipped over certain questions, the cross-tabulations would allow you to see whether any males actually answered any of those questions. If they did, then there may be a flaw in the skip pattern. Running a cross-tabulation is an easy way to see whether the skip patterns are working without having to go through each respondent's answers.

A soft launch is an important final check of the questionnaire's quality. However, we do have one final word of caution. Do not use a soft launch as a substitute for pretesting the questionnaire. The most important step in pretesting is sitting down with your respondents and finding out which questions need adjustments. Use the soft launch as fine tuning, the final step in detecting problems that you may have missed when you walked through the questionnaire with respondents.

PART 5. CONCLUDING THOUGHTS AND NEXT STEPS

Writing an effective questionnaire matters. Whether you work in the public or private sector, the information you collect will shape your understanding of the world and in many cases will affect important decision-making. Your work will often affect how your organization or the public at large thinks about a topic. The difference between a poorly written questionnaire and a well-written questionnaire is the difference between blurry pictures that mislead and accurate pictures that reveal key truths. Ultimately it means the difference between poor decisions and good ones.

Although there is no such thing as a perfect questionnaire, almost all of the ones discussed have the kinds of errors described in this book. In a way, this is no surprise because questionnaire writing has somehow escaped the scrutiny that most other forms of writing benefit from. Few people I know have spent more than a day or two in training on how to write questionnaires. And few have a book on their desks that addresses how to write them.

Consider the critical importance of legal documents—everything hinges on how things are worded. Advertising gurus may spend days sharpening a single phrase intended for a billboard. Why shouldn't the same serious effort be extended to questionnaires, the results of which can affect important governmental, business, and public-health decisions—all decisions affecting the daily lives of ordinary people?

I wrote this book because there is an enormous need for it. I wanted everyone involved in writing questionnaires to have a guide that would make the process easier, more effective, and more meaningful. This book offers two major themes and a framework for writing questionnaires that will do just that.

Theme 1: Organizing Research to Support Decision-Making

The first theme in this book is the importance of starting every research project with a clear understanding of the decisions the research will support. Most research projects are initiated for some larger purpose, perhaps to increase early detection of breast cancer, improve employee morale and productivity, or improve satisfaction among customers. Whenever you are asked to collect data, something important is at stake. Our work is more effective and more meaningful when we start by working through the decisions that the research will ultimately support.

Many times you will be asked to go out and do a survey or study without first having any discussion of the decisions the research will support. Some colleagues or clients will be very impressed that you want to work through the decisions the research will support, while others will not want to work through such long-term implications. It is helpful to think of the possible decisions the research might support and to pitch them to whoever commissioned the survey. You might say, "Are you guys thinking of cancelling the program, or are you thinking that you might just adjust it?" For an advertising study, you might say, "Are you considering cancelling both advertisements altogether, or are you thinking about keeping one of them, or is there something else you are considering?" Ask "What do you hope the research will show, and why?" Such questions can help guide people to the decisions, or choices, that are on the table.

Nailing down ahead of time the decisions that need to be made takes effort, but the payoff is enormous. Like throwing darts, you might get lucky and hit the bull's-eye without really trying, but if you do try and you aim carefully, you are more likely to get a good result. When researchers take the time to identify their objective very clearly, the questionnaire that follows is invariably more effective. The organization that needs the information can use the data to take action confidently and with measurable results.

Keep track of the decisions people are actually making. Find out what is in the organization's budget. That often reveals how the company prioritizes its decision-making! As you become experienced with the kinds of decisions your clients or colleagues are making, you will be better able to help the next time the task of writing a questionnaire lands on your desk.

Theme 2: The Importance of Qualitative Research

Writing a good questionnaire must begin and end with qualitative research. Knowing your subject is critical to executing an effective questionnaire. Qualitative research is your way inside your respondents' thinking. It will offer you numerous insights into the subject, which will in turn give you a kind of expertise in designing the resulting questionnaire that you simply wouldn't have without it. Doing qualitative research both *before* you write the questionnaire and *after* you write it is best. Pretesting the questionnaire with a smaller group of respondents will help you tweak and revise it before launching it.

Many researchers skip one or both steps, justifying their choice by saying, "We *don't need* to talk to people—the questions are pretty straightforward" or "We *don't have time* to pretest the questionnaire." These two attitudes are the kiss of death for gathering reliable information. In the long run, making the effort to talk to your target audience will save you time and deliver better results.

As you take the time to conduct qualitative research, you will improve your ability to write questionnaires. During pretesting, you will see how people respond to questions and gain a better understanding of how to clearly present concepts, label endpoints in scales, ask open-ended questions, and so on. The more time you can spend asking respondents, "Tell me in your own words what you think that question was asking" and "How did you come up with your answer?" the more you will refine your ability to write an excellent questionnaire.

A Framework to Use as a Guide

When I was starting to develop the guidelines on how to write questions, I realized we needed a framework that would help us keep track of them. Early in the process, my goal was simply to write down all the guidelines in plain English, avoiding any jargon, so that they would be clear to anyone. After about two years of editing and sorting the guidelines into categories, I came up with this conceptual framework.

This framework organizes these guidelines for writing questions into four categories: make questions clear, answerable, easy, and unbiased. It also provides three additional categories for special cases—selecting items from a list, rating items on a scale, and asking open-ended questions.

I rounded out the framework with chapters on planning research to support decision-making, conducting qualitative research, planning the questionnaire before writing questions and a chapter on pretesting at the end. The result is a user-friendly framework with the steps in sequential order, which makes it really easy to remember what you have read in this book and apply it to your work.

This framework will also assist you in working with colleagues. You might find yourself saying, "I want to make sure the questions are clear, answerable, easy, and unbiased." Who would quarrel with that? And in the end, they won't quarrel with your results.

Next Steps

I have focused my career on helping organizations get the information they need in order to make sound decisions that help their organizations move forward in a positive way. Now that you are armed with the skills to help your organization make better decisions, we encourage you to build upon your knowledge of this topic. Some of this will happen automatically in the course of conducting the qualitative research we recommend and pretesting questionnaires.

I encourage you to take as many questionnaires and surveys as you can. Surely you get many requests to participate in questionnaires. Being a respondent gives you additional insight into all the issues we discuss in this book. I have learned a lot over the years by taking questionnaires and struggling to really understand the questions. Some of these questions appear as examples in this book. Please take the time to respond to questionnaires. It will help you refine your skills.

As you work towards improving your ability to design research and write questionnaires, please visit the website listed below. This website offers additional information and insights since the time when this book was written. Please also sign up to receive information about additional issues in questionnaire design.

http://www.davidfharris.com

APPENDIX: GUIDELINES

Part 1 **PLAN RESEARCH**

  1 *Plan Research to Support Decision-Making*
     Plan research to support decision-making. (Research Planning #1)

  2 *Qualitative versus Quantitative Research*
     Conduct qualitative research before writing a questionnaire.
        (Research Planning #2)

  3 *The Research Plan*
     Write a Research Plan. (Research Planning #3)

Part 2 **PLAN THE QUESTIONNAIRE**

  4 *The Questionnaire Plan*
     Use a Questionnaire Plan for designing the questionnaire.
        (Questionnaire Planning #1)
     Determine the information needed before deciding how to write
        the questions. (Questionnaire Planning #2)
     Determine how to analyze the data while planning the
        questionnaire. (Questionnaire Planning #3)

  5 *Organize the Order of Questions*
     Organize the categories of information you will collect in the
        questionnaire. (Questionnaire Planning #4)
     Do not begin the questionnaire with difficult or sensitive questions.
        (Questionnaire Planning #5)
     Organize the order of questions to avoid order bias. (Questionnaire
        Planning #6)
     To reduce misunderstanding in a sequence of questions, order
        questions from the general to the more specific. (Questionnaire
        Planning #7)
     Use a transition statement if the topic of questions will change
        abruptly. (Questionnaire Planning #8)

PART 3   WRITE QUESTIONS

6   *Make Questions Clear*

State the unit of measurement. (Clear #1)

Use the vocabulary of respondents. (Clear #2)

Use precise words and phrases. (Clear #3)

When using the word *you*, make sure respondents know to whom you are referring. (Clear #4)

Make sure the question is really asking only one question. (Clear #5)

When asking for percentages, make sure the base is clear. (Clear #6)

Make sure the question stem and the answer choices match each other. (Clear #7)

Use bold, underlining, italics, and/or capitalization to highlight key words and phrases. (Clear #8)

7   *Make Questions Answerable*

State time frames in which people can recall the information you need. (Answerable #1)

Don't assume regularity of behavior. (Answerable #2)

Don't ask people for information they simply don't have. (Answerable #3)

Screen respondents to make sure each question applies to them. (Answerable #4)

Make "Don't Know" an answer choice if some respondents simply don't know the answer to your question. (Answerable #5)

8   *Make Questions Easy*

Keep the question stem under twenty-five words. (Easy #1)

When writing questions, say the question out loud as if you were talking to someone. (Easy #2)

Limit the length of the questionnaire. (Easy #3)

Don't ask for more detail than you really need. (Easy #4)

Soften questions with phrases such as *approximately, your best estimate,* or *as best you can remember.* (Easy #5)

Don't ask questions in the form of complex grids. (Easy #6)

Add labels to answer categories. (Easy #7)

9   *Make Questions Unbiased*

Do not introduce ideas or opinions in questions that will influence responses. (Unbiased #1)

Make sure that none of the answer choices is more loaded than any of the others. (Unbiased #2)

Make clear that either a positive or a negative answer is equally acceptable. (Unbiased #3)

Randomize answer choices if there is a possibility of order bias. (Unbiased #4)

To get sensitive information, consider disguising the question, shifting the focus away from the respondent, softening the question, or collecting correlated data. (Unbiased #5)

10 Presenting Lists

Make sure the list includes all possible answer choices. (Lists #1)

Make sure numeric categories are as broad and detailed as needed. (Lists #2)

Make sure items on the list do not overlap. (Lists #3)

Consider using forced choice instead of "Check All That Apply." (Lists #4)

Use the question to direct respondents to the list. (Lists #5)

11 Presenting Rating Scales

Make the scale match how people think about the topic. (Scales #1)

Ask the question before describing the scale. (Scales #2)

Consider using bipolar scales, unless what you are measuring does not have a clear opposite. (Scales #3)

For bipolar scales, decide whether you want a midpoint and what to call it. (Scales #4)

Whether to label the middle points is usually a practical decision. (Scales #5)

Limit the number of times you ask respondents to rate things. (Scales #6)

Make the scale length reasonable—shorter is usually better. (Scales #7)

Don't make the endpoints too extreme. (Scales #8)

Make sure bipolar scales are balanced. (Scales #9)

Replace agree/disagree scales with direct questions about what you really want to measure. (Scales #10)

If you are naming only the endpoints, present the scale horizontally with the positive endpoint and higher numbers to the right. (Scales #11)

When naming all the points on the scale, put the more positive labels at the top when displayed vertically or to the right when displayed horizontally. (Scales #12)

12 Asking Open-Ended Questions

Format and label answer boxes to help respondents understand the response task. (Open-Ended #1)

Provide an appropriate space for answers. (Open-Ended #2)

Do not use exploratory open-ended questions as a substitute for qualitative research. (Open-Ended #3)

Recognize the limitations of exploratory open-ended questions. (Open-Ended #4)

Make exploratory open-ended questions specific. (Open-Ended #5)

Consider adding an introductory statement to improve the quality of responses. (Open-Ended #6)

PART 4 PRETEST AND REVISE THE QUESTIONNAIRE

13 Internal Pretesting

Make sure the skip patterns work properly. (Pretesting #1)

Examine the questionnaire with colleagues to find and fix flaws. (Pretesting #2)

14 Pretesting with Respondents

Develop a plan for pretesting (Pretesting #3)

Pretest the questionnaire in the mode in which it will be given to respondents. (Pretesting #4)

Pretest the questionnaire with 3 to 10 respondents per segment, and consider more than one round of pretesting. (Pretesting #5)

Conduct a soft launch of the questionnaire as a final step in quality control. (Pretesting #6)

REFERENCES

Converse, Jean M., and Stanley Presser. 1986. *Survey Questions: Handcrafting the Standardized Questionnaire.* Beverly Hills, CA: Sage Publications Inc.

Cooperative Institutional Research Program (CIRP). 2010. *Freshman Survey.* Administered by the Higher Education Research Institute at the University of California at Los Angeles. http://www.heri.ucla.edu/cirpoverview.php.

Dillman, Don A., Jolene D. Smyth, and Leah Melani Christian. 2009. *Internet, Mail, and Mixed-Mode Surveys: The Tailored Design Method.* 3rd ed. Hoboken, NJ: John Wiley & Sons, Inc.

Goldman, Alfred E., and Susan Schwartz McDonald. 1987. *The Group Depth Interview: Principles and Practice.* Englewood Cliffs, NJ: Prentice-Hall.

Krosnick, Jon A. 1991. "Response Strategies for Coping with Cognitive Demands of Attitude Measures in Surveys." *Applied Cognitive Psychology* 5 (3): 213–36.

Miller, Peter V., and Charles F. Cannell. 1982. "A Study of Experimental Techniques for Telephone Interviewing." *Public Opinion Quarterly* 46: 250–69.

Moore, David W. 2002. "Measuring New Types of Question Order Effects: Additive and Subtractive." *Public Opinion Quarterly* 66: 80–91.

Rockwood, T. H., R. L. Sangster, and D. A. Dillman. 1997. "The Effect of Response Categories in Questionnaire Answers: Context and Mode Effects." *Sociological Methods and Research* 26 (1): 118–40.

Schuman, Howard. 2008. *Method and Meaning in Polls and Surveys.* Cambridge, MA: Harvard University Press.

Smyth, Jolene D., Don A. Dillman, Leah Melani Christian, and Michael J. Stern. 2005. "Comparing Check-All and Forced-Choice Question Formats in Web Surveys: The Role of Satisficing, Depth of Processing, and Acquiescence in Explaining Differences." *Social and Economic Sciences Research Center Technical Report* #05-029, Washington State University. http://survey.sesrc.wsu.edu/dillman/papers/htm.

Smyth, Jolene D., Don A. Dillman, and Leah M. Christian. 2007. "Context Effects in Web Surveys: New Issues and Evidence." In *The Oxford Handbook of Internet Psychology,* edited by Adam Joinson, Katelyn McKenna, Tom Postmes, and Ulf-Dietrich Reips, 427–43. New York: Oxford University Press.

Smyth, Jolene D., Don A. Dillman, Leah Melani Christian, and Mallory McBride. 2009. "Open-Ended Questions in Web Surveys: Can Increasing the Size of Answer Spaces and Providing Extra Verbal Instructions Improve Response Quality?" *Public Opinion Quarterly* 73: 325–37.

Sudman, S., and N. Bradburn. 1982. *Asking Questions: A Practical Guide to Questionnaire Design.* San Francisco: Jossey-Bass.

Willis, Gordon B. 2005. *Cognitive Interviewing: A Tool for Improving Questionnaire Design.* Thousand Oaks, CA: Sage Publications Inc.